OUTDOOR ENTERTAINING

OUTDOOR ENTERTAINING

General editor Lynn Humphries

The essential guide for any outdoor occasion—with menu ideas, useful tips, and more than 300 tempting recipes

CollinsPublishersSanFrancisco

A Division of HarperCollins*Publishers*

First published in USA 1992 by
Collins Publishers San Francisco

Produced by Weldon Russell Pty Ltd
107 Union Street
North Sydney NSW 2060 Australia

A member of the Weldon International Group of companies

Library of Congress Cataloging-in-Publication Data
Outdoor entertaining / general editor, Lynn Humphries.
     p.   cm.
   Includes index.
   ISBN 0-00-255053-9
   1. Outdoor cookery. 2. Menus. I. Humphries, Lynn, date.
TX823.097 1992
641.5'78—dc20   91–44554
                                      CIP

Publisher: Elaine Russell
Managing editor: Dawn Titmus
Editor: Ariana Klepac
Editorial assistant: Margaret Whiskin
Home economists: Carolyn Fienberg, Jacki Passmore, Suzie Smith
Food stylists: Carolyn Fienberg, Consuelo Guinness,
   Jacki Passmore, Suzie Smith
Photographers: Mark Burgin, Rowan Fotheringham, Mike Hallson,
   Ashley Mackevicius
Contributors: Alan Hill, Jane Sheard
Design concept: Catherine Martin
Finished artist: Jean Meynert
Copy editor: Jo Jarrah
US cooking consultant: Mardee Haidin Regan
Indexer: Garry Cousins
Production: Jane Hazell

Printed by Griffin Press, Netley, South Australia, Australia

A KEVIN WELDON PRODUCTION

*Opposite: barbecued fish in wine and herb marinade
(left, marinade page 137); festive coleslaw (far top right, page 84);
wild berry and apricot trifle (far center right, page 209); avocado
and mushroom salad (far bottom right, page 80)*

*Page 2: Veal and wine terrine (left, page 46); wild rice salad
(right, page 87)*

Page 6: Mediterranean layered bread (page 64)

Contents

Introduction

As many of us spend our workdays indoors, it's not surprising that entertaining outside on weekends and summer evenings has such allure. Whatever the occasion—whether a special celebratory dinner, a sports event or an informal get-together at the end of a workday—it is enhanced if the setting is out-of-doors, with a beautiful view, fine weather and delicious food.

There's something about fresh air that makes even the most basic food taste delicious, and meals that are actually cooked out-of-doors seem to have an extra charm. Perhaps it's the fact that the general atmosphere—and therefore the cook—is more relaxed; formalities are abandoned, timing is less important and we are free to enjoy the simple things of life.

Today, when everyone seems so busy, recipes that leave us free to enjoy the company of our guests are more than welcome. *Outdoor Entertaining*, with its wealth of full-color photographs, recipes and hints, presents options that take the hard work out of preparing and presenting stylish meals for entertaining out-of-doors.

Opposite, clockwise from front: marinated fruits (page 222); sun-dried tomato and pasta salad with pesto dressing (page 87); fresh garden salad with tarragon dressing (page 88)

THE BASICS

Each occasion and venue calls for a different treatment regarding food and its accessories. With this in mind, *Outdoor Entertaining* includes twelve special menus and shows you how to set the scene with table settings, flowers, furnishings and, where appropriate, lighting. There's food for a sunny day's boating, a country picnic, a backyard barbecue, and a poolside gathering for a crowd. For something a little less casual, the book also includes a Mexican lunch, an Italian supper, a romantic dinner for two and a weekend brunch. And there's also a family supper, a supper for unexpected guests, a tailgate picnic, and a barbecue among the sand dunes as dusk falls.

If you want to plan a menu of your own for a particular occasion, there are over 300 recipes in *Outdoor Entertaining* from which to choose. Compile your menu so that the courses complement one another—smooth following crunchy, spicy following mild. Take the recipes given in this book as a starting point. Once you understand their basic principles, you are free to adapt and expand them to suit your own requirements. Most recipes can be scaled up or down, depending on how many guests there are. Almost all the recipes are illustrated and have been specially selected for their simplicity and suitability for outdoor entertaining.

To ensure that your meals under the sun or the stars are every bit as magical as they should be, whatever the occasion and whatever the number of guests, this book provides the recipes and advice to smooth the way to success.

A WELL-STOCKED KITCHEN

One of the most useful assets for the busy cook is a well-stocked pantry filled with indispensable stand-bys, both homemade and purchased, that can be the basis of a meal which can be created in just minutes. *Outdoor Entertaining* includes a chapter of recipes for these essential items.

Always keep a well-stocked liquor cabinet if you entertain frequently. A dash of alcohol in a sauce or marinade can turn the dull into the delicious. Marinades add flavor and variety to foods in one of the simplest ways possible. For more details on the appropriate wines and spirits to drink with your meal, see the chapter on drinks and how to store and serve alcohol.

Another great help to a busy cook are quality kitchen implements. They won't necessarily turn you into a better cook but they will help ensure a good result. Knives should be well maintained and at their sharpest; saucepans should be made from metals for conducting heat evenly without sticking; food processors with juicer, slicer and dough-making attachments are also extremely useful. You don't have to go overboard on gadgets. A microwave oven is useful if you're determined to learn how to use it to its maximum potential, not just as a means of defrosting meat in a hurry. And do check out the many pasta-making machines available if your family thrives on all things Italian.

For successful entertaining you should know your shops and suppliers. A good butcher, fish shop and fruit and vegetable market are worth seeking out, even if they are farther afield than your local shops. Fine food requires fine ingredients, and you're handicapped from the start if you settle for anything less.

Investigate the wealth of specialty international ingredients on your supermarket shelves. There are many intriguing items to be found in Asian and Continental delicatessens that will help broaden your culinary horizons and delight your guests.

COOKING OUT-OF-DOORS

Hot weather and outdoor eating often call for rapid methods of cooking such as stir-frying, sautéing, barbecuing and poaching. This book also gives advice on the best ways to barbecue and the kind of equipment to look for.

Surprising as it may seem, you often don't have to cook at all in order to eat well. A variety of salad ingredients dressed with oil and lemon juice and served with platters of cooked meat and seafood can team up with fruits marinated in liqueur-laced sugar syrup and chilled, whipped cream. Choose the freshest and best fruits of the season and be generous with your servings—fresh air does wonders for the appetite. Concentrate on the kind of meal that is strong on presentation and light on perspiration.

The food that is most pleasing to contemplate is presented stylishly with minimum frills—the beauty and variety of the great outdoors is the finest backdrop of all.

With the obvious exception of spur-of-the-moment meals, it is useful to draw up a step-by-step plan of action so that you can purchase all the necessary items and, except for fresh fruit and vegetables, start preparation ahead of time. For impressive, grand occasions, choose tried and tested recipes—this is not the time to experiment.

Orchestrating the perfect meal does take time and experience, but by building your own "library" of ideas, the process will become simpler and more pleasurable every time. Eating outdoors, whether at home or further afield, presents certain constraints. For picnics, forget about anything that requires last-minute difficult preparation or dishes that are likely to fall apart in transit.

Broiled lamb chops with ratatouille sauce (page 158)

Picnics, one of the most popular forms of outdoor entertaining, require advance planning. Make sure that the menu includes easy-to-handle foods that won't spoil in transit.

Unless you have very well-chilled, insulated containers, seafood will not survive a long, hot journey. Will you be far from a water supply? Take moist towelettes to cope with sticky fingers. And include the necessary sprays and balms for insects.

If you're serving finger food before dinner or around the pool as a meal in itself, make sure it lives up to its name. It should be small, light and compact, easily consumed in one or two bites, with no runny sauces to spoil clothes.

Consider the weather. If it's a very gusty day, clip the edges of the tablecloth in place and don't put anything tall or lightweight that might blow over on the table. If it is

extremely hot, find the coolest spot, set up garden umbrellas and check that your guests aren't going to have the sun baking on their backs or glinting in their eyes. Keep a supply of straw hats, shawls and sunglasses handy if you do a great deal of outdoor entertaining. Guests who have unthinkingly come without their own protection from the elements will thank you for it. And, in the event of a sudden downpour, have your "evacuation plan" worked out for a speedy dash undercover.

Dining outdoors at nighttime is particularly pleasurable but requires a judicious choice of lighting. Candles are wonderful, but not when it's windy, and lights strung through the trees need plenty of advance planning. There should be sufficient light to see what you are eating, but not so much that it defeats the whole point of being outside in the first place. Oil lamps also create a wonderful ambience but they must be positioned with safety in mind.

DISHES AND FLATWARE

The function of table accessories—china, linen, glass and silverware, plants, flowers, and any other decorations—is to enhance the food, not to overwhelm it.

If your budget is limited, simple white china is the best option and shows food off to its best advantage. You can add color with rustic patterned platters and bowls or with bright napkins and cloths. Be careful though as anything too bold can vie for supremacy with the food.

Flowers can be chosen to match or contrast. Make sure that their fragrance, however lovely, does not mask the aroma of the meal. Small plants, candlesticks or small sculptures can replace floral arrangements.

BARBECUES

Barbecue grills have come a long way since the old camp fire and some models now look like very close cousins of the kitchen stove. The new breed of barbecues makes it possible to add succulent roasts, spicy curries, casseroles, seafood and extravagant desserts to your outdoor menu. It was inevitable that the growing interest in different cooking methods should find its way outside and a welcome spin-off is that traditional favorites stand a better chance of being cooked well. There can at last be an end to those blackened steaks, burnt sausages and dried-out chops as people learn to appreciate the art of barbecue cooking.

TYPES OF BARBECUE GRILL

At its most basic, a barbecue grill can comprise an old oven shelf supported by a couple of rocks. To raise or lower the grill, just use larger or smaller rocks. It works perfectly well, so why look further?

Most people buy or build a barbecue to improve on two aspects of their cooking: convenience and control. With prices ranging from tens of dollars to hundreds of dollars, there is a model to suit every budget. The secret to buying wisely is finding a model that offers you the options you want without making you pay for features you will never use—easier said than done when the range available is positively daunting.

The first and most important decision you have to make is whether you want an open barbecue or a covered one. The latter can be used as a conventional barbecue and as an outdoor oven. You also need to consider how many people you will be serving, how important portability is and, of course, whether you prefer to cook with gas or solid fuel.

Open barbecues
These range from the small hibachi type with one, two or three sections to permanent brick or stone constructions. The small portable models are ideal for camping and picnics. Features worth looking for are a sturdy stand to raise the barbecue to table height, a movable wind shield and several height settings for the grill rack. Both solid- and gas-fueled models are available.

Large barbecues may have wheels but can't really be called portable. Many are extremely cumbersome. If you need to be able to move the barbecue in and out of the garage or from one shady spot to another, test drive before you buy. Check the following points: handle comfort, wheels that give adequate ground clearance, and effective gas-bottle restraints (if applicable). If you are buying a gas grill, look for easy-to-use controls and electronic ignition.

Many barbecue grills are designed to provide plenty of worktop and storage space. Barbecues left permanently outside should have a dry compartment for storing fuel, be it a gas bottle, a bag of charcoal or just a pile of wood.

Covered barbecues
Some people have reservations about cooking in a covered barbecue. If it's like an oven, why not use the one in the kitchen? One reason is that, if you are entertaining, it is convenient to be able to cook, eat and socialize in one area—and in summer, when kitchens can get unpleasantly hot, it is more pleasant to do this outdoors. More importantly, you just can't create that same smoky, woody flavor in a conventional oven.

Covered barbecues fall into two categories: the kettle type, which can be fueled either by gas or by charcoal or briquets, and the covered gas grill. Both types can be used like conventional barbecues for direct cooking and like ovens for indirect cooking. There are now even some smaller, very portable kettle barbecues available on the market.

If you are using the kettle as an ordinary barbecue (that is, without the lid), wait until the charcoal is glowing and ash covered, replace the top rack and start cooking. If you are using the kettle as an oven you may have to leave it a further 15 minutes or so to let the heat build up. Some models have a heat indicator but with most, you can gauge the temperature by hand. This is not as painful as it sounds! Hold your hand just above the rack: if you can leave it there for 6 or more seconds, the heat is still low; if you whisk it away after a couple of seconds, it's hot. For best results when cooking indirectly, the fuel is arranged on one side while the food is placed opposite it, on the rack above. This means that the food is cooked by convection, as in an ordinary oven, rather than by radiant heat.

Kettles get very hot when in use so they should be situated at least 2 feet (60 cm) from combustible materials and well away from any traffic area. Always wear oven mitts when removing the lid or adjusting the vents. Some models incorporate hooks on which to hang the lid and utensils when not in use.

Gas barbecue grills can look similar to the charcoal kettle but often have extra refinements like a temperature indicator. Two gas burners at the bottom of the bowl heat lava stones. For direct cooking, the food is placed on the rack over the hot lava rocks; for indirect cooking, one burner is turned off and the food is placed on the cooking rack opposite the heat, above the unlit burner.

Covered gas grills come in many models and the number of burners is the most significant difference. Gas grills are generally bigger than the kettles and, as they are often built into a trolley or table, they provide work and storage space. They may have temperature indicators and some have warming racks, a useful addition doubling as a high shelf for browning foods.

BARBECUE FUELS

There are quite a few different types of barbecue fuel available. Purists maintain that there is simply no substitute for wood; charcoal enthusiasts extol its flavorful virtues; advocates of the briquet praise the enduring heat; gas fans love its instant response. The truth is that no one fuel is better than the other. Each has its advantages and each gives good results, provided it is used properly.

Opposite: Asparagus with olive oil and Parmesan (page 169)

Wood
Cooking over a wood fire always seems to bring out the survival instinct in us all. Apart from the fact that wood is fun to gather (a great way to keep the kids occupied) and often free, there is something wonderfully evocative about the fragrance of wood smoke. Different woods give different smells and flavors. Vine prunings, fruit wood, oak and, of course, hickory and mesquite are all suitable for cooking. More resinous woods like pine and eucalyptus may smell fabulous but can impart a bitter taste to the food. Be wary of wood from old building materials—wood that has been painted or treated can give off poisonous fumes.

Whatever wood you use for fuel, make sure it is truly dry; green or wet wood just won't burn properly. No firestarter should be necessary if you use dry wood—just some scrunched-up paper, twigs for kindling and then the bigger pieces. If you have positioned the fire correctly to let the breeze flow through, the flames should flare up and quickly die down to form embers. Don't be in too much of a hurry to start cooking—if you put food on before all the flames have died down it will be singed on the outside and undercooked in the center. Wait until there is a bed of glowing embers before starting to cook.

Charcoal
Charcoal is made commercially by burning wood slowly with limited oxygen. It has several advantages over wood when it comes to barbecues. It may not be free, but it is readily available and easy to store. It also bypasses the flaming bonfire stage—instead of having a huge pile of wood that burns down to a bed of embers that may or may not be sufficient for your cooking needs, you can calculate exactly how much charcoal you will need. Once it is glowing, charcoal gives off excellent heat. As far as taste goes, charcoal imparts a wood-smoky flavor to foods. If you are cooking foods such as shrimp or mussels that take only a few minutes, you can save the charcoal for future use by pouring water over it.

Its disadvantages are that it can be hard to light—you may have to use a firestarter—and that it may not last long enough to cook large pieces of meat. This problem can be overcome by using charcoal in conjunction with briquets.

Charcoal briquets
Charcoal briquets are made of compressed

Seafood is delicious barbecued whether marinated in wine and herbs (page 137) or served with savory butters (page 145)

charcoal. Because the size, density and flavor imparted vary, it pays to become familiar with particular brands. It is very frustrating to find that the new type you have bought takes a good hour to reach the right temperature while the ones you used before took only 30 minutes. Briquets generally take a while to get going (a firestarter is usually essential) but they also burn for a long time. A 10 lb (5 kg) bag should give about 10 hours of cooking heat. This makes them ideal for marathon barbecue sessions and long-cooking meat cuts but not as practical for faster-cooking foods.

Gas

Gas has truly revolutionized the barbecue. Though it is possible to have a gas barbecue connected to your home's gas line, it is far more common to use bottled liquid propane gas. No matter how romantic the notion of gathering a few bits of wood and cooking a simple meal may be, there is no denying that, at the end of a hard day, turning a knob, pressing an ignition button and having almost instant heat is a great deal easier. Maybe the gas barbecue will never fully simulate the lovely woody taste of a barbecue, but it's coming very close, and it means that even people in a hurry can enjoy the pleasures of food cooked outside.

Most gas barbecues have two or more burners with independent controls, which means that you don't have to heat up the entire cooking area for just one chop. The food is not cooked directly over the gas flame, but over some form of heat distributor. Some models use metal bars coated with porcelain or vitreous enamel to distribute the heat but the more usual material is chunks of natural lava or compressed lava compounds. Meat

Firestarters

The safest and most controllable firestarters are the solid bar types based on kerosene or gasoline. Never be tempted to use these substances in their liquid form, or any other flammable liquids, as they can flare up dangerously. Solid firestarters burn with a hot flame for about 15 minutes and during this time they give off fumes. Do not put the grill rack in place or start cooking until the firestarter has burned out and the charcoal or wood is ash covered.

SMOKING

Lovely smoky flavors can be added to foods cooked in a covered barbecue. Soak chips of fragrant wood or cuttings in a pail of water for about 30 minutes. Throw the soaked chips on the charcoals or lava rocks during the last 15 minutes or so of cooking and cover the grill to intensify the flavor.

OPTIONAL EXTRAS

While it is not strictly necessary to have any special equipment for barbecuing, there are a few utensils that make life easier and safer. Start with a box of long matches to make lighting up as easy as possible. Invest in a couple of pairs of long-handled tongs—one set for moving hot coals and wood around, the other for turning food. Long oven mitts protect arms as well as hands.

A water spray is good for dousing flare-ups on solid fuel barbecues but *should never be used on a gas barbecue*—move the food away from the flame and make a mental note to clean the lava.

Small items of food are more manageable if threaded on skewers. Choose bamboo or wooden-handled skewers as all-metal ones get too hot to touch. Soak bamboo skewers in water for about 30 minutes before use or they will burn. Hinged fish baskets are good for turning fish or several chops or sausages at one time.

Keep your grill rack clean with a combined scraper/spatula. A wire brush is the best tool for cleaning the grill section. A good-size brush for basting is handy, as is a selection of unmeltable, unbreakable plates and bowls. And of course, you need somewhere to put the food and utensils while you cook: if your barbecue does not have work space, a small side table is invaluable.

juices and fats falling onto the hot volcanic rock create steam and smoke that fill the air with the familiar barbecue smell and give flavor to the food. Frequent flare-ups indicate that the distributor needs cleaning. Soak the lava rocks overnight in a bucket of hot water and dishwashing detergent, rinse thoroughly under running water and leave in the sun to dry.

It is always a good idea to keep a spare bottle of gas so you don't run out in the middle of a party. Another option is to buy a cylinder fitted with a gauge, but most people get by with testing the weight of the bottle before starting to cook. You need scales to begin: weigh the bottle when empty and again just after it has been filled up to give you the weight of the gas itself. If you put it on the scales before you start to cook you'll be able to work out how much gas you have used so far and how much remains.

Menus

The following pages include twelve thematic menus designed to inspire ideas for outdoor entertaining—from casual backyard affairs and picnics to more sophisticated suppers and meals with a more exotic flavor.

Besides providing a menu of recipes suitable for the occasion, accompanying photographs show you how to set the scene with table settings, flowers, furnishings and, where appropriate, lighting.

Page references are given for all the recipes. Under the twelve miniature photographs are references to the pages where the photographs are shown full size.

Photograph pages 22–23

A Picnic in the Country

Veal and Wine Terrine—page 46

❖

Grapefruit and Watercress Salad—page 80
Wild Rice Salad—page 87

Chicken Thighs Stuffed with Leeks and Cream Cheese—page 135

❖

Apple and Poppy Seed Cake—page 197

Photograph pages 40–41

Tailgate Picnic

Mediterranean Layered Bread—page 64

❖

Potato and Egg Salad in Creamy Dressing—page 87

Beet and Emmenthaler Salad—page 84

Marinated Peppercorn and Mustard Beef with Horseradish Mayonnaise—page 151

❖

Pear and Raspberry Pie—page 220

Photograph pages 58–59

Mexican Fiesta

Chili Corn Soup—page 56

❖

Guacamole—page 50

Nachos—page 73

Beef Tacos—page 73

Mexican Rice—page 102

Stuffed Chili Peppers—page 170

❖

Mexican Flan—page 214

Photograph pages 90–91

Beach Barbecue

Lemon–Ginger Shrimp—page 49

❖

*Red Onion Salad with Avocado
Dressing—page 87*

Sherried Noodle and Cashew Salad—page 104

Corn-on-the-Cob with Sweet Butter—page 175

*Marinated Whole Trout with Olives and
Chili—page 122*

Marinated Honeyed Pork Spareribs—page 156

Photograph pages 74–75

Italian Supper

Eggplant Appetizer—page 52

Roasted Bell Peppers—page 53

Marinated Olives—page 52

❖

Onion and Herb Frittata—page 55

❖

*Spinach and Radicchio Salad with Anchovy
Dressing—page 84*

*Sun-dried Tomato and Pasta Salad with
Pesto Dressing—page 87*

Squab with Ricotta and Herbs— page 134

❖

Zuccotto—page 217

Photograph pages 106–107

Boating Fare

Marinated Octopus—page 113

❖

*Arugula Salad with Caper and Olive
Dressing—page 88*

Marinated Tuna with Fried Vegetables—page 112

Marinated Beets—page 178

Pickled Cucumber—page 178

Marinated Red Onions—page 178

❖

Pumpkin Pie—page 215

Photograph pages 124–25

Family Supper

Apple and Parsley Salad with Tomato
Dressing—page 84

Bacon and Asparagus Salad—page 79

Turkey, Leek and Potato Pie—page 138

❖

Caramel–Nut Self-saucing Pudding—page 218

Photograph pages 164–65

Supper for Unexpected Guests

Artichoke Hearts with Bacon—page 168

❖

Pear Salad with Walnuts and Blue
Cheese—page 79

Tagliatelle with Lemon and Parsley—page 97

❖

Mocha Zabaglione—page 222

Photograph pages 140–41

Garden Barbecue for Twenty

Avocado and Mushroom Salad—page 80

Festive Coleslaw—page 84

Curried Mango Rice Salad—page 80

Marinated Steaks with Savory
Butters—page 145

Sausages Marinated in Beer—page 147

Olive and Herb Bread—page 190

Cheese and Scallion Bread—page 190

❖

Wild Berry and Apricot Trifle—page 209

Photograph pages 184–85

Romantic Dinner for Two

Seafood in Saffron and Lemon Sauce with
Salmon Roe—page 120

❖

Filet of Beef with Red Wine and Pear—page 150

Crisp Potato Cakes—page 175

Braised Scallions—page 178

❖

Individual Chocolate Truffle Cakes—page 202

Photograph pages 204–205

Weekend Brunch

Photograph pages 226–27

Poolside Snacks for a Crowd

*Photograph on following pages, "A Picnic in the Country," from left: apple and poppy seed cake (page 197); grapefruit
and watercress salad (page 80); veal and wine terrine (page 46);   chicken thighs stuffed with leeks and cream cheese
(page 135); wild rice salad (page 87)*

The Pantry

Behind every prudent cook there is often a well-stocked pantry with many useful ingredients that can quickly be transformed into an impromptu meal when guests arrive unexpectedly or decide to stay late, or for those times when cooking is the last thing you feel like doing.

A garlic or lemon mayonnaise can be quickly pressed into service as a dip with shrimp fresh from the market, or with slivers of rare roast beef. Thick, fruity jams and preserves make an instant dessert when spooned into the little pastry shells kept on stand-by in the freezer, and chocolate sauce can dress up good-quality, store-bought ice cream. A piquant spice mixture, finely ground, retains its wonderful flavors for many months when stored in an airtight container. Use it generously to turn a motley selection of vegetables into an aromatic stir-fry.

When you have time to spare, take the trouble to stock your pantry shelves with flavored oils and vinegars, preserved fruits and sauces of all descriptions. Then, when you need to transform basic ingredients at short notice, you can rise to the occasion with a flourish.

The simplest repast can please the palate and the eye. Our enjoyment of food has a lot to do with how we present it. Arrange thinly sliced prosciutto fashioned into rolls or fans on a boldly patterned plate and serve with pickled vegetables from your pantry and a variety of unusual breads.

Opposite, clockwise from front: tapenade (page 36); oven-dried tomatoes (page 35); oven-dried zucchini (page 36); garlic in balsamic vinegar (page 27); rosemary oil (page 28); feta in olive oil (page 37)

Rosemary Vinegar

Use in marinades—especially for lamb—or for deglazing pans for sauces, or salad dressings.

3 rosemary sprigs
2 cups (16 fl oz/500 ml) champagne vinegar
2 tablespoons honey

Makes 2 cups (16 fl oz/500 ml)

Crush the rosemary sprigs slightly and gently tuck into sterilized bottles. (Slightly crushing the rosemary sprigs helps to release the volatile oils, thus enhancing the flavor.) Heat the vinegar and honey over low heat and stir to dissolve. Cool and pour into the bottles. Stand the bottles in a sunny spot for a few weeks before using. Will keep indefinitely.

Blueberry Vinegar

4 cups (1 lb/500 g) blueberries
2 cups (16 fl oz/500 ml) white wine vinegar
1³/₄ cups (12 oz/375 g) sugar

Makes 2¹/₂ cups (20 fl oz/625 ml)

Stir a little thick coconut cream into mayonnaise to serve with freshly cooked shrimp. Coconut cream is also good when spread onto pork chops for barbecuing.

Put blueberries and vinegar into a jar with a plastic lid. Cover and leave in a dark place for 1 week, giving the jar a shake every day. Strain through a fine sieve or double layer of dampened cheesecloth or muslin into a saucepan. Add sugar, stir and bring slowly to a boil. Simmer for 10 minutes. Cool and pour into sterilized bottles. Will keep indefinitely.

Chili Vinegar

Use for chutneys, pickles or dressings, or use a little bit to add heat and tang to sauces.

12 small red chilis
3 large shreds lemon zest
2 cups (16 fl oz/500 ml) white wine vinegar

Makes 2 cups (16 fl oz/500 ml)

Place chilis and lemon zest in a bottle. Top with vinegar, seal and store in a dark cupboard for 2 weeks. The more chilis used, the hotter this vinegar will be; if you prefer a milder vinegar, use fewer chilis.

Raspberry Vinegar

This vinegar used to be drunk as a cordial. You can sprinkle it on a fruit salad or a fresh berry mixture served with heavy (double) cream.

2 cups (8 oz/250 g) raspberries
1¹/₂ cups (12 fl oz/375 ml) white wine vinegar
1¹/₂ cups (10¹/₂ oz/330 g) sugar

Makes 2 cups (16 fl oz/500 ml)

In a big china or glass bowl, combine raspberries and vinegar. Cover and allow to sit for at least 24 hours. Strain the liquid through a double layer of dampened cheesecloth or muslin. Do not press on the solids or the vinegar will not be clear. Discard solids, reserving any raspberries for decoration.

Place liquid in a large pan and add sugar. Stir to dissolve sugar. Bring to a boil and simmer for 10 minutes. Remove from heat and cool. Decorate with any reserved raspberries and pour into sterilized bottles and seal. Will keep indefinitely.

From left: raspberry vinegar; mustard–pepper oil (page 28); chili vinegar; blueberry vinegar; garlic olive oil; rosemary vinegar; red bell pepper oil (page 28)

Garlic in Balsamic Vinegar

Serve with antipasti, chopped in salads or dressings, or chopped and combined with oil for cooking meats.

2 cups garlic cloves (approx. 40 cloves), peeled
1 cup (8 fl oz/250 ml) balsamic vinegar

Makes 1¹/2 cups (12 fl oz/375 ml)

Combine ingredients in a saucepan. Bring to a boil and let simmer for 25–30 minutes. Pour into a sterilized jar and seal. Will keep for up to 1 month in the refrigerator (photograph page 24).

Garlic Olive Oil

Use as bruschetta spread brushed on a slice of bread and topped with diced tomatoes, fresh herbs and cracked black pepper, or for garlic croûtons.

6 garlic cloves, bruised
4 cups (1 qt/1 l) olive oil

Makes 4 cups (1 qt/1 l)

Place bruised garlic and oil in a saucepan. Heat until mixture is aromatic and just warm to the touch. Cool and pour the oil into bottles with the garlic cloves. Seal.

Red Bell Pepper Oil

Use for frying, stir-frying or basting, or in salad dressings.

6 red bell peppers
6 cups (1¹/₂ qt/1.5 l) vegetable oil (or other oil of
your choice)

Makes 6 cups (1¹/2 qt/1.5 l)

Extract juice from bell peppers in a juice extractor. Place juice in a saucepan, bring to a boil and simmer for 30 minutes, or until juice becomes thick and syrupy and has been reduced by half. Pour into the bowl of a food processor or blender, with motor running slowly, and add the oil. Strain mixture through a double layer of dampened cheesecloth or muslin—do not press on solids but allow oil to drip through slowly. Cover and store. Will keep indefinitely (photograph pages 26–27).

Rosemary Oil

Good for dressing salads, basting meats, or with sautéed lamb fillets.

1 bunch rosemary (about 8 sprigs)
4 cups (1 qt/1 l) olive oil

Makes 4 cups (1 qt/1 l)

Wash and dry rosemary thoroughly. Remove leaves and place in the bowl of a food processor. With the motor running, add oil slowly and process until plant fiber breaks up and purée is smooth.

Heat mixture very gently for 20 minutes. Strain through a double layer of dampened cheesecloth or muslin. Do not press on solids but allow oil to drip through slowly. Will keep indefinitely (photograph page 24).

Basil Pesto

Can be heated and served with pasta, stirred into a ratatouille or used as a layer in lasagne.

1 large bunch basil
2 garlic cloves, chopped
¹/₄ cup (2 oz/60 g) pine nuts
³/₄ cup (6 fl oz/185 ml) olive oil
¹/₂ cup (2 oz/60 g) grated Parmesan cheese

Makes 1¹/2 cups (12 fl oz/375 ml)

Remove basil leaves from stems, handling as little as possible to prevent leaves from discoloring. Place leaves, garlic, pine nuts and oil in a food processor and process for 20 seconds. Scrape down the sides of the bowl and process for another 10 seconds. Add the Parmesan and blend to combine. Cover and refrigerate in a glass bowl for 2 hours to allow flavors to develop. Taste for salt before serving. Will keep for up to 1 week in refrigerator.

Mustard–Pepper Oil

Use in marinades, for cooking meats, or in mayonnaise.

1 tablespoon yellow mustard seeds
1 tablespoon black mustard seeds
1 tablespoon black peppercorns
4 cups (1 qt/1 l) olive oil

Makes 4 cups (1 qt/1 l)

Heat mustard seeds and peppercorns in a heavy-based pan until aromatic. Add to oil. Pour into bottles and seal. Will keep indefinitely (photograph pages 26–27).

Chili Paste

Use this paste in recipes that call for fresh chilis. Use sparingly as it is very hot!

3 small onions, in their skins
6 garlic cloves, unpeeled
15 small red chilis
1 tablespoon sugar
2 tablespoons vegetable oil

Makes ²/₃ cup (5 fl oz/155 ml)

Preheat oven to 350°F (180°C).

Place onions and garlic, in their skins, onto a baking sheet. Bake for 30 minutes. Remove from oven, cool, then discard skins and roughly chop. Chop chilis roughly.

Place the onions, garlic, chilis and sugar in a food processor and process into a smooth paste (if necessary, add some oil to help bind ingredients together).

Fry the paste in the remaining oil in a small saucepan and cook for 15 minutes, stirring occasionally so the paste doesn't stick or burn. Store in a sterilized jar with a tight-fitting lid. Keeps for several months in refrigerator.

Green Curry Paste

Use in Thai curries.

2 tablespoons roughly chopped lemon grass
1 piece (2 in/5 cm) galangal, chopped and
    soaked for 30 minutes
3 garlic cloves, roughly chopped
¹/₃ bunch fresh coriander (cilantro), including
    the root and stem, roughly chopped
1 teaspoon grated lemon or lime zest
7 long green chilis (or 15 small green chilis)
1 teaspoon ground coriander
1 teaspoon ground cumin
1 teaspoon shrimp paste
2 bay leaves
black pepper
salt
2 tablespoons vegetable oil

Makes 1 cup (8 fl oz/250 ml)

Place all ingredients in a blender and blend to a smooth paste, using extra oil if necessary. Place into a jar with a screw-top lid and store in the refrigerator for up to 3 weeks. Alternatively, place half in the fridge and freeze the rest, as you need only about 1 tablespoon per recipe.

Coriander Pesto

Serve with grilled fish or with steaks as a condiment.

2 large bunches fresh coriander (cilantro)
¹/₄ cup (2¹/₂ oz/75 g) pepitas (edible pumpkin seeds)
2 garlic cloves, chopped
2 tablespoons lime juice
¹/₂ cup (4 fl oz/125 ml) olive oil
¹/₂ cup (2 oz/60 g) grated Parmesan cheese

Makes 1 cup (8 fl oz/250 ml)

Remove leaves from coriander stems. Place leaves, pepitas, garlic, lime juice and oil in a food processor and process for 20 seconds. Scrape down the sides of the bowl and process for another 10 seconds. Add the Parmesan and blend to combine. Cover and refrigerate in a glass bowl. Taste for salt before serving. Will keep for up to 1 week in refrigerator.

Clockwise from front: chili paste; green curry paste; basil pesto; onion confit (page 37); satay sauce (page 32); coriander pesto

Garam masala

Mayonnaise

6 egg yolks
2 teaspoons Dijon mustard
1 tablespoon lemon juice
salt and white pepper
1 cup (8 fl oz/250 ml) olive oil
1 cup (8 fl oz/250 ml) peanut oil

Makes 2¹/₂ cups (20 fl oz/625 ml)

Place egg yolks, mustard, lemon juice, salt and pepper in the bowl of a food processor. Process for 1 minute. Combine the 2 oils and, with motor running, gradually add the oil in a thin steady stream and process until mayonnaise is thick. Store in a jar and seal. Will keep in refrigerator for 2 weeks (photograph pages 36–37).
NOTE: For watercress-flavored mayonnaise take 2 cups (2 oz/60 g) watercress leaves and 1 quantity of the above mayonnaise recipe. Place watercress leaves in boiling, salted water. Leave for 1 minute (or until water reboils) and drain. Place in ice-cold water. Drain thoroughly, pressing out excess water. Blend until it is a smooth purée and either stir into mayonnaise or blend in while mayonnaise is in the processor.

Béarnaise Mayonnaise

This mayonnaise goes well with chicken salads.

1 cup (8 fl oz/250 ml) mayonnaise, preferably homemade
1 tablespoon Dijon mustard
1 garlic clove, finely chopped
1 tablespoon finely chopped scallions (spring onions)

1 tablespoon lemon juice
3 tablespoons chopped fresh tarragon
1 tablespoon tarragon vinegar
black pepper to taste

Makes 1½ cups (12 fl oz/375 ml)

Combine all ingredients and mix well. Chill to allow flavors to blend. Will keep for 2 weeks refrigerated (photograph pages 36–37).

Garam Masala

¾ cup (2⅓ oz/75 g) coriander seeds
⅓ cup (1½ oz/45 g) cumin seeds
⅓ cup (2 oz/60 g) black peppercorns
18 whole cloves
seeds from 20 green cardamom pods
2 cinnamon sticks
½ nutmeg, grated

Makes 1 cup (8 oz/250 g)

Spread the coriander seeds, cumin seeds and peppercorns in a baking pan and toast in a hot oven for about 8 minutes, or until aromatic. Transfer to a spice grinder and grind to a fine powder. Place in a jar.

Add the remaining spices to the grinder and grind finely. Mix with the first batch, close the container and shake vigorously to mix thoroughly. Will keep for 2–3 months.

NOTE: For maximum freshness, store in an airtight jar in the refrigerator.

Chicken Stock

This stock makes an excellent base for any soup or sauce.

1 chicken (4–5 lb/2–2.5 kg)
3 qt (3 l) water
1 tablespoon salt
2 medium yellow onions, chopped
4 stalks celery, including leaves, chopped
3 large carrots, peeled and chopped
1 cup (1 oz/30 g) loosely packed parsley leaves
6 peppercorns

Makes 2½ qt (2.5 l)

Rinse chicken and trim off any excess fat. Cut chicken into quarters and place in a large pot. Add water and salt. Cover and bring to a boil. Uncover and skim off any scum. Add onions, celery, carrots, parsley and peppercorns. Simmer for 1½ hours, occasionally removing any scum. Remove chicken from pot and reserve for another use. Strain the rest of the liquid. Cool and refrigerate or freeze. Remove any solidified fat before using. Will keep in refrigerator for up to 3 days or, if frozen, will keep indefinitely.

Beef Stock

This stock makes an excellent base for sauces for meat.

4 lb (2 kg) beef bones, preferably meaty ones
½ cup (4 fl oz/125 ml) oil
4 onions, finely chopped
2 leeks, chopped
2 large carrots, chopped
3 stalks celery, including leaves, chopped
1½ tablespoons dried thyme
4 bay leaves
12 black peppercorns
1 cup (1 oz/30 g) parsley leaves, loosely packed
2 teaspoons salt
½ cup (4 fl oz/125 ml) tomato paste
water as needed

Makes 2–3 qt (2–3 l)

Preheat oven to 400°F (200°C).

Spread bones in a single layer on a large baking sheet. Bake for 1½ hours, turning occasionally.

Heat oil in a large pot. Add onions, leeks, carrots and celery and cook over high heat, stirring often. Add browned bones and remaining ingredients.

Pour 1 cup (8 fl oz/250 ml) water into pan in which bones were cooked; scrape caramelized parts from base and sides.

Add water and meat particles to stock. Add additional water to cover all ingredients. Set pot over medium heat, bring to a boil and simmer for 4 hours, skimming occasionally. Strain and discard solids. Cool and refrigerate or freeze. Remove any solidified fat before using. Will keep up to 3 days in the refrigerator or, if frozen, will keep indefinitely.

Fish Stock

This stock makes an excellent base for a hearty fish soup.

½ cup (4 oz/125 g) butter
2 carrots, peeled and chopped
1 large onion, chopped
bones and heads of 2 white-fleshed fish
6 peppercorns
1 bay leaf
1 small bunch parsley
½ cup (4 fl oz/125 ml) white wine
water to cover

Makes 2 qt (2 l)

Heat the butter in a large saucepan and gently cook carrots and onion for 20 minutes. Add fish bones and heads, peppercorns, bay leaf, parsley, and wine, and enough water to cover. Bring to a boil and simmer for 30 minutes only. Strain through dampened cheesecloth or muslin, refrigerate and use within 3 days. If frozen, will keep indefinitely.

Apricot–Strawberry Sauce

Serve with ice cream, or as an accompaniment to an almond or sponge cake.

¹/₂ cup (4 oz/125 g) sugar
³/₄ cup (6 fl oz/185 ml) water
8 fresh apricots, pitted and chopped
1 tablespoon fresh lemon juice
1 cup (4 oz/125 g) chopped strawberries

Makes 1¹/₂ cups (12 fl oz/375 ml)

In a large saucepan, combine the sugar and water. Stir over heat to dissolve sugar. Bring to a boil and simmer for 5 minutes. Add the apricots and cook mixture at a slow boil, stirring occasionally, for about 15 minutes, or until apricots are soft and fall apart. Transfer the mixture to a food processor and process until mixture is a smooth purée. Sieve.

In a saucepan, combine resulting purée with lemon juice and bring to a boil. Add strawberries and simmer for 1 minute, being careful not to let the strawberries fall apart. Transfer the mixture to a bowl, let cool then refrigerate. Serve cold. Will keep in the refrigerator for 3 days (photograph page 34).

Chocolate Sauce

Serve cold with ice cream, or warm with a chocolate fudge cake or brownies.

1 cup (8 fl oz/250 ml) heavy (double) cream
1 tablespoon (¹/₂ oz/15 g) unsalted butter
4 squares (4 oz/125 g) semisweet cooking
  chocolate, chopped
1 tablespoon dark rum, brandy or liqueur of
  your choice

Makes 1¹/₂ cups (12 fl oz/375 ml)

Bring cream and butter to a boil in a small saucepan. Add chocolate and rum, remove from heat and stir until chocolate is melted. Will keep in refrigerator for 3 days but is best served immediately (photograph page 34).

Lemon Sauce

This sauce is tangy and light. It is delicious served with a fresh sponge cake filled with jam and cream.

3 eggs
1 cup (8 oz/250 g) sugar
2 teaspoons freshly grated lemon zest
¹/₂ cup (4 fl oz/125 ml) fresh lemon juice
1 cup (8 fl oz/250 ml) water
pinch salt

Makes 2 cups (16 fl oz/500 ml)

Beat eggs in a large bowl until foamy; add the sugar in a stream and continue beating mixture for 3 minutes or until thick and pale. Transfer the egg mixture to the top of a double boiler. Whisk together the egg mixture, zest and juice, water and salt. Set bowl over boiling water and whisk gently for 10 minutes, cooking the mixture until it thickens around edge. Transfer mixture to a bowl to cool. Cover and refrigerate. Will keep in the refrigerator for 3 days (photograph page 34).

Fresh Tomato Sauce

Add to stews and casseroles instead of stock. Thin with stock or cream to serve hot or cold as a soup. Serve over pasta, or use as the base of pasta sauces, adding meatballs, seafood, olives, etc.

1 medium onion
2¹/₂ tablespoons olive oil
3 garlic cloves, finely chopped
5 large, very red tomatoes
1 tablespoon finely chopped parsley
1 teaspoon chopped oregano
³/₄ teaspoon salt
¹/₂ teaspoon black pepper

Makes 2 cups (16 fl oz/500 ml)

Very finely chop the onion and sauté in the oil until softened and only lightly golden. Add the garlic when almost done. In the meantime, drop the tomatoes into a pan of simmering water, leave for about 10 seconds, then remove with a slotted spoon and peel. Cut the tomatoes in halves and squeeze out the seeds, then chop finely. Add to the onions and cook gently until reduced to a pulp, stirring frequently. Add the herbs and seasonings. Pass through a sieve or purée in a food processor; then sieve to make a smooth sauce. Will keep in the refrigerator for up to 5 days.
NOTE: Can be frozen in small plastic containers of no more than 1¹/₂ cup (12 fl oz/375 ml) capacity.

Satay Sauce

Serve with barbecued beef or chicken skewers, or as a dip with crudités.

1 cup (8 oz/250 g) finely crushed peanuts
1¹/₂ tablespoons olive oil
1 medium onion, finely chopped
1 garlic clove, finely chopped
2 teaspoons curry paste or powder
2 small red chilis, finely chopped
1 tablespoon soy sauce
1 tablespoon lemon juice
2 cups (16 fl oz/500 ml) water

Makes 2 cups (16 fl oz/500 ml)

Always keep some empty 12 fl oz (375 ml) wine bottles in the kitchen. If you have half a bottle of wine left over, instead of putting the cork back and leaving the wine in contact with half a bottle of air (which will cause it to deteriorate quickly), fill the smaller bottle, lessening the air space.

Place crushed peanuts in bowl of a food processor and process until very finely chopped. Heat oil in large heavy-based pan, add onion and garlic and cook for 1 minute. Add curry paste, and cook until aromatic. Add peanuts and cook for 2 minutes, stirring continuously. Add chilis, soy sauce, lemon juice and water. Bring to a boil and simmer uncovered for 15 minutes (photograph pages 28–29).

Sweet Chili and Garlic Sauce

Serve with broiled or roasted meats, fried or steamed snacks, or cold meats such as ham, pork and chicken. Stir a little into mayonnaise or salad dres-sings. Add to gravy or hot sauces.

4 large garlic cloves
1 large red chili
¹/₂ cup (4 fl oz/125 ml) white vinegar
²/₃ cup (5 oz/155 g) sugar
¹/₂ cup (4 oz/125 g) plum jam
1 tablespoon cornstarch (cornflour)
1¹/₂ tablespoons water

Makes 1¹/₂ cups (12 fl oz/375 ml)

In a food processor or blender, chop the garlic and chili. Transfer to a small saucepan and add the remaining ingredients. Boil until smooth, stirring frequently. Cool, then pour into a tightly capped bottle. Will keep for several weeks in the refrigerator.

From left: fresh tomato sauce; sweet chili and garlic sauce

Crème Fraîche

Clockwise from front:
tartlet shells (page 38)
with crème fraîche;
lemon sauce (page 32);
apricot–strawberry
sauce (page 32);
blackberry jam; apricot
jam; brandy fruit
liqueurs (page 38);
chocolate sauce (page
32); sugar cookies
(page 38)

Crème fraîche is a cream that naturally thickens itself. Fill tartlet shells with it and top with fresh fruit.

1¼ cups (10 fl oz/300 ml) heavy (double) cream
2 tablespoons buttermilk

Makes 1½ cups (12 fl oz/375 ml)

Combine the cream and buttermilk in a screw-top jar. Cover tightly and shake for 1 minute. Let stand at room temperature until mixture becomes thick—about 6–9 hours. Will keep up to 1 week in the refrigerator.

Apricot Jam

3 lb (1.5 kg) apricots, pitted
2 cups (16 fl oz/500 ml) water
2 tablespoons lemon juice
2 lb (1 kg) sugar

Makes 6 1-cup (8 fl oz/250 ml) jars

Place apricots, water and lemon juice in a large saucepan. Bring to a boil and simmer for 20 minutes. Add sugar and stir to dissolve. Bring to a boil and boil vigorously until jam reaches the desired consistency—about 20 minutes. Stir continuously to prevent jam from sticking and burning.

Blackberry Jam

4 cups (1 lb/500 g) blackberries
2 cups (1 lb/500 g) sugar
¹/₂ cup (4 fl oz/125 ml) lemon juice

Makes 3 1-cup (8 fl oz/250 ml) jars

Combine ingredients in a large, heavy-based saucepan. Stir over low heat to dissolve sugar. Cook at a slow boil for 30 minutes, or until jam is thick and at desired consistency. Will keep indefinitely.

Red Currant and Rosemary Jelly

This jelly is delicious with lamb roasts or spread on leftover lamb sandwiches. It adds flavor to sauces or marinades for meat (add 1 or 2 teaspoons) or you can rub it over lamb before barbecuing.

2¹/₄ cups (1 lb/500 g) red currants
leaves from 5 rosemary sprigs
¹/₄ cup (2 fl oz/60 ml) water
¹/₃ cup (3 fl oz/90 ml) cider vinegar
1 cup (8 oz/250 g) sugar

Makes 1 cup (8 fl oz/250 ml)

Place red currants and rosemary leaves in a saucepan with water. Bring to a boil and simmer for 10 minutes. Strain through a double layer of dampened cheesecloth or muslin. (Do not press or force liquid through.)

Combine vinegar and sugar in a saucepan over heat. Stir to dissolve the sugar. Add red currant juice. Bring to a boil, boil slowly for 5 minutes and then simmer until jelly thickens. Pour into a sterilized jar, cool and seal. Will keep indefinitely (photograph pages 36–37).

Sweet Mango Chutney

Use with cold meats or add 1 or 2 tablespoons to curry.

2 mangoes
2 tablespoons salt
water to cover
2 cups (16 oz/500 g) sugar
2¹/₂ cups (20 fl oz/600 ml) white vinegar
1 piece (2 in/5 cm) fresh ginger, peeled and finely chopped
6 garlic cloves, finely chopped
1 teaspoon chili flakes
²/₃ cup (3¹/₂ oz/100 g) chopped, pitted dates
²/₃ cup (3¹/₂ oz/100 g) raisins

Makes 3 1-cup (8 fl oz/250 ml) jars

Peel and chop the mangoes. Place in a bowl with salt. Pour in enough water to cover and let stand for 2–3 hours. Strain, discarding the liquid.

Place sugar and vinegar in a saucepan and bring to a boil, stirring until sugar has dissolved. Add mangoes to the sugar–vinegar syrup with all remaining ingredients and bring to a boil. Reduce heat and simmer for about 1¹/₂ hours, stirring occasionally, or until chutney is of a thick consistency. Ladle the chutney into warm, sterilized jars. Cool and seal. Will keep indefinitely (photograph pages 36–37).

Lemon Chutney

Can be used with any cold meats.

4 medium onions
6 medium lemons
2 tablespoons salt
2¹/₂ cups (20 fl oz/600 ml) cider vinegar
5 small red chilis
¹/₄ cup (2 oz/60 g) mustard seeds
2 cups (16 oz/500 g) sugar
1 cup (5 oz/155 g) raisins

Makes 3 1-cup (8 fl oz/250 ml) jars

Peel and chop onions finely. Wash lemons and cut into small pieces, removing all the pips. Place onions and lemons in a bowl and sprinkle with salt. Allow to stand overnight. Drain.

Combine all ingredients in a heavy-based saucepan. Bring to a boil. Simmer for about 1 hour, or until chutney is thick and full of flavor. Spoon into sterilized jars, cool and seal. Store for 1 week before using. Will keep indefinitely (photograph pages 36–37).

Oven-dried Tomatoes

Use in salads, antipasti platters or sandwiches. The oil assumes the delicious flavor of the tomatoes, so keep it and use it as you would a good quality olive oil. Especially good for dressings.

2 lb (1 kg) firm ripe plum tomatoes
sea salt
olive oil

Makes 2 cups (16 fl oz/500 ml)

Cut tomatoes in half lengthwise and place onto a wire rack, cut-side up. Sprinkle with salt. Leave for 4 hours. Resprinkle with salt and turn tomatoes over. Leave for another 2 hours. Place the tomatoes in a very low 220°F (100°C) oven for 3–4 hours, or until the tomatoes are dried but not shriveled and burnt. Will keep indefinitely if packed into a sterilized jar and kept covered with olive oil (photograph page 24).

Use fruit as a centerpiece in place of flowers. Or, try an arrangement of attractive stones or shells in a bowl. Only have a centerpiece if space allows.

Oven-dried Zucchini

Use in sandwiches or as part of an antipasti platter.

1 lb (500 g) small tender zucchinis (courgettes)
sea salt
olive oil

Makes 1 cup (8 fl oz/250 ml)

Slice zucchinis and place onto a wire rack. Sprinkle with salt; leave for 3 hours. Turn over and resprinkle with salt. Leave for another 2 hours. Rinse zucchinis and pat dry. Place in a very low oven (220°F/100°C). Bake for 2 hours, or until dry but not shriveled and burnt. Will keep indefinitely if packed into a sterilized jar and kept covered with olive oil (photograph page 24).

Tapenade

Use as a bruschetta spread or as a pizza base.

1¹/₂ cups (7 oz/220 g) pitted black olives in brine,
*   patted dry*
5 anchovy fillets
¹/₄ cup (2 oz/60 g) canned tuna (preferably
*   packed in oil), drained*
3 tablespoons capers
3 tablespoons extra-virgin olive oil

Makes 1¹/₂ cups (12 oz/375 g)

Place olives in bowl of food processor. Purée until smooth. Add anchovies, tuna, capers and oil. Process for 25 seconds. Will keep refrigerated for 1 week (photograph page 24).

Clockwise from left: pickled vegetables; béarnaise mayonnaise (page 30); mayonnaise (page 30); sweet mango chutney (page 35); lemon chutney (page 35); muesli (page 38); red currant and rosemary jelly (page 35); spiced nuts (page 38); pretzel crackers (page 39)

Preserved Fresh Herbs

A supply of preserved herbs is especially good in winter when supplies of fresh ones are limited.

In a jar with a tight-fitting lid, place alternate layers of coarse-grained salt with the herbs of your choice that have been cleaned with a towel (do not wash them), ending with a layer of salt. Seal the jar and refrigerate. Wash herbs before cooking. Will keep indefinitely.

Pickled Vegetables

³/₄ cup (8 oz/250 g) small cauliflower florets
³/₄ cup (6 oz/185 g) small broccoli florets
¹/₂ cup (2¹/₂ oz /75 g) sliced, peeled carrots

¹/₄ cup (1¹/₂ oz /45 g) chopped green beans
¹/₄ cup (1¹/₂ oz /45 g) chopped red bell pepper
¹/₄ cup (1¹/₂ oz /45 g) chopped yellow bell pepper
1¹/₂ medium stalks celery, sliced
¹/₃ cup (¹/₂ oz/15 g) sliced fennel
1¹/₂ cups (12 fl oz/375 ml) white vinegar
1 cup (8 fl oz/250 ml) water
³/₄ cup (6 oz/185 g) sugar
3 bay leaves
1 teaspoon black mustard seeds
1 teaspoon white mustard seeds
1 tablespoon chopped red chilis

Makes 3 cups (24 fl oz/750 ml)

Bring a large saucepan of salted water to a boil. Blanch all vegetables separately, using a slotted spoon to remove to a bowl of very cold water. Drain the vegetables and pat dry. Spoon vegetables into a sterilized jar.

Combine vinegar, water, sugar, bay leaves and mustard seeds in a pan. Set over heat and stir to dissolve sugar. Bring to a boil, reduce heat, add chilis and simmer for 5 minutes. Pour vinegar mixture into jar to cover vegetables completely. Cool and seal.

Feta in Olive Oil

2 tablespoons finely chopped red bell pepper
2 tablespoons finely chopped yellow bell pepper
¹/₃ cup (¹/₂ oz/15 g) chopped fresh herbs
  (rosemary, tarragon, thyme)
freshly ground black pepper
1¹/₂ lb (750 g) feta cheese, cut into pieces
1¹/₂ cups (12 fl oz/375 ml) light olive oil

Makes 3 cups (1¹/₂ lb/750 g)

Dry the bell peppers completely by placing them between 2 pieces of cloth and pressing out moisture. Place herbs, pepper and bell peppers in a bowl and combine. Roll each piece of feta in the herb mixture. Fill a sterilized jar with the feta, sprinkling in the extra herb mixture. Top with olive oil. Cover and refrigerate. Will keep for 2 weeks (photograph page 24).

Onion Confit

Use as a condiment for barbecued steak and chicken.

¹/₄ cup (2 fl oz/60 ml) olive oil
3 red (Spanish) onions, thinly sliced
1 teaspoon sugar
2 tablespoons balsamic vinegar

Makes 1¹/₂ cups (12 fl oz/375 ml)

Heat olive oil in a heavy-based pan. Add onions and cook gently until soft. Add sugar and balsamic vinegar and simmer for 10 minutes. Cover and refrigerate. Will keep for 3 days covered in refrigerator. Return to room temperature or reheat before use (photograph pages 28–29).

Brandy Fruit Liqueurs

Use for a quick dessert with fresh cream or to fill pastry shells.

²⁄₃ cup (4 oz/125 g) dried figs
²⁄₃ cup (4 oz/125 g) dried pears
³⁄₄ cup (5 oz/155 g) dried peaches
¹⁄₂ cup (3 oz/90 g) dried apples
1 cup (6 oz/185 g) prunes
¹⁄₂ cup (3 oz/90 g) raisins
²⁄₃ cup (4 oz/125 g) apricots, peeled, pitted and chopped
1 vanilla bean
3 cups (24 fl oz/750 ml) brandy

Makes 1 qt (1 l)

Fill jar with fruits and vanilla bean. Cover completely with brandy. Seal and store in a dark cupboard for at least 2 weeks—the longer, the better. If you prefer a sweeter brandy, add sugar to taste. Will keep indefinitely: keep adding more fruit and brandy as needed (photograph page 34).

Spiced Nuts

¹⁄₂ cup (2 oz/60 g) pecan halves
¹⁄₂ cup (2 oz/60 g) walnut halves
¹⁄₃ cup (1¹⁄₂ oz/45 g) unsalted cashews
¹⁄₃ cup (1¹⁄₂ oz/45 g) unsalted peanuts
2 tablespoons vegetable oil
1 teaspoon curry powder
¹⁄₂ teaspoon chili powder
salt to taste

Makes 1¹⁄₂ cups (12 oz/375 g)

Preheat oven to 350°F (180°C).

Combine nuts in a large bowl. Heat oil in a pan over moderate heat. Stir in curry powder and chili powder. Heat until aromatic. Pour oil over nuts and cover nuts completely by stirring.

Place nuts on a large baking sheet. Roast in the oven for 15 minutes, stirring occasionally. Serve warm or at room temperature. Store in a sealed jar (photograph pages 36–37).

Sugar Cookies

2¹⁄₂ cups (9 oz/280 g) all-purpose (plain) flour
²⁄₃ cup (5¹⁄₂ oz/170 g) unsalted butter
pinch salt
3 tablespoons superfine (caster) sugar
2 egg yolks beaten with 5 tablespoons (2¹⁄₂ fl oz/ 75 ml) ice-cold water

Makes 40

Place flour and butter in bowl of a food processor. Process until butter is coarse; add salt and sugar

Ready-made frozen puff pastry is a very useful product to have on hand in the freezer. Always thaw it at room temperature or in the refrigerator. Don't try to speed things up by placing it in the microwave or oven, or the pastry will spoil. Roll out about ¹⁄₄ in (3 mm). If it is too thick, the top layers will be cooked while the center is still doughy.

and process again. Do not overprocess the mixture. With the motor running, add the egg yolk mixture and process until pastry forms a ball. Wrap and chill for 30 minutes.

Preheat oven to 400°F (200°C).

Roll pastry out to ¹⁄₄-in (0.5 cm) thickness. Cut into desired shapes. Place on a baking sheet lined with parchment (baking paper). Bake for 10–15 minutes or until golden. Cool and store in an airtight container. Serve with coffee, ice cream, or mascarpone and berries. If desired, when serving, sprinkle with confectioners' sugar. Will keep in an airtight container for 4 days (photograph page 34).

NOTE: Pastry will freeze, lightly wrapped.

Muesli

3 cups (9 oz/280 g) rolled oats
2 cups (10 oz/315 g) coarse oat bran
³⁄₄ cup (2 oz/60 g) unsweetened (desiccated) coconut
¹⁄₃ cup (2 oz/60 g) currants
¹⁄₃ cup (2 oz/60 g) golden raisins (sultanas)
¹⁄₄ cup (1 oz/30 g) chopped dried mango
¹⁄₃ cup (1¹⁄₂ oz/45 g) chopped dried apple
¹⁄₃ cup (1¹⁄₂ oz/45 g) chopped dried apricots
¹⁄₂ cup (2 oz/60 g) chopped almonds
¹⁄₄ cup (1 oz/30 g) chopped raw cashews
¹⁄₃ cup (2¹⁄₂ oz/75 g) pepitas (edible pumpkin seeds)
¹⁄₃ cup (2¹⁄₂ oz/75 g) sunflower kernels

Makes 4 lb (2 kg)

Combine all the ingredients in a large bowl, then transfer to an airtight container to store. Serve with milk, yogurt, honey or berries. Will keep for up to a month in airtight container (photograph pages 36–37).

Tartlet Shells

These can be filled with a dollop of jam, crème fraîche and fresh berries, or any number of sweet ingredients. A variety of savory fillings can be used as well, including antipasti, ratatouille or pâtés. They can even be used to make small quiches.

1¹⁄₂ cups (6 oz/185 g) all-purpose (plain) flour
¹⁄₂ teaspoon salt
¹⁄₂ cup (4 oz/125 g) unsalted butter, very cold and cubed
¹⁄₄ cup (2 fl oz/60 ml) ice water

Makes 3–6 small tart shells, or 12 cocktail-size tart shells

Preheat oven to 350°F (180°C).

Place flour and salt in bowl of food processor. Process for 20 seconds to combine, then sift. Add butter and process, chopping for 10 seconds at a time, until mixture resembles coarse meal. With machine running, add the water and switch processor off as soon as the pastry forms a ball. Turn dough out of machine and wrap in plastic wrap. Refrigerate for at least 30 minutes. Roll pastry out to ¼ in (0.5 cm) thickness. Line tart tins with pastry. Prick several times with a fork and bake in oven for 15 minutes, or until golden. Cool on wire racks. When completely cool, store in an airtight container (photograph page 34).

NOTE: Can be frozen in airtight container.

Pretzel Crackers

Serve with cheese or topped with savory fillings as a snack.

2 cups (8 oz/250 g) all-purpose (plain) flour
¼ teaspoon table salt
freshly ground pepper
¼ cup (1 oz/30 g) grated Parmesan cheese
3 tablespoons butter
1 tablespoon sugar
½ cup (4 fl oz/125 ml) milk
¼ cup (2 oz/60 g) coarse salt
¼ cup (2 oz/60 g) poppy seeds

Makes 48

½ teaspoon salt
⅓ teaspoon hot paprika

Makes 2½ cups (10 oz/315 g)

Seasoned bread crumbs (left); praline (right)

Preheat oven to 400°F (200°C).

Place flour, table salt, pepper and Parmesan in the bowl of a food processor. Process for 15 seconds. Add butter and sugar and process until mixture resembles bread crumbs. Transfer to a large bowl and add milk, mixing to a firm dough. Wrap in plastic and refrigerate for 1 hour.

Roll dough out thinly, cut into desired shapes and press each shape with salt or poppy seeds. Before baking, you can top these with a variety of ingredients, including pepper, extra Parmesan, dried herbs or caraway seeds. Place on an baking sheet lined with parchment (baking paper) and bake for 10–15 minutes. Will keep in an airtight container for 4 days (photograph pages 36–37).

Combine all ingredients and store in an airtight container.

You can use these to make savory crisps to accompany soup: brush melted butter over puff pastry, sprinkle with seasoned bread crumbs and roll gently. Cut into fingers and bake in a hot oven. Will keep for 4–6 weeks.

Seasoned Bread Crumbs

May be used to coat chicken drumsticks, cutlets, veal steaks, etc. before pan-frying or broiling. Sprinkle over cauliflower cheese or broccoli in béchamel sauce and bake until crisp. Sprinkle over casseroled meats and bake until crisp. Good to sprinkle over pie tops before baking.

2 cups (8 oz/250 g) fine dry bread crumbs
½ cup (2 oz/60 g) finely grated Parmesan cheese
1 tablespoon dried mixed herbs
½ teaspoon ground rosemary
½ teaspoon ground oregano

Praline

1 cup (5 oz/155 g) whole almonds (or an equal mix of whole hazelnuts and almonds)
1 cup (8 oz/250 g) superfine (caster) sugar
3 tablespoons water
1 teaspoon almond or peanut oil

Makes 2 cups (12 oz/375 g)

Spread the nuts in a baking dish and brown in a hot oven until well toasted. Remove and cool.

Make a syrup of the sugar and water and cook without stirring over moderate heat until it turns a golden caramel color. Add the nuts and stir in evenly.

Brush a baking sheet with oil, pour in the praline mixture and leave to cool and harden. Break up and store in an airtight jar. Usually praline is ground to a semi-fine powder before use. Will keep for several months in a dry cupboard.

Photograph following pages "Tailgate Picnic:" marinated peppercorn and mustard beef with horseradish mayonnaise (front, page 151); pear and raspberry pie (left, page 220); Mediterranean layered bread (center, page 64); potato and egg salad in creamy dressing (back, page 87); beet and Emmenthaler salad (right, page 84)

Starters and Soups

Where starters or appetizers are concerned, a light touch is called for in the amount you serve. You're just whetting your guests' appetites for the dishes to follow, so make sure you don't fill them up to the extent that they can't manage the later courses.

If the hors d'oeuvre are to be handed around with drinks before the guests seat themselves at the table, make sure the finger food lives up to its name. It should be something that can be handled easily without having to use a knife, fork or plate, especially for people encumbered with wine glasses, handbags or small children.

Soup can be a meal in itself when served with fresh crusty bread and a salad. Chilled soups are fresh-air, hot-weather favorites and are easily prepared in advance. But if they're only intended as a start to a meal, keep servings on the small side.

If you're serving starters in the tapas tradition, aim for recipes that you can prepare in advance. With the exception, perhaps, of one item, last-minute fiddling and cooking is out for this type of approach, especially when you have a main course and dessert still to organize. Of four items, for example, only one need be hot.

And don't feel obliged to cook. Oysters and shrimp bought fresh from the fish market, or slivers of smoked foods such as chicken, salmon, beef or turkey, only need dressing up with a good sauce or mayonnaise—one you may already have on hand in your pantry or refrigerator. Start effortlessly and the rest of the meal will be smooth sailing.

Opposite: seafood gazpacho (left, page 56); chilled cucumber and dill soup (right, page 56)

Clockwise from front right: smoked trout pâté; chicken pâté; crab dip

Crab Dip

Serve with crudités and biscuits or use it to fill little pastry shells.

¹/₄ cup (2 oz/60 g) cream cheese, softened
1 tablespoon mayonnaise
¹/₃ cup (2 oz/60 g) finely chopped red bell pepper
¹/₃ cup (2 oz/60 g) finely chopped green bell pepper
2 tablespoons finely chopped yellow bell pepper
2 scallions (spring onions), finely chopped
1 garlic clove, finely chopped
1 tablespoon lemon juice
dash Tabasco sauce
salt
pepper
¹/₂ cup (4 oz/125 g) crabmeat
1 tablespoon chopped fresh dill

Makes 2 cups (16 oz/500 g)

Combine the cream cheese and mayonnaise. Add bell peppers, scallions and garlic and stir to combine. Add the lemon juice and Tabasco. Mix thoroughly and season with salt and pepper. Stir in the drained crabmeat and dill. Allow to stand for 1 hour before serving. Re-season just before serving.
NOTE: Can be made 1 day in advance (keep in the refrigerator).

Smoked Trout Pâté

4 oz (125 g) filleted smoked trout meat
2 tablespoons drained, prepared horseradish
¹/₃ cup (3 fl oz/90 ml) sour cream
¹/₄ cup (2 fl oz/60 ml) heavy (double) cream
1 tablespoon capers
dill, for decoration

Makes 1¹/₃ cups (12 oz/375 g)

Place smoked trout and horseradish in bowl of a food processor. Process for 1 minute. Add creams and process to combine. Stir in capers. Serve on small toasts. Will keep refrigerated for 3 days.

Chicken Pâté

3 tablespoons (1¹/₂ oz/45 g) unsalted butter
3 tablespoons olive oil
1 lb (500 g) chicken livers, trimmed and patted dry
3 medium onions, chopped
¹/₂ cup (4 fl oz/125 ml) dry white wine
2 garlic cloves, coarsely chopped
1 tablespoon dried sage
1 tablespoon chopped fresh rosemary
freshly ground black pepper
3 tablespoons capers
5 anchovy fillets
2 teaspoons tomato paste

Makes 2 cups (16 oz/500 g)

Heat butter and oil in a heavy-based pan over moderate heat. Sauté chicken livers and onions until browned—about 10 minutes. Add wine, garlic, sage, rosemary and pepper, and cook until liquid has reduced—about 3 minutes. Add capers, anchovies and tomato paste. Stir well and cook for another minute. Cool mixture. Transfer to a food processor and process until mixture is almost smooth. Remove to a bowl, cover and refrigerate for at least 2 hours before serving. Serve with crackers or toast or on fresh crusty bread.

Salmon Mousse with Blanched Cucumber

1 tablespoon unflavored gelatin
2 tablespoons water
3 cans (each 8 oz/250 g) red salmon
¹/₂ cup (4 oz/125 g) cream cheese
1 egg white
1 tablespoon lemon juice
salt
pepper
¹/₂ cup (2 oz/60 g) diced, seeded cucumber
¹/₄ cup (¹/₂ oz/15 g) finely chopped scallions (spring onions)
³/₄ cup (6 fl oz/185 ml) heavy (double) cream
dash Tabasco sauce
1 large cucumber, finely sliced

Serves 10—or more if handed around with drinks

Oil a large fish mold. Soften gelatin in water and dissolve over boiling water. Remove skin and bones from salmon, reserving liquid. Beat salmon and liquid with an electric mixer for 1 minute. Gradually add cream cheese; beat until completely combined. Add egg white, lemon juice, salt and pepper. Beat thoroughly. Fold in gelatin, diced cucumber and scallions. Whip cream until thick and fold into salmon mixture. Pour into oiled mold and refrigerate until firm. Place sliced cucumber in a bowl. Pour on 1 cup (8 fl oz/250 ml) boiling water; drain. Decorate unmolded mousse with the slices to resemble fish scales. Serve with lemon wedges.

At the height of summer, keep food light and fresh-tasting. Balance creamy with crunchy, sour with sweet, spicy and hot with mild.

Salmon mousse with blanched cucumber

Veal and Wine Terrine

This recipe is best made 2 days ahead so the flavors have time to develop.

¹/₄ cup (2 oz/60 g) butter, melted
2 lb (1 kg) sliced bacon, rind removed
2 cups (2 oz/60 g) chopped flat-leafed (Italian) parsley
1 cup (1 oz/30 g) chopped fresh chives
1 cup (1 oz/30 g) chopped fresh basil
3 tablespoons chopped fresh sage
2 tablespoons chopped fresh tarragon
3 onions, chopped
1¹/₂ lb (750 g) veal cutlets, thinly sliced
¹/₂ cup (4 fl oz/125 ml) dry white wine

Serves 6

Preheat oven to 350°F (180°C).

Line the base and sides of a 9 x 5 in (22 x 12 cm) loaf pan with foil, making sure foil overlaps sides. Brush foil with butter, arrange bacon to completely cover base and sides of tin (bacon should overlap sides of tin). Combine herbs and onions.

Arrange slices of veal on top of bacon, making sure bacon is completely covered. Spoon about one-quarter of the herb mixture evenly onto veal. Then place a layer of bacon lengthwise along the top of herb mixture. Keep layering the ingredients until all are used, finishing terrine with a layer of veal.

Pour wine into terrine and wait until it is absorbed (about 5 minutes). Seal the terrine with overlapping bacon strips. Cover terrine with foil and place in baking dish. Pour water into baking dish to come halfway up the sides of the pan. Bake terrine in oven for about 1¹/₂ hours or until cooked. Remove from oven; cool. When completely cooled, place weight on terrine and refrigerate overnight.

Before serving, remove terrine from pan, remove foil and slice (photograph page 2).

Oysters with lemon vinaigrette

*Mussels in half shells
with coriander and
tomato*

Mussels in Half Shells with Coriander and Tomato

30 small mussels
3 tomatoes, peeled, seeded and chopped
salt and pepper
1 red bell pepper, finely chopped
¹/₃ cup finely chopped coriander (cilantro)
¹/₄ cup (2 fl oz/60 ml) balsamic vinegar

Serves 15 as cocktail food, or 5 as an appetizer

Scrub mussels, removing any beards that may still be attached. Steam until they just open; discard any that remain closed. Pull each mussel open, being careful not to tear the shell apart. Onto each mussel put a teaspoon of tomato sea-soned with salt and pepper. Sprinkle with bell pepper and coriander and finish with a small drizzle of balsamic vinegar. Serve hot or cold.

Oysters with Lemon Vinaigrette

¹/₂ cup (4 fl oz/125 ml) olive oil
3 tablespoons lemon juice
2 teaspoons grainy mustard
1 teaspoon sugar
36 oysters, shucked

Serves 3 as an appetizer

Combine oil, juice, mustard and sugar in a jar. Shake well and serve with oysters.

Lemon–Ginger Shrimp

3 lb (1.5 kg) jumbo shrimp
1/2 cup (4 fl oz/125 ml) olive oil
2 teaspoons sesame oil
1/4 cup (2 fl oz/60 ml) lemon juice
1 onion, chopped
2 garlic cloves, peeled
2 tablespoons grated ginger
2 tablespoons fresh coriander (cilantro) leaves

Serves 8

Shell shrimp, leaving tails intact, and remove vein. Pour oils into bowl of food processor, add remaining ingredients and process until puréed. Place shrimp in bowl, pour on marinade and let stand in refrigerator for at least 2 hours. Thread the shrimp on metal skewers or bamboo skewers that have been soaked in water for at least an hour. Barbecue shrimp for about 5 minutes, turning and basting frequently with marinade. Just before serving, brush shrimp with the remaining marinade (photograph pages 90–91).

Deep-fried Whitebait

1/2 cup (2 oz/60 g) all-purpose (plain) flour
salt
pepper
oil for deep-frying
1 lb (500 g) whitebait
lemon wedges

Serves 4 as an appetizer

Season the flour with salt and generously with freshly cracked black pepper. Heat the oil in a large saucepan or deep fryer. Roll whitebait in flour and, in batches, fry until golden. Serve with lemon wedges.

Tabouleh

Serve with hummus and pita chips

1/4 cup (2 oz/60 g) bulgar (cracked wheat)
1 cup (8 fl oz/250 ml) water
3/4 cup (6 oz/185 g) pine nuts
1 cup (1 oz/30 g) finely chopped mint leaves
2 cups (2 oz/60 g) finely chopped parsley
8 small tomatoes, chopped
1/4 cup (1 oz/30 g) peeled, seeded and chopped
   cucumber
1/4 cup (1/2 oz/15 g) finely chopped scallions (spring
   onions)
2 tablespoons lemon juice
salt
2 garlic cloves, finely chopped
1/4 cup (2 fl oz/60 ml) olive oil
freshly ground black pepper

Serves 6

Preheat oven to 350°F (180°C).

Soak cracked wheat in the water for 20 minutes. Place pine nuts on a baking sheet and toast in oven for 5 minutes. Remove from oven and allow to cool.

Place mint, parsley, tomatoes, cucumber and scallions in a large bowl. In a separate bowl combine the lemon juice, salt and garlic. Slowly whisk in the oil. Stir in pepper. Add cracked wheat and pine nuts to parsley mixture. Pour on the dressing and toss well.

The dressing and parsley mixtures can be prepared up to 3 hours ahead and combined just before serving (photograph page 50).

Hummus

1 3/4 cups (13 oz/400 g) garbanzo beans (chick-peas)
6 cups (1 1/2 qt/1.5 l) water
3 garlic cloves, peeled
1 1/4 cups (10 oz/315 g) tahini paste
1 teaspoon dried cumin
1 teaspoon chili powder (or to taste)
salt
1/3 cup (3 fl oz/90 ml) lemon juice
2 tablespoons olive oil

Makes 3 cups

Wash garbanzo beans (chick peas) and soak in cold water for 24 hours. Place garbanzo beans, with their soaking liquid, in a large saucepan and bring to a boil. Simmer for 2 hours, skimming off any scum that may surface. Drain garbanzo beans, reserving 1/4 cup (2 fl oz/60 ml) liquid, and refresh in cold water.

Place garbanzo beans and reserved liquid in bowl of a food processor. Process until smooth. Add garlic, tahini, spices and salt, lemon juice and olive oil. Reprocess and adjust seasoning. Serve drizzled with additional olive oil with pita chips, tabouleh and taramasalata (photograph page 50).

Taramasalata

1 lb (500 g) tarama (carp roe), red or golden
   whitefish caviar, or smoked cod roe
1 lb (500 g) cream cheese, at room temperature
1 garlic clove, chopped
2 tablespoons lemon juice
freshly ground black pepper
1/4 cup (2 fl oz/60 ml) olive oil
2 tablespoons heavy (double) cream

Makes 3 cups

In the bowl of a food processor, combine tarama (roe), cream cheese, garlic, lemon juice and pepper. Process until just smooth. With motor running, add the olive oil and cream and process until just blended. Transfer to a bowl, cover and refrigerate (photograph page 50).

Opposite: deep-fried whitebait (left); mozzarella in carozza (right, page 52)

Don't feel you have to serve three courses. Serve substantial nibbles with pre-meal drinks (savory profiteroles, dips, tiny vol-au-vent shells with various fillings) and you can dispense with the first course.

Pita Chips

4 pita pockets (Lebanese bread)
olive oil
paprika

Preheat oven to 375°F (200°C).
   Cut the pita pockets into triangles. Brush both sides of the bread with a little olive oil and sprinkle with paprika. Place in a single layer on a baking sheet and bake for 10–15 minutes, or until golden brown.

Guacamole

4 ripe avocados
1 large onion, chopped
2 garlic cloves, peeled
2 tablespoons olive oil
2 tablespoons lemon juice
$^{1}/_{4}$ cup (2 fl oz/60 ml) sour cream
2 teaspoons Tabasco sauce

From left: pita chips;
taramasalata (page 49);
hummus (page 49);
tabouleh (page 49)

$^{1}/_{4}$ teaspoon chili powder
corn tortillas (corn chips), for serving

Serves 10

Cut avocados in half, remove skin and seeds. Place in bowl of food processor with onion, garlic, oil, lemon juice, sour cream, Tabasco sauce, and chili powder and process until puréed. Transfer guacamole to a serving bowl and serve with corn tortillas (photograph pages 58–59).

Satay-flavored Stuffed Eggs

6 large eggs
baking soda (bicarbonate of soda)
1 tablespoon heavy (double) cream
1 tablespoon store-bought, prepared satay sauce
2 teaspoons finely chopped parsley
12 small shrimp, peeled
3 lemon slices, quartered
2 cups (6 oz/185 g) finely shredded lettuce

Makes 12

Satay-flavored stuffed eggs (left); Indonesian spiced eggs (right)

Place the eggs in a saucepan of cold water, add a pinch of baking soda and bring to a boil. Simmer for 8 minutes, then cool under running cold water. Drain.

Peel the eggs and cut in halves lengthwise. Scoop the yolks into a small mixing bowl and mash until smooth. Add the cream, satay sauce and parsley and beat to a smooth paste. Spoon into a piping bag. Pipe a large rosette of the filling into each egg white and decorate each with a shrimp and a piece of lemon.

Arrange the eggs on top of the lettuce on a large platter.

Indonesian Spiced Eggs

6 large eggs
baking soda (bicarbonate of soda)
1 medium onion, grated and drained
2 garlic cloves, crushed
2 teaspoons grated fresh ginger
2 tablespoons vegetable oil
2 teaspoons ground coriander
1/2 teaspoon powdered lemon grass
1/2 teaspoon turmeric

1/2 teaspoon blachan (dried shrimp paste)
2 teaspoons tomato paste
1 tablespoon dark brown sugar
2 tablespoons sambal ulek or other hot chili sauce
3/4 cup (6 fl oz/185 ml) thick coconut milk
salt
pepper
1 scallion (spring onion) or 1 small bunch fresh coriander (cilantro), finely chopped

Serves 6

Place the eggs in a saucepan of cold water, add a pinch of baking soda and bring to a boil. Simmer for 8 minutes, then remove from the heat and cool under running cold water.

Separately sauté the onion, garlic and ginger in the oil until very well colored. Add the spices, blachan (dried shrimp paste) and tomato paste and cook briefly, then add the sugar, chili sauce and coconut milk. Simmer for 15 minutes over moderate heat, stirring frequently, until the sauce is thick and aromatic. Add a little cold water if necessary. Add salt and pepper.

Peel the eggs and cut in halves. Heat gently in the sauce before serving. Scatter the scallion over the eggs.

Bread and Butter Cucumbers

Serve with cheese and crackers with pre-dinner drinks.

2 large cucumbers
2 tablespoons cooking salt
1¹/₂ cups (12 fl oz/375 ml) white vinegar
1 cup (8 fl oz/250 ml) water
³/₄ cup (6 oz/185 g) sugar
1 teaspoon black mustard seeds
1 teaspoon white mustard seeds

Makes 3 1-cup (8 fl oz/250 ml) jars

Slice cucumbers thinly. Place slices in layers in a large shallow dish, sprinkling each layer with salt. Cover and stand overnight. Rinse cucumbers well under cold water. Drain. Combine vinegar, water, sugar and mustard seeds in a pan. Set over heat and stir to dissolve sugar. Bring to a boil, reduce heat and simmer for 5 minutes. Add cucumbers, bring to a boil and remove from heat. Working quickly, with a pair of tongs, transfer cucumber slices to a sterilized jar. Fill the jar with the vinegar mixture. Cool and seal. Will keep indefinitely (photograph page 193).

Mozzarella in Carozza

Plan a menu that involves as little last-minute preparation as possible. A chilled soup for a first course leaves you free to attend to a hot main course. Many desserts can be made a day or more ahead.

6¹/₂ oz (200 g) mozzarella cheese
8 slices white bread
1 tablespoon dried oregano
freshly ground black pepper
2 eggs, beaten
³/₄ cup (3 oz/90 g) fine, dry bread crumbs
oil, for deep frying

Serves 6

Slice the mozzarella ¹/₂ in (1 cm) thick. Cut crusts off the bread, sprinkle mozzarella with the oregano and pepper and place between 2 slices of bread. Press down firmly. Cut each piece into 4 smaller squares. Dip each piece in egg, then bread crumbs, and deep-fry until golden (photograph page 48).

Figs and Prosciutto with Strawberry Vinaigrette

³/₄ cup (6 oz/185 g) strawberries
2 tablespoons balsamic vinegar
¹/₂ cup (4 fl oz/125 ml) olive oil
12 large figs
6 slices prosciutto, cut in half lengthwise
¹/₄ cup (2 fl oz/60 ml) brandy
freshly ground black pepper

Makes 12

Preheat oven to 300°F (150°C).

For vinaigrette: place strawberries and vinegar in a blender. Blend until smooth. With motor running, add oil in a slow steady stream. Blend until combined, adding more vinegar if you prefer a sharper vinaigrette.

Wrap a piece of prosciutto around each fig. Make a cross-shaped incision in the top of each fig and drizzle on a little brandy. Sprinkle with pepper and bake in oven for 10 minutes. Serve warm, with strawberry vinaigrette.

Marinated Olives

12 oz (375 g) black olives
2 cups (16 fl oz/500 ml) olive oil
3 garlic cloves
dried rosemary
dried oregano

Serves 6

Marinate olives in olive oil with garlic, rosemary and oregano. Serve as an antipasto (photograph pages 74–75).

Eggplant Appetizer

2 large eggplants (aubergines) cut into 2¹/₂ in (6 cm) lengths
salt
1¹/₄ cups (10 fl oz/315 ml) olive oil
1 onion, peeled and chopped
4 tomatoes, chopped
2 garlic cloves, crushed
1 tablespoon tomato paste
¹/₂ cup (4 fl oz/125 ml) water
2 teaspoons dried rosemary

Serves 6

Sprinkle the eggplant with salt and leave in a colander for 30 minutes. Rinse under cold water and dry.

Heat 1 cup (8 fl oz/250 ml) of the oil in a frying-pan. Add half the eggplant and cook for 5 minutes, or until softened. Remove from pan with slotted spoon. Repeat with the remaining eggplant.

Heat the remaining oil in pan, add onion, tomatoes and garlic and cook over low heat for 5 minutes. Add tomato paste and water and cook for a further 10 minutes. Add eggplant and rosemary and cook for a few more minutes. Serve hot or cold as an antipasto (photograph pages 74–75).

Deep-fried Chorizo with Eggplant

12 small eggplants (aubergines)
8 oz (250 g) chorizo sausage
2 tablespoons olive oil
1 small red (Spanish) onion, finely chopped
2 garlic cloves, finely chopped

¹/₄ cup finely chopped parsley
salt
¹/₂ teaspoon paprika
¹/₄ cup (1 oz/30 g) grated Parmesan cheese

Makes 12

Preheat oven to 350°F (180°C).

Place eggplants on a greased baking sheet and bake in oven for 15–20 minutes (depending on size), or until soft. Alternatively, microwave on HIGH for 5–7 minutes. Remove from oven and cool slightly. Slice off one long side of each eggplant and scoop out the flesh. Reserve the flesh and the eggplant cases.

Remove the sausage casings and crumble the sausage in a bowl.

Heat oil in a heavy-based pan. Add onion and garlic and cook until onion is soft. Add chorizo and cook for 2 minutes, stirring constantly. Add parsley, salt and paprika and combine thoroughly. Stir in eggplant pulp.

Fill each eggplant "case" with a little of the mixture. Sprinkle with Parmesan and bake for 5 minutes, or until Parmesan is melted and bubbling. Serve hot.

Roasted Bell Peppers

8 red bell peppers
olive oil

Makes 1 cup (8 fl oz/250 ml)

Preheat oven to 350°F (180°C).

Rub bell peppers with olive oil. Roast in the oven for 40 minutes, or until skins blister. Place in a covered bowl until cool enough to handle, then peel, seed and chop flesh into chunky strips. Place strips in a sterilized jar and cover completely with olive oil and seal. Serve as an antipasto (photograph pages 74–75).

Deep-fried chorizo with eggplant (left); figs and prosciutto with strawberry vinaigrette (right)

Tomato and Bell Pepper Soup with Chili Cream

2 red bell peppers
2 tablespoons oil
1 large onion, chopped
2 garlic cloves, chopped
³/₄ cup (6 fl oz/185 ml) sherry
8 medium tomatoes, peeled and seeded
4 cups (1 qt/1 l) chicken stock
1 bay leaf
1 tablespoon black peppercorns
3 thyme sprigs
1 basil sprig
1 large parsley sprig
1 cup (8 fl oz/250 ml) heavy (double) cream
juice of ¹/₂ lemon
salt and pepper

Chili cream
1 long green chili
1 garlic clove

Tomato and bell pepper soup with chili cream

5 spinach leaves, blanched in hot water
¹/₃ cup (3 fl oz/90 ml) cold heavy (double) cream
1 tablespoon lime juice
salt and pepper

Serves 6

Roast bell peppers, peel off and discard skins and chop.

In a large pan, heat oil and sauté onion and garlic. Add sherry and cook until liquid evaporates. Add tomatoes and stock. Tie herbs together in cheesecloth or muslin and add to the pan. Cook for 10 minutes, or until reduced by one-third. Add cream and bell peppers. Bring to a simmer and cook for 15 minutes, or until liquid is slightly reduced. Remove herb bag. Transfer mixture to a processor and blend until smooth. Season to taste with lime juice, salt and pepper.

For chili cream: blend chili, garlic and spinach in a food processor. Add cream and blend until combined. Season to taste with lime juice, salt and pepper.

*Feta cheese and onion
soufflé*

Feta Cheese and Onion Soufflé

*butter and very fine, dry bread crumbs for the
    soufflé dish*
1 very large onion
3 tablespoons olive oil or butter
1¹/₂ cups (12 fl oz/375 ml) milk
1 bay leaf
3¹/₂ tablespoons (1³/₄ oz/50 g) butter
3 tablespoons all-purpose (plain) flour
3 tablespoons heavy (double) cream
salt
pepper
grated nutmeg
3 egg yolks
1 tablespoon fine fresh white bread crumbs
³/₄ cup (3 oz/90 g) feta cheese, finely grated
1 tablespoon grated Parmesan cheese
4 egg whites

Serves 4

Preheat oven to 375°F (190°C).

Butter a 2 qt (2 l) soufflé dish and coat the
inside with very fine dry bread crumb. Tie a
greased and floured parchment (baking paper)
collar around the rim to extend about 2 in (5 cm)
above the top of the mold.

Peel and very thinly slice the onion. Sauté in the
oil for about 15 minutes. Reduce the heat to low
and cook for a further 20 minutes, stirring frequently, until onions are caramelized. Cool.

Pour milk into a small pan and add the bay leaf.
Heat until almost boiling then remove from the
heat. Melt 3 tablespoons (1¹/₂ oz/45 g) of the butter

in a medium-size heavy pan and stir in the flour,
cooking until lightly golden. Add the milk, cream,
salt, pepper and nutmeg and stir over gentle heat
until very thick. Remove from the heat and whisk
in the egg yolks. Set aside to partially cool.

Fry the bread crumbs in the remaining butter
until golden. Stir onions and cheeses into the batter. Beat the egg whites to form firm peaks. Fold
into batter, then spoon into the prepared soufflé
dish. Scatter the fried bread crumbs over the top.
Bake for 35 minutes, or until the center is still
slightly runny.

Onion and Herb Frittata

1 tablespoon olive oil
2 onions, chopped
4 eggs
2 tablespoons chopped sage
2 tablespoons chopped parsley
2 tablespoons chopped basil
2 tablespoons chopped oregano
¹/₄ cup (2 oz/60 g) butter

Serves 6

Heat oil in a frying-pan, add onions and cook over
low heat until softened. Remove from pan. Beat
eggs in a bowl, add onions and herbs and mix
well. Heat butter in an ovenproof nonstick frying-
pan; add egg mixture and cook over moderate
heat until base is golden and omelet starts to set.
Place top of omelet under hot broiler and cook
until top is set. Remove from pan, allow to cool
and cut into wedges. Serve as antipasti (photograph pages 74–75).

Opposite: summer vegetable soup with pesto

Chilled Cucumber and Dill Soup

3 cucumbers, peeled, seeded and chopped
1 onion, chopped
2 tablespoons chopped dill
3 cups (24 fl oz/750 ml) chicken stock
$^1/_2$ cup (4 fl oz/125 ml) heavy (double) cream

Serves 6

Place cucumbers, onion, dill and chicken stock in a saucepan. Bring to a boil over moderate heat, turn down to a simmer and cook until soft. Allow to cool then purée in a food processor. Return to saucepan, add cream and reheat slowly. Do not boil. Serve garnished with dill (photograph page 42).

Chili Corn Soup

6 long, green sweet chilis
$^1/_4$ cup (2 fl oz/60 ml) oil
2 onions, chopped
3 garlic cloves, crushed
4 tomatoes, peeled, seeded and chopped
10 cups (2$^1/_2$ qt/2.5 l) chicken stock
2 cups (8 oz/250 g) fresh corn kernels
1 cup (8 oz/250 g) mild cheese, shredded

Serves 10

Robust soups need robust bowls such as those made of earthenware. Reserve porcelain and bone china for more elegant fare.

Roast the chilis over a hot gas flame or broil until the skin blisters. Wrap in tea towel and let stand for 30 minutes. Remove and discard the skin from chilis and cut them into strips.

Heat oil in a large saucepan, add onions and cook over low heat for 5 minutes, or until softened. Add garlic and cook for a further minute. Add tomatoes and cook until mixture forms a smooth paste. Add chicken stock and bring to a boil. Add corn, reduce heat and simmer soup for another 10 minutes, or until corn is tender. Serve soup in hot bowls and garnish with cheese (photograph pages 58–59).

Seafood Gazpacho

Photograph pages 58–59, "Mexican Fiesta," clockwise from front: stuffed chili peppers (page 170); chili corn soup (page 56); guacamole (page 50); beef tacos (page 73); nachos (page 73); Mexican rice (page 102); Mexican flan (page 214)

4 tomatoes, peeled and seeded
1 medium cucumber, peeled and seeded
1 small red bell pepper
1 yellow pimiento
1 medium-size red onion
2 garlic cloves, finely chopped
dash of Tabasco sauce
1 teaspoon ground cumin
juice of 1 lime
4 cups (1 qt/1 l) tomato juice
2 tablespoons balsamic vinegar
$^1/_2$ cup (4 fl oz/125 ml) olive oil
salt
pepper
$^1/_4$ cup chopped fresh coriander (cilantro)
1 avocado
1 cup (8 oz/250 g) chopped combined shrimp and crab meat
coriander leaves, for serving

Serves 8

Finely chop all vegetables and combine them all, except the avocado, in a large bowl. Add garlic, Tabasco, cumin and lime juice. Add tomato juice and balsamic vinegar and stir to combine. Stir in the oil. Season with salt and pepper, add coriander (cilantro) and refrigerate until very cold.

Just before serving, stir in the finely chopped avocado and combined shrimp and crab meat. Sprinkle with coriander leaves and serve (photograph page 42).

Summer Vegetable Soup with Pesto

1 tablespoon vegetable oil
2 onions, coarsely chopped
1 can (16 oz/500 g) tomatoes, chopped
2 qt (2 l) chicken or vegetable stock
4 carrots, thinly sliced
2 potatoes, diced
4 leeks (white parts only), thinly sliced
2 large stalks celery with leaves, thinly sliced
2 cups (10 oz/315 g) sliced green beans
1 medium zucchini (courgette), cut into $^1/_2$ in (1 cm) slices
$^3/_4$ cup (3 oz/90 g) broken spaghetti (2$^1/_2$ in/6 cm lengths)
1 cup (6 oz/185 g) dried haricot (navy) beans, soaked, cooked until tender and drained

Pesto
2 garlic cloves
$^3/_4$ cup fresh basil leaves
$^1/_2$ cup (2 oz/60 g) freshly grated Parmesan cheese
2 tablespoons olive oil

Serves 8

Place oil in a frying-pan over moderate heat, add onions and cook, stirring, until tender. Add tomatoes and cook, stirring, for 8 minutes. Bring stock to a boil in a large saucepan. Add carrots, potatoes, leeks, celery and onion and tomato mixture. Simmer for 15 minutes. Add green beans, zucchini, spaghetti and cooked beans. Simmer until vegetables are tender.

For pesto sauce: place garlic, basil, cheese, oil and $^1/_4$ cup (2 fl oz/60 ml) of the hot soup liquid in a food processor and blend until smooth. Serve soup topped with a dollop of pesto.

Light Meals

A light meal is not a small portion of something that is better suited to a banquet, but rather food in a class all of its own. A light meal is satisfying (not overly substantial), comprised of first-class ingredients, quick to prepare and, above all, imaginative.

The "packaging" is the quick-to-prepare part. Bagels, baguettes, focaccia, brioches and croissants are instant containers, while a good honest slice of whole wheat bread is the perfect foundation for open-face sandwiches. Taco shells are envelopes just ready for filling, and pastry shells (on stand-by in the freezer) give the impression you've gone to a lot of trouble.

Ensure you use first-class ingredients: cheeses, eggs and the freshest vegetables and salad greens, with a lot of treats such as prosciutto, smoked fish and pickled vegetables thrown in with a generous hand. Cooking is minimal—either do-ahead or last-minute quick-and-easy. Foods such as pissaladière and pizza are perfect examples of light meals. Their flavors and colors are brilliant and they are popular with guests of all ages.

Much of this type of food is transportable, the ideal stuff for picnics or boating expeditions. Pack a rug, a few utensils and enjoy *al fresco* dining with minimum effort and maximum style.

Opposite: escabèche of trout (page 73)

Pizza Base

This dough can be used to make several small pizzettas or one big pizza. The list of toppings for a pizza is endless!

²/₃ cup (5 fl oz/155 ml) warm water
1¹/₂ teaspoons dry yeast
³/₄ teaspoon salt
2 cups (8 oz/250 g) all-purpose (plain) flour
2 tablespoons cornmeal (optional)

Makes 1 large or 6 small bases

Preheat oven to 400°F (200°C).

Place water in a large, warm mixing bowl. Sprinkle yeast over water and let stand for 3–4 minutes. Whisk gently. Add salt and mix again. Add flour to liquid and start kneading. When dough pulls away from sides of the bowl (it should be fairly sticky), remove from bowl to a floured surface. Knead for 12 minutes, adding more flour only if mixture remains sticky. Place dough in a lightly floured bowl, cover with a clean tea towel and a thick, folded bath towel and leave in a warm place for 2 hours.

Punch down and return covers and leave for another 2–3 hours. Remove from bowl and divide dough into 6 equal portions (if making pizzettas). Lightly oil a pizza pan or baking sheet and sprinkle with cornmeal. Roll each portion into a small round shape and place on pan. Prick several times with a fork and bake in the oven for 10–15 minutes, or until golden.

If you wish to top your pizza and reheat to melt the topping, shorten cooking time by 5 minutes.

Smoked Salmon and Mascarpone Pizzettas

1 quantity Pizza Base recipe, made into 6 bases
1 cup (8 oz/250 g) mascarpone cheese, at room temperature
10 slices smoked salmon
¹/₄ cup chopped chives
2 tablespoons extra-virgin olive oil
freshly ground black pepper

Serves 6

Spread each pizzetta base with 2–3 tablespoons of mascarpone. Divide salmon into equal portions and arrange over mascarpone. Sprinkle with chives and drizzle with oil. Sprinkle with pepper and serve.

Spinach and Pine Nut Pizzettas

8 leaves spinach, stems removed
1 tablespoon water
1 tablespoon olive oil

6 garlic cloves, halved
¹/₄ cup (2 oz/60 g) pine nuts
2 oz (60 g) Parmesan cheese
1 quantity Pizza Base recipe, made into 6 bases

Serves 6

Place spinach in a saucepan. Add the water and cook, covered, for 4–5 minutes, or until wilted. Drain and squeeze out excess water.

Heat oil in a pan, add garlic halves and fry until golden.

Refresh pine nuts by placing on a baking sheet and toasting in a preheated 350°F (180°C) oven for 4 minutes. Shave the Parmesan cheese.

Assemble pizzettas by layering ingredients on top of warm bases. Place under a broiler just to melt the Parmesan.

Tomato, Olive and Anchovy Pizzettas

1 quantity Pizza Base recipe, made into 6 bases
1¹/₂ cups (12 fl oz/375 ml) cooked Fresh Tomato Sauce (see recipe, page 32)
12 olives, pitted and quartered
6 anchovy fillets
¹/₄ cup small fresh basil leaves, or 6 large basil leaves, shredded
freshly ground black pepper

Serves 6

Warm pizzetta bases and top with tomato sauce, olives and 1 anchovy fillet per pizzetta. Sprinkle with basil and pepper and serve.

Sun-dried Tomato, Mushroom and Bell Pepper Pizzettas

12 sun-dried tomatoes
2 tablespoons olive oil
2 garlic cloves, finely chopped
6 mushrooms, sliced
1 quantity Pizza Base recipe, made into 6 bases
1¹/₂ cups (12 fl oz/375 ml) cooked Fresh Tomato Sauce (see recipe, page 32)
1 bell pepper, roasted, seeded and peeled
¹/₂ cup (60 g/2 oz) grated Parmesan cheese
freshly ground black pepper

Serves 6

Chop tomatoes into strips and set aside. Heat oil in a pan (including any extra oil from sun-dried tomatoes), add garlic and mushrooms and cook until mushrooms are tender. Top pizzetta bases with warmed tomato sauce and then the rest of the ingredients, ending with the Parmesan and pepper. Place under a broiler to melt the Parmesan and serve.

A picnic for a sports event such as racing or tennis calls for rather more formal food than that for a country-style picnic. It must be special, but still easily transportable and not messy. Roulades, pâtés, smoked or barbecued meats or fish (served cold), rice salads and chicken breasts, wings or thighs cooked in a variety of ways are ideal.

Chicken and Walnut on Rye

¹/₄ cup (2 oz/60 g) butter
1 tablespoon Dijon mustard
1 tablespoon chopped chives
6 slices rye bread
6 slices cooked chicken
6 oz (185 g) Camembert cheese, sliced
1 avocado, sliced
1 tomato, sliced
¹/₄ cup (2 fl oz/60 ml) mayonnaise
2 tablespoons sour cream
2 tablespoons chopped walnuts

Makes 6 sandwiches

Combine butter, mustard and chives; spread onto bread. Arrange chicken, Camembert, avocado and tomato on bread. Combine mayonnaise, sour cream, and walnuts and spoon on top (photograph pages 226–27).

Prosciutto and Sun-dried Tomato Focaccia

¹/₄ cup (2 oz/60 g) butter
1 garlic clove, crushed
2 tablespoons chopped fresh basil
6 triangles focaccia bread
6 slices prosciutto
¹/₂ cup (3 oz/90 g) sun-dried tomatoes
12 slices mozzarella cheese
3 canned artichoke hearts, cut in half
¹/₄ cup (1¹/₂ oz/45 g) pitted black olives
1 tablespoon olive oil

Makes 6 sandwiches

Combine butter, garlic and basil; spread onto focaccia. Arrange prosciutto, tomatoes, mozzarella, artichoke hearts and black olives onto bread. Drizzle on olive oil (photograph pages 226–27).

Clockwise from back: smoked salmon and mascarpone pizzetta; sun-dried tomato, mushroom and bell pepper pizzetta; tomato, olive and anchovy pizzetta; spinach and pine nut pizzetta

Pissaladière

Pissaladière is best served hot but is also good cold. It is very easy to reheat.

1 lb (500 g) puff pastry, or 2 sheets ready rolled
1/4 cup (2 fl oz/60 ml) olive oil
4 medium onions, sliced into rings
2 tablespoons balsamic vinegar
2 large tomatoes, sliced
1 large red bell pepper, roasted and cut into strips
6 black olives, pitted and halved
2 anchovy fillets

Serves 8

Preheat oven to 350°F (180°C).

Roll out pastry and line a 10-in (25 cm) round pie dish. Line pastry shell with foil and weigh down with pie weights or dried beans and bake in oven for 15 minutes. Leave oven turned on.

Meanwhile, heat oil in a large pan. Add onions and cook gently for 10 minutes. Add balsamic vinegar and simmer for another 10 minutes. Remove from heat and drain onions.

Fill pastry case with onions; arrange tomato, bell pepper strips, olives and anchovies on top. Bake in oven for 30 minutes. Serve.

Mediterranean Layered Bread

1 round cottage loaf (10 in/25 cm in diameter)
1/4 cup (2 oz/60 g) butter, melted
1 garlic clove
2 teaspoons dried rosemary
1 medium eggplant (aubergine), sliced
1 cup (8 oz/250 g) ricotta cheese
1/4 cup (1 oz/30 g) grated Parmesan cheese
1 cup (4 oz/125 g) black olives, pitted
1 cup (4 oz/125 g) stuffed olives
2 tablespoons chopped fresh basil
8 oz (250 g) can pimientos, drained
8 oz (250 g) sliced salami
7 oz (220 g) Cheddar cheese, thinly sliced

Serves 8

Slice top off bread, and remove insides, leaving a 3/4-in (2 cm) shell. Combine butter, garlic and rosemary and brush inside of bread shell. Place sliced eggplant under hot broiler and broil on both sides until golden brown. Allow to cool. Combine ricotta and Parmesan in bowl. Combine olives and basil in another bowl. Cut whole pimientos in half.

Spread base and sides of loaf with cheese mixture, place half the eggplant slices in bread, then half the olive mixture, half the pimiento, half the salami, then all the Cheddar. Repeat with remaining eggplant, olive mixture, pimiento and salami. Replace top, wrap loaf in foil, place on baking sheet, top with another baking sheet, and place a weight on tray to flatten slightly. Refrigerate for at least an hour. To serve, remove foil and cut into wedges with a serrated knife (photograph page 6).

Opposite: pissaladière

Ham, Asparagus and Mustard Cream Open Sandwich

¹/₄ cup (2 oz/60 g) butter
2 tablespoons ricotta cheese
1 scallion (spring onion), chopped
1 tablespoon chopped parsley
6 slices whole wheat bread
6 medium lettuce leaves (about 1 oz/30 g)
12 slices ham
1 bunch asparagus, washed, trimmed and cooked
3 hard-boiled eggs, sliced

Mustard cream
2 tablespoons Dijon mustard
¹/₄ cup (2 fl oz/60 ml) mayonnaise
2 tablespoons sour cream

Makes 6 sandwiches

Combine the butter, ricotta, scallion and parsley, then spread onto bread slices. Place the lettuce over the butter mixture. Arrange the ham, asparagus, and sliced eggs on the lettuce. Combine mustard, mayonnaise and sour cream. Spoon on top (photograph pages 226–27).

Cheese and Egg Scramble with Chives and Bacon

3 strips bacon
6 eggs
2 tablespoons finely chopped chives
¹/₂ teaspoon salt
¹/₄ teaspoon coarsely ground black pepper
¹/₄ cup (1 oz/30 g) grated Cheddar cheese
4 slices whole wheat
  bread, toasted and buttered

Serves 4

Very finely shred the bacon. Heat a small pan and sauté the bacon until lightly crisped. Remove with a slotted spoon. Beat the eggs, adding half the chives, the salt and pepper and the bacon, reserving a little for garnish. Stir in the cheese. Pour the bacon drippings into an omelet or nonstick pan and heat to moderate. Pour in the egg mixture and stir slowly until just set. Serve over buttered toast and garnish with the remaining chives and reserved bacon.

Cheese and egg scramble with chives and bacon

66

Spanish omelet

Spanish Omelet

3 large (about 1 lb/500 g) potatoes
1 small onion
1/4 cup (2 fl oz/60 ml) olive oil
5 eggs
3/4 teaspoon salt
1/4 teaspoon black pepper
2 teaspoons chopped parsley (optional)

Serves 4–6

Peel the potatoes and slice very thinly. Rinse in cold water and drain well. Thinly slice the onion. Heat half the oil in a cast-iron pan and fry the potatoes and onion over gentle heat until softened. Remove vegetables from pan.

Beat the eggs with the salt, pepper and parsley, if used. Break up the potato and onion with a sharp spatula, or leave in layers, as preferred. Heat the remaining oil in the pan over moderate heat. Pour egg over the potato, then transfer to the pan. Cook gently until firm and golden brown underneath. To turn the omelet, use a plate that will just fit inside the rim of the pan. Place it over the omelet, invert the pan and remove the omelet onto the plate; then slide it back into the pan to cook the other side. Take care it does not burn. Invert back onto a serving plate, cut into wedges and serve hot or cold.

NOTE: While the omelet cooks, form the sides by pressing right around the edge with a narrow spatula so the finished omelet is evenly thick and not tapering off at the edges.

Herbed Soufflé Omelet

1/4 cup (2 oz/60 g) butter
1/4 cup (1 oz/30 g) all-purpose (plain) flour
1 cup (8 fl oz/250 ml) milk
10 eggs, separated
1 tablespoon chopped fresh sage
1/2 cup (1/2 oz/15 g) chopped fresh chives
1/2 cup (1/2 oz/15 g) chopped fresh parsley
2 tablespoons chopped fresh tarragon
sage leaves, for garnish

Serves 8

Preheat oven to 425°F (220°C).

Melt butter in saucepan, add flour and cook, stirring, for 1 minute. Gradually add milk and stir until mixture boils and thickens. Remove from heat, transfer to large bowl and cool. Add egg yolks and herbs and mix well.

Beat egg whites in large bowl until soft peaks form. Fold half of the whites into yolk mixture, then fold in remaining whites. Pour mixture carefully into a large ovenproof oval serving dish. Bake in oven for about 20 minutes, or until well risen, golden and firm to touch. Serve immediately, garnished with sage (photograph pages 204–205).

NOTE: The roux for this omelet may be made ahead of time.

Minted Cheese Flan

This slightly sweet flan goes well with sliced tomatoes dressed with a tangy dressing of vinegar and olive oil. You can also serve it in very thin wedges with pre-dinner drinks.

Pastry
1½ cups (6 oz/185 g) all-purpose (plain) flour
¾ teaspoon salt
⅓ cup (3 oz/90 g) butter or margarine
1 small egg

Filling
4 oz (125 g) pecorino cheese (or any firm, slightly salty cheese)
5 eggs
2 teaspoons sugar
2 teaspoons finely chopped fresh mint

Serves 4–6

Preheat oven to 375°F (190°C).

To make the pastry: sift flour onto a board, make a well in the center and add salt. Add butter or margarine and egg, and work in, gradually drawing in flour. Add enough ice water to make a firm dough and knead briefly until smooth. Wrap in plastic wrap or aluminum foil and chill for 2 hours.

Roll out to line a shallow pie dish or quiche mold. Prick the base thoroughly. Line with foil and cover with pie weights or beans. Bake in oven for 6 minutes. Remove foil and beans; cool.

For the filling: arrange cheese in the pie shell. Beat eggs with the sugar and mint, and pour over the cheese. Bake until well risen and firm to the touch, about 25 minutes. Serve warm or cold, cut into wedges.

Don't serve foods that are difficult to handle in formal situations. Corn-on-the-cob, small birds such as quail that need to be picked up with the fingers and eaten, asparagus, spaghetti and globe artichokes fall into this category. For an informal gathering, no one minds tackling items such as these; but you should provide your guests with plenty of napkins or finger-bowls to rinse their fingers.

Egg and Mushroom Flan

Serve warm or cold, cut into wedges, as a light meal or as a vegetable accompaniment to broiled or roasted meats.

1 lb (500 g) fresh button mushrooms
3 tablespoons butter
2 teaspoons chopped fresh herbs (parsley, oregano, thyme)
salt
black pepper
4 large eggs

Serves 4–6

Preheat oven to 350°F (180°C).

Very thinly slice the mushrooms and sauté in the butter until tender. Process in a blender or food processor to form a smooth paste. Add the herbs, salt, pepper and eggs and mix to combine. Pour into a buttered quiche mold or pie plate and set in a roasting pan. Add hot water to reach halfway up the sides. Bake for about 30 minutes, or until set.

Rare Roast Beef with Béarnaise on Rye

2 tablespoons water
2 tablespoons white wine vinegar
1 scallion (spring onion), chopped
few sprigs tarragon
1 cup (8 oz/250 g) butter, cubed
4 egg yolks
¼ cup (2 oz/60 g) cream cheese

Minted cheese flan (left); egg and mushroom flan (right)

2 tablespoons fruit chutney
6 slices rye bread
12 slices rare roast beef
6 dill pickles, sliced
6 slices Swiss cheese
1 onion, sliced
snow pea or other sprouts

Makes 6 sandwiches

To make béarnaise sauce, combine water, vinegar, scallion and tarragon in saucepan and bring to a boil. Reduce liquid by half. Strain. Melt butter over low heat; cool. Place egg yolks and strained liquid in top of double boiler and gradually whisk in butter, over simmering water, until mixture thickens.

To assemble sandwich, combine cream cheese and chutney and spread mixture on bread. Arrange roast beef, pickles and Swiss cheese on bread. Sprinkle on onion and sprouts. Spoon on béarnaise sauce (photograph pages 226–27).

Smoked salmon and shrimp open sandwich

Smoked Salmon and Shrimp Open Sandwich

3 tablespoons (1¹/₂ oz/45 g) butter, at room temperature
1 tablespoon drained, prepared horseradish
1 tablespoon sour cream
6 slices whole wheat bread
6 oz (185 g) sliced smoked salmon
6 oz (185 g) cooked baby shrimp, peeled

Caper cream
¹/₄ cup (2 fl oz/60 ml) mayonnaise
¹/₄ cup (2 fl oz/60 ml) sour cream
2 teaspoons capers, chopped
1 tablespoon chopped chives
2 teaspoons chopped dill
2 teaspoons lemon juice
1 teaspoon lemon zest, grated
2 tablespoons black caviar

Makes 6 sandwiches

Combine butter, horseradish and sour cream; spread onto bread. Arrange smoked salmon and shrimp on bread. Combine the rest of the ingredients, except caviar, and mix well. Spoon cream onto smoked salmon and seafood; spoon on caviar.

Smoked Beef

Liquid smoke is a dark liquid made from water and natural hickory smoke that can be used as a marinade ingredient to give food a smoky flavor. It is available from specialty stores.

6 lb (3 kg) beef brisket, trimmed
1/2 cup (4 fl oz/125 ml) liquid smoke
1 teaspoon celery salt
1 teaspoon onion salt
1 tablespoon Worcestershire sauce
1 cup barbecue sauce

Serves 12–14

Place the brisket of beef on a piece of aluminum foil, large enough to enclose it. Mix together the liquid smoke, salts and Worcestershire sauce and pour over the beef. Wrap the beef and marinade in foil and place in the refrigerator for 24 hours.

Preheat oven to 275°F (140°C).

Put wrapped beef in a baking dish in oven for 4 hours. Remove foil from top of beef, brush on barbecue sauce and bake for another 30 minutes, basting often with more of the barbecue sauce.

Cool in the refrigerator, then slice thinly.

Cajun Chicken with Mustard Sauce

1 cup (4 oz/125 g) all-purpose (plain) flour
2 teaspoons dried oregano, crumbled fine
2 teaspoons ground cumin
2 teaspoons ground coriander
1 teaspoon ground thyme
1/2 teaspoon cayenne pepper
salt
5 tablespoons (2 1/2 oz/75 g) unsalted
    butter
4 chicken breast halves, cut into pieces
combination of your favorite mustard
    varieties

Serves 8

Combine flour and all the seasonings in a shallow dish. Melt 3 tablespoons (1 1/2 oz/45 g) butter in a saucepan. Dip each piece of chicken in butter then in flour mixture. Melt remaining butter in a large frying-pan. Add chicken, in batches, and sauté until browned and cooked through. Serve with a dipping sauce made from the mustards.

Cajun chicken with mustard sauce (back); smoked beef (front)

Focaccia with Baked Ricotta

Focaccia with baked ricotta

1 lb (500 g) ricotta cheese
6 tablespoons olive oil
salt
freshly ground black pepper
1 teaspoon paprika

2 onions, thinly sliced
focaccia bread—for 4
8 slices prosciutto
8 oz (250 g) mushrooms, sliced
12 sun-dried tomatoes
4 slices Jarlsberg cheese
basil sprigs for garnish (optional)

Serves 4

Preheat oven to 350°F (180°C).

Place ricotta on an oiled baking dish. Drizzle with 2 tablespoons of the olive oil, salt, pepper and paprika. Place in oven and bake 25–30 minutes.

Heat 2 tablespoons of the oil in a large pan, add onions and cook until soft. Set aside in a warm place.

Divide focaccia slab into 4 equal pieces, slice horizontally in half and brush each side with a little of the remaining olive oil. Assemble by piling all the ingredients onto one side, ending with Jarlsberg cheese. Place under a preheated broiler and broil until cheese melts. Top with the other half and serve immediately, garnished with basil, if desired.

Beef Tacos

2 tablespoons olive or safflower oil
1¹/₂ lb (750 g) ground (minced) beef
1 onion, chopped
1 garlic clove, crushed
1 teaspoon chili powder
1 14-oz (440 g) can peeled whole tomatoes, mashed
¹/₄ cup (1¹/₄ oz/40 g) taco seasoning mix
1 cup (8 fl oz/250 ml) water
2 tablespoons tomato paste
10 taco shells
1 cup (8 oz/250 g) grated Cheddar cheese
3 tomatoes, finely chopped
2 onions, finely sliced
¹/₂ small head of lettuce, shredded

Serves 10

Preheat oven to 350°F (180°C).

Heat oil in pan, add meat and cook over high heat, mashing with a fork until golden brown. Add chopped onion, garlic and chili powder and cook, stirring, for a further 3 minutes. Add tomatoes, seasoning mix, water and tomato paste; stir until combined. Bring to a boil, reduce heat and simmer meat for about 20 minutes, or until mixture is thick and meat is cooked. Place taco shells on baking sheet and bake in the oven for about 5 minutes, or until heated through (or microwave on HIGH for 1 minute).

To assemble tacos, spoon a little cheese in the base of taco, top with meat, then follow with to-mato, sliced onion and lettuce. If desired, serve guacamole (see recipe page 50) and sour cream with tacos (photograph pages 58–59).
NOTE: Beef mixture is suitable to freeze or microwave.

Nachos

2 tablespoons olive or safflower oil
2 onions, chopped
2 garlic cloves, crushed
2 small red chilis, finely chopped
2 14-oz (440 g) cans peeled whole tomatoes, mashed
¹/₄ cup (1¹/₂ oz/45 g) taco seasoning mix
1 teaspoon dried cumin
¹/₂ cup (4 fl oz/125 ml) water
¹/₄ cup (2 oz/60 g) tomato paste
1 15¹/₂-oz (450 g) can red kidney beans, drained and rinsed
8 oz (250 g) tortilla (corn) chips
1 cup (8 oz/250 g) grated Cheddar cheese
¹/₂ cup (4 fl oz/125 ml) sour cream
4 scallions (spring onions), chopped

Serves 10

Heat oil in a saucepan, add onions and cook over low heat for about 5 minutes, or until softened. Add garlic and chilis and cook, stirring, for a further minute. Add tomatoes, seasoning mix, cumin, water and tomato paste; stir until combined. Bring to a boil, reduce heat and simmer for about 15 minutes, or until thick. Add kidney beans and cook for a further 5 minutes, or until heated through.

At serving time, preheat oven to 350°F (180°C). Arrange tortilla chips onto base and edges of an ovenproof serving dish; spoon bean mixture down the center of tortilla chips. Sprinkle with cheese and cook in oven for about 5 minutes or until cheese melts. Remove from oven, top with Guacamole (see recipe page 50), then sour cream, and sprinkle with scallions (photograph pages 58–59).

Escabèche of Trout

2 ocean trout fillets
salt
pepper
paprika
¹/₂ cup (4 fl oz/125 ml) plus 2 tablespoons olive oil
2 teaspoons sherry vinegar, or ¹/₄ cup (2 fl oz/ 60 ml) red wine vinegar
¹/₃ cup (¹/₂ oz/15 g) chopped scallions (spring onions)
1 garlic clove, finely chopped
1 tomato, seeded and finely chopped
1 tablespoon capers
zest of ¹/₄ orange and ¹/₄ lemon, cut into fine strips and blanched
2 tablespoons chopped parsley
fresh thyme

Serves 6

Remove any bones from fish. Cut each fillet into pieces; sprinkle with salt, pepper and paprika. Heat 2 tablespoons of the olive oil in a heavy-based pan. Brown fish on each side and transfer to a deep dish.

Heat the remaining oil, vinegar, scallions and garlic in the same small pan. Sprinkle fish with tomato, capers, zest, parsley and thyme. Pour the oil marinade over fish, cover and store until required. Serve at room temperature (photograph page 60).

If your entertaining area is some distance from the kitchen, set up a table where you can stack china, jugs of ice water, extra napkins and cutlery, clean glasses—anything you might need in a hurry—so that you are not constantly scurrying back indoors to fetch and carry.

Photograph following pages, "Italian Supper," clockwise from left: roasted bell peppers (page 53); marinated olives (page 52); eggplant appetizer (page 52); zuccotto (page 217); sun-dried tomato and pasta salad with pesto dressing (page 87); spinach and radicchio salad with anchovy dressing (page 84); squab with ricotta and herbs (page 134); onion and herb frittata (page 55)

Salads

Salads can be anything you want them to be, and for outdoor entertaining their extraordinary versatility can be exploited to the full. They can be meals in their own right, starters, between-course refreshers, accompaniments to meat, fish and poultry, or fillings for sandwiches. They can be hot, warm or cold. And they can include fruit, grains and pasta depending on the flavor and balance of textures you want to achieve and on how substantial you want the finished dish to be. Even the simplest combination of ingredients creates a deliciously different salad if unusual dressings are added. Olive, sesame, peanut, safflower and walnut are but a few of the many oils now available, each with its own distinctive taste. Vinegars can be flavored with herbs, fruit and spices; the Japanese varieties offer a sweeter, milder alternative to some of the more assertive types. You can buy vinegars ready-made or, with just a little effort, make your own.

Making mayonnaise at home is so easy and quick. For a variation, simply blend in fresh herbs or spices just before serving. Mayonnaise flecked with green parsley or watercress will dress up a basic potato salad, while the addition of spices will turn it into something a little exotic. If you're watching your weight, or just prefer a lighter touch, dressings based on yogurt or crème fraîche are ideal.

With the wealth of seasonal vegetables and herbs now widely available, the exciting salad variations you can come up with are infinite.

Opposite: summer vegetable salad (left, page 78); bean salad with Japanese dressing (right, page 78)

Bean Salad with Japanese Dressing

1 lb (500 g) yard-long beans
1 teaspoon wasabi powder
2 teaspoons water
2 tablespoons rice vinegar
1 garlic clove, finely chopped
1 teaspoon sesame oil
1 teaspoon soy sauce
1 tablespoon sesame seeds, toasted

Serves 4

Bring a pan of salted water to a boil. Add the beans and cook for 3 minutes. Drain and set aside to cool.

Combine wasabi and water in a small bowl. Blend and then let stand for 5 minutes. Place remaining ingredients with the wasabi mixture in a screw-top jar. Shake vigorously to blend.

Toss the beans with the dressing and serve (photograph page 76).

Summer Vegetable Salad

1½ lb (750 g) broccoli, cut into small florets
11 oz (345 g) yellow squash (marrow), quartered
2 carrots, peeled and cut into thick matchsticks
1 red bell pepper, cut into strips

Mustard seed vinaigrette
1½ tablespoons grainy mustard
3 tablespoons tarragon vinegar
salt
freshly ground pepper
¾ cup (6 fl oz/185 ml) extra-virgin olive oil

Bring a large pan of salted water to a boil. Add broccoli, bring back to a boil and simmer over moderate heat for about 5 minutes, or until broccoli is tender. Drain and refresh in cold water. Repeat for squash, shortening cooking time. Place carrots in a saucepan, cover with cold water, bring to a boil and simmer over moderate heat for several minutes, or until tender. Refresh in cold water. Combine all vegetables in a bowl.

Pear salad with walnuts and blue cheese

Bacon and asparagus salad

For the dressing: place mustard in a small bowl. Add vinegar, salt and pepper and whisk well. Slowly add olive oil, whisking constantly until dressing is foamy. Pour dressing over vegetables and toss to coat well (photograph page 76).

Bacon and Asparagus Salad

8 oz (250 g) bacon, sliced
1 tablespoon oil
2 bunches asparagus, trimmed
³/₄ cup (6 fl oz/185 ml) olive oil
¹/₄ cup (2 fl oz/60 ml) lemon juice
¹/₄ cup (2 fl oz/60 ml) tarragon vinegar
2 egg yolks, lightly beaten
2 tablespoons chopped fresh dill
2 shallots, chopped
¹/₄ cup (2 oz/60 g) grated Parmesan cheese

Serves 6

Cook bacon in hot oil until crisp. Drain and cut into pieces. Steam or cook asparagus in water for about 5 minutes, or until tender. Arrange bacon and asparagus on serving platter. For the dressing, combine oil, lemon juice, vinegar, egg yolks, dill and shallots and mix well. Spoon dressing over bacon and asparagus, sprinkle with Parmesan.

NOTE: Bacon and asparagus are also suitable for the microwave.

Pear Salad with Walnuts and Blue Cheese

6 pears, peeled
4 cups (3 oz/90 g) mixed salad leaves—curly
    endive (chicory), watercress, snow pea
    sprouts
3 stalks celery, sliced

Dressing
¹/₄ cup (2 fl oz/60 ml) walnut oil
¹/₄ cup (2 fl oz/60 ml) safflower oil
2 tablespoons lemon juice
2 tablespoons chopped chives

¹/₂ cup (4 oz/125 g) crumbled blue cheese
¹/₂ cup (2 oz/60 g) walnuts, chopped

Serves 6

Cut base of pears flat so as to stand straight. Arrange a pear and some salad leaves in individual bowls. Scatter an equal amount of celery in each bowl. Combine oils, lemon juice and chives and pour over salads. Sprinkle cheese and walnuts on top of each salad.

Seafood and Watercress Salad with Orange and Poppy Seed Dressing

1 lb (500 g) large shrimp
10 oz (315 g) scallops
6 cups (1 lb/500 g) lightly packed watercress sprigs

Orange and poppy seed dressing
¹/₃ cup (3 fl oz/90 ml) honey
1 teaspoon grated orange zest
3 tablespoons orange juice
1 tablespoon poppy seeds
¹/₄ cup (2 fl oz/60 ml) light olive oil
1 tablespoon rice vinegar

Serves 6

Bring a large pan of water to a boil and simmer for 5 minutes before adding shrimp. Cook shrimp for 1¹/₂ minutes. Remove with a slotted spoon and set aside. Add scallops to water and cook for 1 minute. Remove with a slotted spoon and set aside. Peel and devein shrimp. Combine seafood and watercress, stir through dressing and serve.

For dressing: combine all ingredients in a jar and shake well.

Tailor your choice of tablecloth to the occasion. Plain white for a brunch; a floral design for lunch; a lace pattern for a formal dinner or afternoon tea under the trees; a bold print for an Italian meal or child's party—whatever you deem most appropriate. Picnics at the beach or in the countryside call for rugs or blankets that double as something to sit on and a surface on which to place the food.

Avocado and Mushroom Salad

2 tablespoons olive or safflower oil
10 strips bacon, chopped
6 avocados, peeled, seeded and sliced
2 lb (1 kg) tomatoes, sliced
12 oz (375 g) small button mushrooms (champignons), sliced

Dressing
1 cup (8 fl oz/250 ml) vegetable oil
¹/₄ cup (2 fl oz/60 ml) white wine vinegar
¹/₄ cup (2 fl oz/60 ml) cider vinegar
2 teaspoons sugar
¹/₂ cup (¹/₂ oz/15 g) chopped chives

Serves 20

Heat olive oil in a pan, add bacon and cook over high heat until crisp. Remove from pan and set aside. Arrange avocado slices, tomatoes and mushrooms on a serving platter. Combine dressing ingredients and mix well. Spoon dressing over salad and sprinkle on bacon (photograph pages 140–41).

Grapefruit and Watercress Salad

2 grapefruits, peeled and segmented
1¹/₂ cups (1¹/₂ oz/45 g) shredded arugula (rocket)
2 cups (2 oz/60 g) lightly packed watercress leaves

3 scallions (spring onions), chopped
¹/₂ cup (4 fl oz/125 ml) olive or safflower oil
2 tablespoons walnut oil
¹/₄ cup (2 fl oz/60 ml) grapefruit juice
1 tablespoon grated ginger
2 tablespoons chopped mint

Serves 6

Arrange grapefruit, arugula and watercress in a bowl with scallions. Combine remaining ingredients, pour over salad and toss lightly (photograph pages 22–23).

Curried Mango Rice Salad

4 cups (1³/₄ lb/880 g) long-grain white rice
¹/₄ cup (2 oz/60 g) butter

Seafood and watercress salad with orange and poppy seed dressing

3 onions, chopped
2 garlic cloves, crushed
1 tablespoon curry powder
8 stalks celery, chopped
3 apples, sliced
3 green bell peppers, chopped
1 lb (500 g) fresh corn kernels
6 scallions (spring onions), chopped
1 cup (4 oz/125 g) roasted cashews, chopped
¹/₂ cup (¹/₂ oz/15 g) chopped parsley

Mango dressing
2 mangoes, peeled
1 cup (8 fl oz/250 ml) olive or safflower oil
¹/₂ cup (4 fl oz/125 ml) orange juice
¹/₄ cup (2 fl oz/60 ml) walnut oil
¹/₄ cup (2 fl oz/60 ml) white wine vinegar
¹/₄ teaspoon ground cinnamon
¹/₄ teaspoon ground ginger

¹/₂ cup (4 fl oz/125 ml) mayonnaise

Serves 20

Cook the rice in a large pot of boiling water for about 10 minutes, or until tender. Drain, then refresh under cold water. Spread rice out on tea towels to cool and dry out a little. Melt butter in a small pan, add onions and cook until softened. Add garlic and curry powder and cook, stirring, for 1 minute. Place rice in a large bowl, add onion mixture and mix well. Add celery, apples, bell peppers, corn, scallions, cashews and parsley, and mix well.

Remove flesh from mangoes, place in food processor with oil, orange juice, walnut oil and vinegar, and process until puréed. Transfer dressing to bowl, add cinnamon, ginger and mayonnaise and whisk until combined. Add dressing to rice and mix well (photograph pages 140–41).

Niçoise Salad with Tuna

12 tiny new potatoes
8 oz (250 g) green beans, ends removed
1 bunch curly endive (chicory), washed and dried
3 hard-boiled eggs, peeled and halved
8 oz (250 g) cherry tomatoes
12 small black olives
2 cans (each 6¹/₂ oz/200 g) tuna, drained
1 tablespoon olive oil
3 scallions (spring onions), finely chopped
1 tablespoon lemon juice
salt
freshly ground pepper

Dressing
¹/₃ cup (3 fl oz/90 ml) red wine vinegar
2 anchovy fillets
2 teaspoons Dijon mustard
freshly ground pepper
²/₃ cup (5 fl oz/155 ml) extra-virgin olive oil

Serves 6

Place the potatoes in a saucepan. Cover with cold water, bring to a boil, then simmer over moderate heat for 10–12 minutes, or until tender.

Cook beans in boiling salted water for about 4 minutes, or until tender. Arrange the potatoes, beans, endive, eggs, tomatoes and olives on a large platter. Combine the tuna with the oil, scallions, lemon juice, salt and pepper. Arrange on the platter.

For dressing: place vinegar, anchovy fillets, mustard and pepper in a small bowl and whisk until combined. Gradually add oil, whisking until thoroughly incorporated. Reseason with pepper. Pour dressing over salad ingredients.

Serve with lots of crusty bread.

Insalata Mista

Each person pours his or her own dressing, and seasons the salad with salt. Authentic insalata mista is never served with pepper.

2 lettuces: choose from iceberg, Boston, Bibb
    (mignonette), butter or romaine
1 small bunch arugula (rocket)
1 small bunch watercress
1 fennel bulb, thinly sliced
3 stalks celery, sliced
1 cup (8 oz/250 g) small tomatoes
red wine vinegar
olive oil
salt

Serves 8

Combine all the vegetables. Serve with red wine vinegar and olive oil. Season with salt.

Opposite: niçoise salad with tuna

Mushroom and heart of palm salad (left, page 87); insalata mista (right)

Spinach and Radicchio Salad with Anchovy Dressing

12 spinach leaves, washed and dried
12 radicchio leaves, washed and dried
1 fennel bulb, sliced
2 medium onions, sliced

Anchovy dressing
2 anchovy fillets
1/2 cup (4 fl oz/125 ml) olive oil
2 tablespoons lemon juice
2 tablespoons white wine vinegar
1/2 teaspoon sugar
1/4 cup (1 oz/30 g) grated Parmesan cheese

Serves 6

Remove stems from spinach leaves and chop leaves roughly. Arrange spinach, radicchio, fennel and onions on serving platter. Place anchovies, oil, lemon juice, vinegar and sugar in food processor and process until smooth. Spoon dressing on the salad, sprinkle with Parmesan (photograph pages 74-75).

Apple and Parsley Salad with Tomato Dressing

1 onion, chopped
1 small red bell pepper, seeded and chopped
1 garlic clove, peeled
2 tomatoes, peeled and chopped
1/2 cup (4 fl oz/125 ml) olive oil
1/4 cup (2 fl oz/60 ml) white wine vinegar
1 teaspoon sugar
2 large apples, peeled, cored and sliced
1 cucumber, peeled and chopped
3 stalks celery, sliced
3 zucchinis (courgettes), grated
2 cups (2 oz/60 g) chopped parsley

Serves 6

Place onion, bell pepper, garlic, tomatoes, oil, vinegar and sugar in the bowl of a food processor and process until puréed. Pass dressing through a fine sieve. Combine apple slices, cucumber, celery, zucchini and parsley in a bowl. Add dressing and mix well. Transfer salad to serving bowl or platter (photograph pages 124–25).

Festive Coleslaw

1/2 medium green cabbage, shredded
1/2 medium red cabbage, shredded
8 stalks celery, chopped
1 bunch radishes, sliced
6 carrots, peeled and grated
3 onions, chopped
2 green bell peppers, chopped
2 red bell peppers, chopped
2 cups (16 fl oz/500 ml) mayonnaise
1/2 cup (4 fl oz/125 ml) olive or safflower oil
1/4 cup (2 fl oz/60 ml) white wine vinegar

Serves 20

Combine cabbages, celery, radishes, carrots, onions and bell peppers in a large bowl and toss until combined. Combine the remaining ingredients, pour over salad and mix well (photograph pages 140–41).

Potato Salad in Red Wine Vinegar with Onions

8 potatoes, peeled and cubed
1/4 cup (2 fl oz/60 ml) red wine vinegar
2 tablespoons chopped dill
2 small red (Spanish) onions, sliced
1/3 cup (3 fl oz/90 ml) sour cream
1/3 cup (3 fl oz/90 ml) mayonnaise
salt
pepper

Serves 6

Place potatoes in a large saucepan. Cover with water, set over low heat, bring water to a boil and cook potatoes until tender. Drain. Gently toss with vinegar, dill and onions. Cool. Combine the sour cream and the mayonnaise, season with salt and plenty of ground black pepper. Gently fold into potatoes and serve.

Beet and Emmenthaler Salad

4 leeks, cut in rounds
2 bunches asparagus, stems trimmed
3 beets (beetroot), cooked, peeled and quartered
4 oz (125 g) Emmenthaler cheese, very thinly sliced
1/2 cup (4 fl oz/125 ml) olive oil
2 tablespoons hazelnut oil
2 tablespoons white wine vinegar
1 tablespoon balsamic vinegar
2 tablespoons chopped fresh chives
2 teaspoons caraway seeds, crushed
1 garlic clove, crushed

Serves 8

Steam leeks and asparagus until tender. Refresh under cold water. Arrange leeks, asparagus, beets and cheese in a serving bowl or on a platter. Combine oils, vinegars, chives, caraway seeds and garlic. Pour dressing on salad just before

serving (photograph pages 40–41).

NOTE: If taking this salad to a picnic, it is best to prepare it just before leaving. The dressing can be made ahead of time and should be transported in a separate container. Add to salad just before serving.

Chicken and Almond Salad with Lemon Mayonnaise

3 chicken breast halves
salt
pepper
²/₃ cup (5 fl oz/155 ml) water
1 Boston or Bibb (mignonette) lettuce, torn into serving pieces
2 cups (2 oz/60 g) lightly packed watercress sprigs

Lemon mayonnaise
2 eggs
5 tablespoons (2¹/₂ fl oz/75 ml) lemon juice

2 tablespoons Dijon mustard
1 cup (8 fl oz/250 ml) light olive oil
¹/₂ cup (4 fl oz/125 ml) peanut oil
grated zest (rind) of 2 lemons

¹/₃ cup (2 oz/60 g) toasted almonds, for serving
2 tablespoons grated lemon zest, for serving

Serves 6

Preheat oven to 300°F (150°C).

Place chicken breasts in a single layer in a baking dish. Sprinkle with salt and pepper. Add water, place in oven and bake for 30 minutes, until breasts are cooked through. Remove from water and cut into strips. Combine chicken and salad greens in a large bowl.

For mayonnaise: place eggs, lemon juice and mustard in bowl of food processor and process for 1 minute. Combine oils. With motor running, add oils in a slow, steady stream and process until thoroughly combined. Stir in lemon zest.

Toss mayonnaise with greens and chicken and sprinkle with almonds and lemon zest.

Potato salad in red wine vinegar with onions (left); chicken and almond salad with lemon mayonnaise (right)

Layered Salad

1 Boston or Bibb (mignonette) lettuce
1 yellow bell pepper
1 red bell pepper
3 firm ripe tomatoes
1 large cucumber
1 avocado

Dressing
1 egg
³/₄ cup (6 fl oz/185 ml) tomato juice
¹/₂ cup (4 fl oz/125 ml) olive oil
¹/₄ cup (2 fl oz/60 ml) red wine vinegar
Tabasco sauce
salt
pepper
2 tablespoons chopped fresh coriander (cilantro)

Serves 6

Dice all salad ingredients and place in layers in a glass salad bowl.

Combine all dressing ingredients and whisk until smooth. Refrigerate until slightly thick—about 1 hour. Pour dressing over salad and serve.

Garbanzo Salad with Basil Vinaigrette

5 cups (16 oz/500 g) cooked garbanzo beans (chick-peas)
1 red (Spanish) onion, finely chopped
²/₃ cup (3 oz/90 g) pitted black olives, chopped
¹/₃ cup chopped parsley
2 tomatoes, finely diced

Basil vinaigrette
1 garlic clove, finely chopped
1 tablespoon Dijon mustard
¹/₄ cup (2 fl oz/60 ml) red wine vinegar
freshly ground black pepper
¹/₃ cup (3 fl oz/90 ml) extra-virgin olive oil
¹/₄ cup finely chopped basil leaves

Serves 6

Combine all salad ingredients in a bowl.

Combine garlic, mustard, vinegar and pepper in a bowl. Whisk well, then add oil in a slow stream. Whisk constantly until mixture thickens. Stir in the basil. Gently toss dressing with salad.

Garbanzo salad with basil vinaigrette (left); layered salad (right)

Mushroom and Heart of Palm Salad

1/3 cup (3 fl oz/90 ml) olive oil
1 garlic clove, finely chopped
1 lb (500 g) button mushrooms (champignons)
3 tablespoons balsamic vinegar
1 tablespoon red wine (optional)
1/2 cup (1/2 oz/15 g) chopped parsley
1 can (13 1/2 oz/425 g) hearts of palm, sliced
salt
pepper

Serves 6

Heat oil, add garlic and mushrooms. Toss until all mushrooms are coated. Add balsamic vinegar and red wine. Toss over heat for 1 minute. Add parsley and stir thoroughly. Remove to a bowl to cool. Add sliced hearts of palm, season with salt and freshly ground black pepper and serve (photograph page 83).

Red Onion Salad with Avocado Dressing

3 red onions, cut into thin wedges
3 stalks celery, sliced
8 oz (250 g) cherry tomatoes, halved
8 oz (250 g) snow pea sprouts

Avocado dressing
1/2 avocado
1 teaspoon green peppercorns
1/2 cup (4 fl oz/125 ml) olive or safflower oil
2 tablespoons lemon juice
2 tablespoons white wine vinegar

Serves 8

Arrange the onions, celery, tomatoes and snow pea sprouts in a serving bowl. For the dressing, place the avocado in a food processor with the peppercorns, oil, lemon juice and vinegar and process until puréed. Pour over salad (photograph pages 90–91).

Wild Rice Salad

1 cup (6 oz/185 g) wild rice
1/2 cup (3 oz/90 g) long-grain white rice
2 stalks celery, chopped
1 onion, chopped
1 apple, peeled and chopped
1 red bell pepper, chopped
1/2 cup (4 fl oz/125 ml) mayonnaise

2 teaspoons Dijon mustard
1 garlic clove, crushed
1/4 cup (2 fl oz/60 ml) olive or safflower oil
2 tablespoons tarragon vinegar

Serves 6

Cook the wild rice and white rice in 1 qt (1 l) boiling water until just tender—about 30 minutes. Drain and allow to cool. Place rice in bowl with celery, onion, apple and bell pepper and mix well. Combine remaining ingredients, pour over salad and mix well (photograph page 2).

Sun-dried Tomato and Pasta Salad with Pesto Dressing

1 cup (1 oz/30 g) loosely packed basil leaves
1/4 cup (1 1/2 oz/45 g) toasted pine nuts
1 garlic clove, peeled
3/4 cup (6 fl oz/185 ml) olive oil
12 oz (375 g) fettuccine
3/4 cup (4 oz/125 g) sun-dried tomatoes
1/2 cup (3 oz/90 g) black olives, pitted

Serves 6

Place basil leaves, pine nuts and garlic in bowl of food processor and process until very finely chopped. Gradually add oil with motor running and process until puréed. Cook pasta in boiling water until *al dente*. Add a little oil to prevent pasta sticking together. Drain and refresh under cold water. At serving time, place pasta in bowl with dried tomatoes and olives, add basil dressing and mix well (photograph page 8).

If you run out of space in the refrigerator and have bottles of wine you need to chill in a hurry, don't be tempted to put them in the freezer. Instead, simply withdraw the corks slightly and layer the bottles with ice in a large, clean plastic garbage bucket.

Potato and Egg Salad in Creamy Dressing

2 lb (1 kg) baby potatoes, peeled
4 hard-boiled eggs, peeled and quartered
1/2 cup (4 fl oz/125 ml) mayonnaise
2 tablespoons sour cream
1 small onion, chopped
1 garlic clove, crushed
1/4 cup (2 fl oz/60 ml) olive or safflower oil
2 tablespoons vinegar
2 tablespoons chopped dill

Serves 8

Cook the potatoes in boiling water for about 8 minutes, or until tender; drain and refresh under cold water. Cut potatoes in half and arrange on a serving platter with eggs. Combine remaining ingredients in bowl and mix well. Spoon over potatoes and eggs (photograph pages 40–41).

Arugula Salad with Caper and Olive Dressing

oil, for shallow-frying
4 slices white bread, cubed
1½ cups (1½ oz/45 g) arugula (rocket) leaves
4 oz (125 g) snow pea sprouts

Caper and olive dressing
½ cup (2 oz/60 g) green olives, pitted
1 tablespoon capers
1 small onion, chopped
¾ cup (6 fl oz/185 ml) olive oil
¼ cup (2 fl oz/60 ml) grapefruit juice
2 tablespoons white wine vinegar
1 tomato, finely chopped

Serves 8

Heat the oil in a frying-pan, add the bread cubes and fry until golden-brown on all sides. Remove with a slotted spoon and drain on paper towels. Arrange arugula leaves and sprouts in a serving bowl.

For caper and olive dressing: purée olives, capers, onion, oil, grapefruit juice and vinegar in food processor. Refrigerate until ready to serve. Add tomato, pour on dressing and sprinkle with croûtons (photograph pages 106–107).

A table set out on the veranda for an evening meal can be illuminated sufficiently by the back-drop of lighting in the house. If more is needed, use oil lamps and dim them to the brightness required, or set squat candles securely on the table. Lamps can be suspended in the rafters of the veranda.

Rare Roast Beef Salad with Coconut–Mint Dressing

1 beef fillet, rolled with all fat removed
2 tablespoons crushed peppercorns
2 tablespoons olive oil
mixed salad greens

Dressing
juice of 2 limes
¾ cup (6 fl oz/185 ml) coconut milk
2 teaspoons fish sauce
2 tablespoons chopped fresh mint
1 red chili, finely chopped

Serves 6

Preheat oven to 400°F (200°C).

Rub beef fillet with peppercorns. Heat oil in a pan until very hot. Add beef and sear very quickly all over. Place fillet in a roasting pan and cook for 20 minutes. Let fillet cool for 10 minutes. Prepare salad greens and place in a bowl. Slice fillets into strips.

For dressing: place all ingredients in a blender and process until thoroughly combined.

Combine salad greens, beef and dressing. Serve immediately.

Fresh Garden Salad with Tarragon Dressing

16 asparagus spears, stems trimmed
3 green zucchinis (courgettes), very thinly sliced lengthwise
½ cucumber, thinly sliced
4 cups (6 oz/185 g) lettuce leaves (romaine, coral, butter), washed and dried
2 tablespoons sage leaves
2 tablespoons basil leaves

Dressing
2 tablespoons hazelnut oil
½ cup (4 fl oz/125 ml) olive oil
¼ cup (2 fl oz/60 ml) lime juice
2 tablespoons white wine tarragon vinegar
2 teaspoons Dijon mustard
½ teaspoon sugar
2 tablespoons chopped fresh tarragon

Serves 8

Steam asparagus until tender, drain, rinse under cold water and allow to cool.

Place zucchinis in a small pot of boiling water; cook for 1 minute, then refresh under cold running water.

Arrange cucumber, a variety of lettuce, asparagus and zucchini in serving bowl. Sprinkle on sage and basil leaves.

For the dressing: place all ingredients in a bowl and whisk until combined. Pour over salad and serve (photograph page 8).

Caesar Salad

4 slices bread
2 tablespoons garlic-flavored oil or plain olive oil
1 head romaine lettuce
2 tablespoons olive oil
3 strips bacon
1 medium bunch arugula (rocket)

Dressing
2 eggs
1 tablespoon Dijon mustard
3 anchovy fillets
¾ cup (6 fl oz/185 ml) olive oil (including oil anchovies were packed in)
⅓ cup (3 fl oz/90 ml) peanut oil
¼ cup (2 oz/60 g) grated Parmesan cheese
freshly ground black pepper

Serves 6

Preheat oven to 375°F (180°C).

Brush both sides of bread with garlic-flavored oil. Cut into squares. Place on a baking sheet and bake until golden—about 10 minutes. Set aside. Meanwhile, wash lettuce and place in a large bowl. Heat oil in a saucepan, add bacon and cook until crisp. Remove from pan and drain. Add to lettuce.

Photograph following pages, "Beach Barbecue," clockwise from front: marinated honeyed pork spareribs (page 156); corn-on-the-cob with sweet butter (page 175); lemon–ginger shrimp (page 49); marinated whole trout with olives and chili (page 122); red onion salad with avocado dressing (page 87); sherried noodle and cashew salad (page 104)

Caesar salad (back); rare roast beef salad with coconut–mint dressing (front)

For the dressing: bring a small saucepan of water to a boil. Break each egg into the water, one at a time, removing them as soon as the egg white turns opaque. Place in bowl of a food processor. Add mustard and anchovy fillets. Process for 1 minute. Slowly add the combined oils in a thin steady stream. Process until completely combined. Stir in Parmesan and season with pepper. Toss dressing with the salad greens, sprinkle with croûtons and serve.

Pasta, Rice and Noodles

For family meals, impromptu suppers for unexpected visitors, lunches for one or dinners for a crowd, whatever the occasion, pasta, rice and noodles rate as the cook's best friends. They are among the most versatile and widely eaten foods in the world.

The good thing about all these staples is that they can be dressed up or down to suit the occasion. If you can make your own pasta, so much the better (you could even invest in a pasta-making machine), or you can often buy it fresh from your local supermarket. Failing that, there are plenty of excellent-quality, dried varieties available.

Rice can be as humble or as elegant as you want it to be. Try a simple fried rice dish for the family or a creamy risotto or a paella for a relaxed lunch party on the patio. And for something rather grand, noodles deep-fried into "nests" as containers for a rich seafood sauce would not be out of place at a formal occasion.

When time is at a premium, pasta, rice and noodle dishes are sufficiently filling that a salad and some fresh fruit need be the only accompaniments—hence their suitability for spur-of-the-moment entertaining.

Opposite: baked macaroni and cheese with tuna and peas (left, page 102); tricolor pasta with summer vegetables (front and right, page 98)

Rainbow Lasagne

5 tablespoons (2¹/₂ oz/75 g) butter
5 tablespoons (1¹/₂ oz/45 g) all-purpose (plain)
  flour
4 cups (1 qt/1 l) milk
salt
white pepper
¹/₂ teaspoon sharp mustard
2 cups (8 oz/250 g) grated mozzarella cheese
1 lb (500 g) chopped frozen or fresh spinach
¹/₂ teaspoon grated nutmeg
2 medium onions, sliced
3 tablespoons olive oil
1 large red bell pepper, sliced
2 cups (12 oz/375 g) corn kernels
3 large tomatoes, sliced
1 lb (500 g) curly instant lasagne or partially
  cooked dried lasagne
1¹/₂ cups (12 fl oz/375 ml) Fresh Tomato Sauce
  (recipe, page 32)

Serves 6–8

Preheat oven to 350°F (180°C).

In a medium saucepan, melt the butter and stir in the flour. Remove from the heat, add the milk and stir until smooth. Return to moderate heat and stir until thickened. Add salt and pepper to taste and the mustard. Stir in three-quarters of the cheese, cover the top with a piece of plastic wrap to prevent a skin from forming and set aside.

Cook the spinach in a tightly covered pan over low heat, removing the lid and increasing the heat after a short while to boil off the liquid. Season to taste with salt and pepper and add the nutmeg. Sauté the onions in 2 tablespoons of the oil until softened and lightly colored, then sauté the bell pepper in the remaining oil. Mix half the onion with the spinach, and one-third of the cheese sauce. Cook the corn in lightly salted water, drain and mix with the remaining onion and one-third of the cheese sauce.

Grease a large lasagne dish and arrange lasagne in the bottom. Spread the spinach evenly over it. Cover with another layer of pasta, then arrange the sautéed peppers and sliced tomatoes evenly over it and pour on the tomato sauce. Cover with another layer of pasta, then the corn sauce. Top with a final layer of pasta and spread the remaining cheese sauce evenly over the top. Scatter on the remaining grated cheese. Bake for about 45 minutes.

NOTE: The lasagne can be prepared in advance and refrigerated until ready to cook. Assembled, uncooked lasagne can be frozen. Cook in a medium oven for about 1 hour.

Rainbow lasagne

Baked pasta and eggplant

Baked Pasta and Eggplant

3 small eggplants (aubergines) (each
    2 in/5 cm in diameter)
salt
2 lb (1 kg) very ripe tomatoes
3 garlic cloves
2 cups (16 fl oz/500 ml) olive oil
$^{1}/_{2}$ teaspoon black pepper
$^{1}/_{2}$ teaspoon sugar
2 tablespoons finely chopped parsley
1 tablespoon chopped basil
1 lb (500 g) macaroni
4 oz (125 g) spicy salami, diced
4 oz (125 g) mozzarella cheese, diced
$^{2}/_{3}$ cup ($2^{1}/_{2}$ oz/75 g) finely grated pecorino or
    Parmesan cheese
2–3 hard-boiled eggs, peeled and sliced

Serves 6

Preheat oven to 375°F (190°C).

Wipe the eggplants and cut into $^{1}/_{4}$-in (0.5 cm)
slices. Spread on a plate and sprinkle with salt.
Set aside for 15 minutes for the salt to draw off
any bitter juices.

Chop the tomatoes. In a frying-pan, sauté with
garlic in 3 tablespoons of the oil until very soft
and pulpy, then add about $^{3}/_{4}$ teaspoon salt, the
pepper, sugar and herbs and cook for 5 minutes.

Bring a large pan of salted water to a boil, add
the macaroni and 1 tablespoon oil and boil until
tender but still firm. Drain well and place in a
mixing bowl. Add the salami, mozzarella,
Parmesan and the tomato sauce. Set aside.

Grease a pie dish with a little olive oil. Heat
the remaining $1^{3}/_{4}$ cups (14 fl oz/440 ml) oil in a
wide pan. Rinse and thoroughly dry the eggplant
slices. Fry in the oil until lightly colored and softened. Arrange the eggplant slices overlapping
each other, to completely line the pie dish. Place
the sliced eggs over the layer of eggplant, then
pour in the macaroni and press any remaining
eggplant on top. Bake for about 30 minutes, remove from the oven and let stand for about 7
minutes before turning out on a serving dish. Cut
into wedges to serve. Pass around additional
grated Parmesan or pecorino and serve a green
salad to accompany the dish.

NOTE: The eggplant can be fried in advance. Store
in the refrigerator, layered with plastic wrap to
prevent the slices from sticking together. Make
the tomato sauce up to 3 days in advance.

Fettuccine with Asparagus Tips, Ham and Cheese

salt
1 tablespoon olive or vegetable oil
1 lb (500 g) fettuccine
12 fresh asparagus spears
4 oz (125 g) prosciutto or cooked ham, diced
3 oz (90 g) grated fresh pecorino cheese
2 tablespoons butter
1½ teaspoons finely chopped parsley

Serves 4

Bring a large pan of water to a boil; add salt, olive oil and the pasta. Bring to a boil again, then reduce heat to maintain a rolling boil while the pasta cooks—about 8 minutes.

In another saucepan, cook the asparagus in simmering, lightly salted water until tender enough to be easily pierced with a fork. Drain and cut into ¾-in (2 cm) pieces.

Drain the pasta and transfer to a bowl. Cut the ham into small squares. Toss the pasta with the asparagus, ham, half the cheese and the butter. Serve in pasta bowls and top with the remaining cheese and finely chopped parsley.

Spaghetti Bolognese

8 oz (250 g) lean ground (minced) beef
8 oz (250 g) lean ground (minced) veal
4 tablespoons olive oil
4 oz (125 g) bacon, minced
1 large onion, finely chopped
2–3 garlic cloves, finely chopped
2 large chicken livers, finely chopped
1 bay leaf
1 tablespoon finely chopped parsley
1½ lb (750 g) sun-ripened tomatoes
3 tablespoons tomato paste
¾ teaspoon sugar
salt
pepper
1 teaspoon chopped basil
1½ lb (750 g) spaghetti
finely grated Parmesan cheese
chopped parsley

Serves 6

Prepare the sauce several hours in advance if possible to allow time for the flavors to develop. In a large saucepan, sauté the beef and veal in the 3 tablespoons of olive oil over moderately high heat, stirring continually to break up any lumps. In a smaller pan, cook the bacon until well browned, then use a slotted spoon to add it to the meat. Sauté the onion in the bacon fat until soft and golden, then add the garlic and chicken livers and cook until the livers change color. Add to the meat along with the bay leaf and parsley.

Peel the tomatoes by placing in a pan of simmering water for 8–10 seconds to loosen the skin. Cut in halves and squeeze the seeds into a strainer, allowing any liquid to pass through. Finely chop the tomatoes. Add to the sauce and cook for 15 minutes, stirring occasionally to prevent sticking. Add the tomato paste and sugar, with salt and pepper to taste, and simmer for about 40 minutes. It should not be necessary to add liquid to the pan; but if the sauce does become dry, add a little warm water. Stir in the basil a few minutes before the sauce is done.

Bring a large pan of water to a boil, salt it generously and then add the remaining oil. Add the pasta and bring to a boil, then reduce heat so that the water maintains a rolling boil. Cook, stirring occasionally, for about 12 minutes. The pasta should be al dente, barely tender when ready. Drain the pasta thoroughly and transfer it to a serving dish or serve immediately in spaghetti bowls. Spoon the sauce over the top and sprinkle on Parmesan cheese and parsley. Serve immediately.

NOTE: The bolognese sauce can be prepared up to several days in advance and then stored in a covered container in the refrigerator. You can also freeze the pasta sauce in plastic containers. Remove from the freezer 2 or 3 hours ahead of time to thaw.

Tagliatelle with Lemon and Parsley

1 lb (500 g) tagliatelle
2 tablespoons olive oil
¼ cup (2 oz/60 g) butter
2 small onions, chopped
1 tablespoon grated lemon zest
½ cup (2 oz/60 g) pitted, chopped green olives
½ cup (½ oz/15 g) chopped flat leaf (Italian) parsley

Serves 4

Cook the pasta in a large pot of boiling water until al dente. Add a little of the olive oil to the pot to prevent the pasta from sticking together. Drain and return to the pot with the butter, remaining olive oil, onions, lemon zest, olives, and parsley and mix well. Warm gently (photograph pages 164–65).

NOTE: The pasta in this dish can be cooked ahead of time and then reheated in a microwave oven or by covering with boiling water. Pasta on its own freezes well, but avoid freezing this completed dish as the texture of both the asparagus and prosciutto are ruined by freezing.

Opposite: spaghetti bolognese (top); fettuccine with asparagus tips, ham and cheese (bottom)

When inviting people of widely differing ages to a meal (adults, teenagers and children), menu planning needs particular care. Pasta and rice are favorites for all generations; mildly spicy food is acceptable to sophisticated and young palates; and simple meat and fish dishes with sauces that can be served separately to the older members of the gathering are ideal.

Spaghetti with braised pork ribs

Tricolor Pasta with Summer Vegetables

salt
3 tablespoons olive or vegetable oil
4 oz (125 g) tomato-flavored tagliatelle or
    fettuccine
4 oz (125 g) spinach-flavored tagliatelle or
    fettuccine
4 oz (125 g) plain tagliatelle or fettuccine
1 medium zucchini (courgette), sliced
$^1/_2$ cup (3 oz/90 g) green peas
4 spears fresh asparagus
12 cherry tomatoes
12 large snow peas
1 scallion (spring onion)
black pepper
$1^1/_2$ tablespoons ($^3/_4$ oz/20 g) butter (or use extra
    olive oil)

$^1/_4$ cup (1 oz/30 g) finely grated Parmesan cheese
$1^1/_2$ teaspoons very finely chopped fresh basil

Serves 6

Bring a large pan of water to a boil, salt generously and add $1^1/_2$ tablespoons of the olive oil. Add the pasta and cook until just tender—about 9 minutes.

Meanwhile, in a small saucepan, simmer the peas in lightly salted water for about 4 minutes; remove with a slotted spoon. Cut the asparagus into $^3/_4$-in (2 cm) pieces, add to the pan with the zucchini and cook for about 3 minutes, then remove. Add the snowpeas and cook for 30 seconds. Remove and cut into shreds. Cut the scallion into fine shreds.

Drain the pasta and toss with the remaining olive oil, all of the vegetables, the butter and half of the cheese. Serve in pasta bowls and sprinkle on the remaining cheese with the finely chopped basil (photograph page 92).

Spaghetti with Braised Pork Ribs

2¹/₂ lb (1.25 kg) meaty pork spareribs
1 large onion, chopped
3 garlic cloves, chopped
3 tablespoons olive or vegetable oil
1 can (14 oz/440 g) crushed tomatoes
1¹/₂ cups (12 fl oz/375 ml) water
1 cinnamon stick
1 bay leaf
1 whole clove
¹/₂–1 teaspoon paprika
salt
black pepper
3 tablespoons finely chopped parsley
1¹/₂ lb (750 g) spaghetti
¹/₃ cup (³/₄ oz/20 g) pitted black olives
finely grated Parmesan cheese (optional)

Serves 6

Preheat oven to 350°F (180°C).

Place the ribs in a casserole. Sauté the onion and garlic in two-thirds of the oil until lightly colored. Add the tomatoes and water and bring to a boil. Pour over the ribs and add the cinnamon stick, bay leaf and clove. Cover and bake for 2 hours, or until the ribs are very tender.

Remove the meat and cut into small cubes. Transfer the liquid to a saucepan and add paprika, salt and pepper and half the parsley. Boil rapidly to reduce to about 3 cups (24 fl oz/750 ml). Return the meat and keep warm.

Bring a large pan of salted water to a boil and add the remaining oil and pasta. Return to boiling, then cook with the water just simmering for about 12 minutes, or until the pasta is tender. Transfer to a colander to drain, then place in a large serving dish and pour the meat and sauce on top, or serve in deep bowls. Garnish with the olives, Parmesan and remaining parsley.

Linguine with Three Cheeses and Black Olives

3 tablespoons olive oil
1 lb (500 g) linguine
salt
2 tablespoons butter
2 tablespoons finely grated pecorino or
    Parmesan cheese
¹/₂ cup (2 oz/60 g) grated Cheddar cheese
¹/₂ cup (2 oz/60 g) grated mozzarella cheese
³/₄ cup (3 oz/90 g) pitted, small, whole black
    olives
finely chopped parsley or small sprigs fresh
    parsley

Serves 4

Bring a large pan of salted water to a boil and add one-third of the oil. Add the pasta and simmer gently for about 7 minutes, or until just tender. Drain well and transfer to a mixing bowl. Toss through remaining oil, butter, cheeses and olives, and spoon immediately into pasta bowls. Garnish with the parsley and serve at once.

Spaghetti with smoked salmon and cream cheese (left); linguine with three cheeses and black olives (right)

Spaghetti with Smoked Salmon and Cream Cheese

1 tablespoon olive or vegetable oil
1 lb (500 g) spaghetti
6¹/₂ oz (200 g) cream cheese, at room
    temperature
1 tablespoon chopped fresh dill
6¹/₂ oz (200 g) smoked salmon, sliced and diced
lemon slices or wedges
sprigs of fresh dill

Serves 4

Bring a large pan of salted water to a boil, add the oil and spaghetti and boil gently for about 12 minutes, or until *al dente*. In the meantime, beat the cream cheese and dill chopped together. Drain the pasta and stir in the cream cheese. Serve at once, garnished with the salmon, lemon and dill sprigs.

Quick-bake Rice

2 cups (10 oz/315 g) white rice
10 oz (250 g) package frozen spinach
1 large onion, sliced
¼ cup (2 oz/60 g) butter
1 garlic clove, chopped
salt
black pepper
freshly grated nutmeg
5 oz (155 g) peeled, cooked small shrimp
2 tablespoons pine nuts, toasted

Serves 4–6

Preheat oven to 375°F (190°C).

Place the rice in a heavy saucepan with a tightly fitting lid. Add 3 cups (24 fl oz/750 ml) water and bring to a boil. Cover, reduce heat to very low and cook gently for 12 minutes.

Thaw the spinach in a covered saucepan over gentle heat or in a microwave. In a small pan, sauté the onion in half the butter until golden brown. Add garlic and sauté briefly, then add the spinach and cook briefly. Add salt, pepper and nutmeg to taste.

Use some of the remaining butter to thickly grease a casserole or rice mold. Mix the shrimp with half the rice, the pine nuts with the remainder. Place pine nut rice in the bottom of the prepared dish and spread the spinach mixture on top; cover with the shrimp rice. Cut any remaining butter into small cubes and place on top. Bake for 12 minutes. Invert onto a serving plate and garnish with sprigs of fresh herbs.

NOTE: The rice can be made ahead of time and frozen, or assembled and refrigerated for up to 12 hours before cooking. If longer advance preparation is required, omit the shrimp.

Indian Fruity Spiced Rice

3 tablespoons clarified butter
2 cups (10 oz/315 g) long-grain white rice
1 teaspoon salt
1½ teaspoons garam masala
½ cup (3 oz/90 g) dried mixed fruit
¼ cup (2 oz/60 g) finely chopped dried apricots
2 whole cloves
seeds from 2 cardamom pods
1 cinnamon stick

Serves 6

In a medium saucepan with a heavy base and close-fitting lid, melt the clarified butter. Add the rice and stir for 2–3 minutes. Add the remaining ingredients along with 2¾ cups (22 fl oz/685 ml) water. Bring just to a boil, reduce heat to lowest setting, cover, and then cook for approximately 18 minutes, until light and fluffy. Stir well. Discard the cloves and cinnamon stick.

NOTE: Rice reheats well in the microwave oven, so the dish can be prepared ahead of time and reheated on MEDIUM-HIGH. It also can be frozen. Reheat in microwave or place in a low oven.

As you will be surrounded by plants and flowers in the garden, keep the table centerpiece to a simple arrangement of flowers. Alternatively, arrange the flowers on a serving table adjacent to the dining table.

Quick-bake rice

Layered Saffron Rice with Chicken, Peas and Pine Nuts

2 cups (10 oz/315 g) long-grain white rice
1/2 teaspoon powdered saffron (or 1 1/2 teaspoons turmeric)
salt
1 large onion, sliced
1/4 cup (2 fl oz/60 g) clarified butter
8 oz (250 g) boneless chicken breast, cubed
1 1/2 teaspoons garam masala (optional)
black pepper
1 cup (6 oz/185 g) green peas
1/2 cup (2 oz/60 g) toasted pine nuts

Serves 6

Preheat oven to 350°F (180°C).

Place the rice in a medium saucepan with a close-fitting lid and heavy base. Add saffron, 1 1/2 teaspoons salt and 2 3/4 cups (22 fl oz/685 ml) water. Bring just to a boil, stir briefly, then cover tightly and cook over very low heat for 15 minutes.

Meanwhile, sauté the onion in the butter until golden brown; remove with a slotted spoon. Add the chicken and sauté until almost cooked, add the garam masala and season with salt and pepper. Cook the peas in boiling, lightly salted water. Drain.

In a glass casserole, layer rice, onions, chicken, peas and pine nuts, finishing with rice and covering the top with pine nuts. Bake in oven for 15 minutes.

NOTE: The dish can be assembled in advance and reheated in the microwave or in a low oven. The whole dish, or leftovers, can be frozen. Defrost and reheat in a microwave or low oven. Add a little butter to moisten.

Indian fruity spiced rice (left); layered saffron rice with chicken, peas and pine nuts (right)

Baked Macaroni and Cheese with Tuna and Peas

1 tablespoon olive or vegetable oil
1²/₃ cups (8 oz/250 g) macaroni
salt
2 tablespoons (1 oz/30 g) butter
2 tablespoons all-purpose (plain) flour
1¹/₂ cups (12 fl oz/375 ml) milk
*³/₄ cup (3 oz/90 g) grated Gruyère or other mild
    cheese*
¹/₂ teaspoon sharp mustard
2 teaspoons chopped parsley
1 can (6¹/₂ oz/200 g) tuna, drained
1 cup (6 oz/185 g) green peas, cooked
¹/₄ cup (1 oz/30 g) fine dry bread crumbs

Serves 6

Preheat oven to 350°F (180°C).

Cook the macaroni in a large saucepan of gently boiling, salted water to which you have added the olive or vegetable oil (to prevent the pasta from sticking together) and set aside. Ensure the liquid does not boil during cooking. When tender but still holding their form, drain the macaroni and sprinkle on a little vegetable oil or melted butter to prevent them from sticking together.

Melt the butter in a medium saucepan. Add the flour and cook briefly, then whisk in the milk and cook until thick. Add the cheese, mustard and parsley.

Toss the pasta with the tuna and peas and transfer to a buttered ovenproof dish. Pour on the sauce and cover the surface with the bread crumbs. Dot a little extra butter over the surface if desired. Bake in the oven for about 15 minutes, or until the surface is crisp and golden. Serve hot (photograph page 92).

NOTE: This dish can be made a day or two in advance and refrigerated in a covered container. Reheat in a moderate oven. If making in advance, do not bake before storing. To freeze, wrap the container in several layers of plastic wrap to exclude air. Thaw slowly by placing it in the refrigerator at least 5 hours before cooking, or defrost and heat in microwave oven.

Mexican Rice

2¹/₂ cups (1 lb/500 g) short-grain white rice
¹/₂ cup (4 fl oz/125 ml) olive or corn oil
2 onions, chopped
2 garlic cloves, crushed
2 small chilis, finely chopped
4 tomatoes, peeled, seeded and chopped
1 cup (4 oz/125 g) fresh peas
3 carrots, peeled and diced
5 cups (1¹/₄ qt/1.25 l) chicken stock, boiling
3 hard-boiled eggs, peeled and quartered
2 tablespoons chopped parsley

Serves 10

Rinse rice under cold running water to remove starch; drain. Spread rice out over a flat surface to dry.

Heat oil in a large frying-pan, add onions, garlic and chilis and cook, stirring, over moderate heat for 1 minute. Add rice and stir until coated with oil and lightly golden. Add tomatoes, peas, carrots and chicken stock. Bring to a boil, reduce heat and simmer, covered, for about 35 minutes, or until rice is cooked. During cooking time, stir rice frequently to prevent it from sticking to the base of the pan. Spoon rice onto serving platter, garnish with eggs and sprinkle with parsley (photograph page 171).

Paella Valenciana

2 lb (1 kg) fish heads and trimmings
*12 large uncooked shrimp in the shell
    (or 6 shrimp and 6 small crayfish tails)*
12 small fresh mussels, soaked and scrubbed
12 fresh clams, soaked overnight
3 large tomatoes, chopped
12 sea scallops
*8 oz (250 g) white fish fillets (perch, sea bass,
    cod, etc.), cubed*
8 cups (2 qt/2 l) water
4 tablespoons (2 fl oz/60 ml) olive oil
1 medium onion, chopped
2 garlic cloves, chopped
*3 cups (21 oz/650 g) short-grain white or round-
    grain Italian rice*
1 cup (8 fl oz/250 ml) dry white wine
large pinch of saffron threads
salt
pepper

Serves 4–6

Place the fish heads and trimmings in a deep saucepan and add the water, shrimp, mussels and clams. Bring to a boil, then reduce to a simmer. Use a slotted spoon to remove the mussels and clams as soon as their shells open. Remove the top shell of each, if you like, and set aside, covered, to prevent them from drying out. When the shrimp are almost cooked, remove and peel. Return the shells to the saucepan; cover the shrimp to prevent them from drying out. Add 2 of the chopped tomatoes to the stock and simmer gently for 10 minutes. Add the scallops and cubed fish and cook briefly, then remove with a slotted spoon and set aside with the shrimp. Simmer the stock a further 10 minutes, then strain into a pitcher.

Sauté the remaining tomato, the onion and the garlic in 2 tablespoons of the olive oil.

In a *paella* or other suitable wide, shallow pan, stir the rice into the remaining oil for 2 minutes. Add 3 cups (24 fl oz/750 ml) stock and cook on moderate heat for 5–6 minutes. Add the wine and cook for 3–4 minutes, then add the sautéed tomato and onion. Add the remaining stock a little at a time, allowing it to be absorbed before adding more. In total between 5 and 6 cups (1¹/₄ qt/1.25 l

Food always looks best on a plain plate, or one with a simple pattern or neat border. All-over designs are fine for large serving platters but not for individual place settings.

and 1½ qt/1.5 l) of stock will be needed.

When the rice is almost done, add the seafood, pressing it into the rice. Mix the saffron with a little hot stock and pour over the rice, adding salt and pepper to taste. Cook on moderate heat, taking care that the rice does not stick to the bottom of the pan. When done, the rice will be just tender and bright yellow and the seafood cooked but still moist and tender. Serve with wedges of lemon.

NOTE: The stock can be made in advance and refrigerated. *Paella* should not be cooked until ready to serve.

Paella Valenciana

Photograph pages
106–107, "Boating
Fare," clockwise from
front: marinated tuna
with fried vegetables
(page 112); marinated
beets (page 178);
pickled cucumber (page
178); marinated red
onions (page 178);
arugula salad with
caper and olive dress-
ing (page 88); pumpkin
pie (page 215); mari-
nated octopus (page 113)

Sherried Noodle and Cashew Salad

¼ cup (2 fl oz/60 ml) olive or safflower oil
2 teaspoons sesame oil
1 teaspoon chili oil
1 red bell pepper, seeded and chopped
1 lb (500 g) Chinese egg noodles
2 tablespoons chopped fresh coriander (cilantro)
2 tablespoons roasted cashews, chopped
2 tablespoons sherry

Serves 6

Heat oils in a frying-pan, add bell pepper and noodles and cook over high heat for 3 minutes, or until noodles are cooked. Remove from heat, transfer noodles to bowl, stir in coriander (cilantro), cashews and sherry (photograph pages 90–91).

Stir-fried Seafood in Crisp Noodle Nests

Light the fire early for a
barbecue. If you have a
large number of guests
(up to 20), start cooking
the food in good time as
it will have to be cooked
and served in stages.

6–8 oz (185–250 g) thin egg noodles
oil, for deep-frying
1 tablespoon ginger juice or Chinese wine
12 medium fresh shrimp, peeled
12 fresh sea scallops or small pieces of fish
small lobster or crayfish tails, halved (optional)
2 cleaned squid, cut into rings
1 stalk celery
1 medium carrot
1 medium zucchini (courgette)
3 slices fresh ginger
¼ cup (2 fl oz/60 ml) vegetable oil
1 tablespoon light soy sauce
salt
pepper
⅓ cup (3 fl oz/90 ml) fish or chicken stock
1 teaspoon cornstarch (cornflour)
parsley

Serves 4

Soak the noodles in boiling water for a few minutes to soften. Drain and spread on a tray to partially dry. Heat oil for deep-frying. Dip a noodle nest basket (or 2 wire-mesh strainers, one slightly smaller than the other) into the hot oil to thoroughly coat them with oil. Remove and cool.

Arrange one-quarter of the noodles in a layer in the larger basket, allowing some to protrude over the edge. Press the top or smaller basket into the nest and clip or tie the two handles together. Place in the hot oil to fry until crisp and golden. Separate the baskets, then use a narrow-bladed knife to gently ease the noodle "nest" from the metal basket. Drain on paper towels. Prepare 4 nests in this way.

Opposite: Thai-style
stir-fried rice noodles
(left); stir-fried seafood
in crisp noodle nests

Sprinkle the wine over the combined seafood and set aside. Thinly slice celery, carrot and zucchini. Shred the ginger. Stir-fry the vegetables in the vegetable oil for about 2 minutes, or until cooked but still crisp. Set aside.

Stir-fry the seafood for about 2 minutes, or until it changes color. Add the soy sauce and cook briefly, stirring. Return the vegetables to the pan and add salt and pepper to taste. Mix together the stock and cornstarch, pour into the pan and stir until thickened.

Stand the noodle nests on a platter, individual plates or shallow bowls and surround with parsley. Spoon in the filling and serve at once.
NOTE: The nests can be made ahead of time and stored in an airtight container. Surround them with tissue or paper towels to prevent breakage.

Thai-style Stir-fried Rice Noodles

6 oz (185 g) rice stick noodles
6 oz (185 g) boneless chicken breast
6 oz (185 g) fresh bean sprouts
1 small carrot
½ stalk celery
2 scallions (spring onions)
3 slices ginger, finely shredded
3 tablespoons vegetable oil
1 small fresh red chili, finely shredded
½ teaspoon sugar
2 tablespoons fish sauce
salt
pepper
fresh coriander (cilantro) sprigs
1–2 teaspoons toasted sesame seeds

Serves 4

Cover noodles with boiling water and set aside for 5–6 minutes to soften. Drain well and set aside.

Cut the chicken into small cubes. Rinse and drain the bean sprouts. Cut the carrot and celery into matchstick shreds. Shred the white part of the scallions. Finely chop the scallion greens and set aside for garnish.

Sauté the chicken and ginger in the vegetable oil for about 1½ minutes, or until the chicken changes color. Push to one side of the pan and sauté the vegetables, half the onion and half the chili for about 2 minutes. Remove.

Add noodles to the pan and toss in the oil, adding sugar, fish sauce, salt and pepper. Return the meat and vegetables and toss with the noodles. Transfer to a serving dish and garnish with sprigs of fresh coriander (cilantro), the remaining chili and scallion greens. Scatter on the sesame seeds.
NOTE: Noodles can be softened in advance, covered with cold water and refrigerated until needed. Drain well before using.

Fish and Seafood

Delicately flavored or wonderfully rich, seafood is ideal on a balmy day when the last thing you want to do is spend hours in a hot kitchen. Broiled with butter and lemon juice, cooked on skewers or, more exotically, wrapped in foil and baked in a pit over hot coals, seafood is both light and luscious.

Barbecued, broiled or pan-fried, fillets and small fish, shrimp and squid need only be cooked for a few minutes. Seafood tastes delicious cooked over a barbecue and smells wonderful in the process. Oily varieties are the easiest to cook this way.

Avoid fish with small bones. In this instance, a blander, firm-fleshed fish is preferable to a more flavorful one that has to be picked over carefully. It can be enlivened with marinades and sauces for more sophisticated palates.

Crabs, shrimp and lobsters look and taste marvelous. You can even buy them ready-cooked. As guests will be using their hands while eating, make sure you provide plenty of fingerbowls filled with water and lemon.

Smoked salmon never goes out of fashion and is excellent served with a simple garnish as a starter or made into a pâté. Smoked trout and tuna are equally delicious and versatile, while smoked cod is perfect baked with a sauce and topped with cheese and bread crumbs.

Be prepared to change your menu according to what's best at your local fish market that day. Spontaneity is one of the keys to successful entertaining.

Opposite: steamed whole fish Chinese style (bottom, page 122); tea- and orange-smoked shrimp (top, page 110)

Tea- and Orange-smoked Shrimp

16 large fresh shrimp in their shells
$^1/_2$ teaspoon salt
2 teaspoons ginger wine or sweet sherry
3 tablespoons jasmine tea leaves
4 pieces Chinese dried orange zest (or the
    zest of $^1/_2$ orange)
1 tablespoon sugar
1 small fresh mango, peeled and cut off the pit
2 teaspoons sweet chili sauce (or to taste)
1 teaspoon finely chopped fresh basil
1 large ripe avocado
sprigs of fresh basil

Serves 4

Rinse and dry the shrimp. Use a sharp knife to cut through the shell along the center back. Lift out the dark vein and discard. Sprinkle the shrimp along the cut area with salt and ginger wine.

Fold a double thickness of aluminum foil into a 7-in (18 cm) square and place inside a large wok. Place the tea leaves, orange zest and sugar on the foil and position a metal rack over them. Arrange the shrimp on the rack. Cover with the lid and place over high heat. When the contents begin to smoke, the heat may be reduced. Smoke-cook for about 12 minutes (cooking time will depend on the size of the shrimp), or until the shrimp are firm and cooked through but have not begun to dry out. Remove from the wok. Remove heads and shells. Arrange the shrimp in fan shapes on large plates.

Purée the mango in a food processor or blender; stir in the chili sauce and basil. Place a spoonful of the sauce on each plate and garnish with thinly sliced avocado and basil (photograph page 108).

Slicing meat, fish and poultry neatly into thin strips or cubes before cooking is often a laborious business. Food will slice better (and more quickly) if it has been chilled for about 30 minutes in the freezer. Cucumbers and tomatoes also slice well when chilled.

Stir-fried Shrimp with Shredded Vegetables

12 large shrimp in their shells
1 medium onion
1 medium red bell pepper
2 scallions (spring onions)
3 tablespoons vegetable oil
1 medium carrot, thinly sliced
3 thin slices fresh ginger, shredded
12 snow peas (optional)
$^1/_2$ cup (4 fl oz/125 ml) light chicken stock or water
1 tablespoon light or low-salt soy sauce
1 teaspoon cornstarch (cornflour)
salt
white pepper

Serves 4

Shell the shrimp, leaving the last section of the shell and the tail intact. Cut the onion and bell pepper into narrow strips cutting from top to base; separate the pieces.

Cut the scallions into $1^3/_4$-in (4 cm) lengths and shred finely lengthwise.

Heat a wok or large pan, add the oil and stir-fry the onion, bell pepper and carrot until they begin to soften, then remove to a plate. Stir-fry the shrimp until they change color and are barely cooked through; remove. Add scallions, ginger and snow peas and stir-fry for 30 seconds. Return the shrimp and vegetables. Add the stock mixed with soy sauce and cornstarch and stir on high heat until the sauce thickens. Season to taste with salt and pepper. Serve at once over white rice.

NOTE: The vegetables can be cut up several hours in advance and stored in a plastic container in the refrigerator. Do not cook until just before serving time.

Chili Crab

1 large fresh crab (2–3 lb/1–1.5 kg)
3 tablespoons vegetable oil
1 large onion, finely chopped
6 slices fresh ginger, shredded
3 garlic cloves, chopped
2 fresh red chilis, seeded and chopped
1 red bell pepper, diced
2 tablespoons white or brown sugar
2 tablespoons white wine vinegar
¹/₂ cup (4 fl oz/125 ml) tomato ketchup
salt
pepper

Serves 4–6

Use a cleaver to chop the crab claws in halves. Remove the undershell and scrape away the inedible parts, then cut into the body between each leg, so that a portion of the body meat remains attached to each leg. Crack the leg shells with the butt of the cleaver. Heat the oil in a wok or large pan and stir-fry the crab pieces until the shell is bright red and the flesh partially cooked—about 3 minutes. Remove and set aside.

Stir-fry the onion until lightly colored, then add the ginger, garlic, chilis and bell pepper and stir-fry until just tender. Add the sugar, vinegar and ketchup and stir on high heat for 45 seconds, then return the crab and add seasonings. Toss the crab in the sauce for 2–3 minutes, then transfer to a serving dish. Spoon on the sauce and serve immediately with white rice.

Stir-fried shrimp with shredded vegetables (left); chili crab (right)

Marinated Tuna with Fried Vegetables

Serves 8

3½ lb (1.75 kg) tuna, in one piece, skin removed
½ cup (½ oz /15 g) chopped parsley
2 tablespoons chopped fresh coriander (cilantro)
2 tablespoons cracked black peppercorns
1½ cups (12 fl oz/375 ml) olive oil
2 garlic cloves, crushed
1 lemon, sliced
olive oil, for shallow-frying
2 eggplants (aubergines), thinly sliced
2 zucchinis (courgettes), thinly sliced lengthwise
1 red bell pepper, cut into thick strips
1 green bell pepper, cut into thick strips

Marinated tuna with fried vegetables (left); marinated octopus (right)

Preheat oven to 350°F (180°C).

Roll tuna in parsley, coriander and pepper. Place tuna in baking dish; add oil, garlic and lemon slices. Cover with foil and bake in oven for about 30 minutes, or until cooked through. While cooking, turn and baste tuna with oil. Remove from oven; allow tuna to cool in oil. Refrigerate for several hours or overnight.

Shallow-fry vegetables in batches; drain on paper towels and allow to cool. At serving time, remove tuna from oil (reserving oil) and discard garlic and lemon. Using a sharp knife, slice tuna into 8 steaks. Arrange on a serving platter with vegetables; drizzle on reserved oil.

Cod poached in coconut milk (left); Indonesian-style fish (right)

least 2 hours to marinate, turning several times.

Drain well. Brush the barbecue grill with oil to prevent the fish from sticking, and cook over gently glowing coals until the fish is tender. Brush occasionally with the marinade during cooking.

If desired, the marinade can be simmered on low heat while fish is cooking, to serve as a sauce.
NOTE: The fish can be marinated overnight, if required, but use slightly less fresh basil in this case.

Cod Poached in Coconut Milk

2–2¹/₂ lb (1–1.25 kg) cod or other thick white fish
  fillets
1 large onion, sliced
1¹/₂ tablespoons vegetable oil
2 stalks lemon grass
1 fresh red chili, seeded
3 cups (24 fl oz/750 ml) thick coconut milk
2 tablespoons light soy, Thai fish sauce or salt
white pepper

Serves 6

Cut the fish into 2-in (5 cm) squares and place in a medium saucepan.

Sauté the onion in the oil until well colored; add to the fish. Cut the lemon grass stalks into 4-in (10 cm) lengths and slit in halves lengthwise. Add all of the ingredients to the fish and cook over moderate heat for about 10 minutes, or until the fish is just cooked through. Do not overcook. Serve with rice flavored with turmeric, salt and chopped garlic.
NOTE: Cracked crabs or whole peeled shrimp are both delicious cooked this way.

Rolled fillets of sole with grapes in white wine sauce

Barbecued Fresh Sardines with Garlic Oil Dressing

12 fresh sardines
1¹/₂ teaspoons coarse salt
3 tablespoons vegetable or olive oil
3–4 garlic cloves, finely chopped
fresh herbs
lemon

Serves 4

Sprinkle the sardines with salt about 20 minutes before cooking. Brush lightly with oil and cook on a barbecue grill until just done. In a small pan heat the remaining oil and add the garlic. Pour the hot garlic oil over the fish and serve at once garnished with herbs and lemon.

Spicy Barbecued Snapper with Dill

1 or 2 snapper or bream (about 2 lb/1 kg total weight)
salt
black pepper
2 tablespoons (1 oz/30 g) butter, or olive or vegetable oil
1 lemon, sliced
3–4 fresh dill sprigs

Serves 4

Clean the fish and make several diagonal slashes on each side. Season inside and out with salt and pepper. On a piece of aluminum foil large enough to enclose the fish, spread or brush the butter over an area the same size as the fish and place the fish on it. Place several lemon slices and a sprig or two of dill in the cavity of the fish and arrange the remaining lemon and herbs over the fish. Wrap the foil around the fish, folding the edges over to seal. Place on the barbecue grill over moderate heat to cook until tender—about 25 minutes for 1 large fish or 15 for 2 smaller fish. Test during cooking by inserting a skewer into the thickest part of the fish. If the flesh is tender and white, the fish is done. Serve.

Rolled Fillets of Sole with Grapes in White Wine Sauce

21 oz (650 g) sole fillets (or whiting or sea perch)
1 cup (8 fl oz/250 ml) dry white wine
salt
white pepper
1 cup (8 fl oz/250 ml) light (single) cream
³/₄ cup (4 oz/125 g) white grapes, halved
dill sprigs

Serves 4

Skin the fillets and season lightly. Roll up each one separately, starting at the narrow end. Stand the fish rolls in a microwave-safe dish. Add half the wine and cover with plastic wrap. Microwave on HIGH for 6 minutes.

Drain the liquid from the dish into a small saucepan and add the remaining wine, salt and pepper. Bring to a boil and simmer for about 6 minutes, then add the cream and simmer gently until the sauce thickens. Add the grapes and pour over the fish. Garnish with sprigs of dill. Serve.

Barbecues are synonymous with relaxed informality. Virtually all the preparation can be done ahead of time. Marinate meat and fish overnight; prepare salad dressings and store in screw-top jars in the refrigerator 2 or 3 days beforehand; make savory butters and the dessert a day or more ahead and store in the refrigerator or freezer. Buy salad ingredients on the day.

Opposite: barbecued fresh sardines with garlic oil dressing (left); spicy barbecued snapper with dill (right)

Pan-fried sea perch with lemon juice and herb butter

Pan-fried Sea Perch with Lemon Juice and Herb Butter

4 sea perch fillets
2 lemons
¼ cup (2 oz/60 g) butter
½ teaspoon salt
⅓ teaspoon black pepper
2 teaspoons finely chopped parsley
1 teaspoon chopped dill
1 teaspoon chopped chives
1 tablespoon very finely chopped red bell pepper
1 garlic clove, finely chopped
4 small zucchinis (courgettes)
dill sprigs for serving

Serves 4

Cut one lemon in two and squeeze half over the fish. Cut the remaining half into 2 wedges and the other lemon into 4 wedges and set aside. Mash the butter with salt, pepper, herbs, bell pepper and garlic. Spread over the fish and pan-fry until cooked through, turning once.

Slice zucchinis lengthwise without cutting through the stalk end. Drop into boiling, lightly salted water to simmer until just tender. Drain well. Arrange fish and zucchini on plates with white rice, lemon wedges and sprigs of dill. Spoon any sauce left in the pan evenly over the fish.

NOTE: Parsley and dill can be replaced with 2 teaspoons of fresh coriander.

118

Fish, Asparagus and Pea Casserole

2 lb (1 kg) cod or other thick white fish fillets
1 cup (8 fl oz/250 ml) dry white wine
1 bunch thin green asparagus
1 cup (6 oz/185 g) green peas
salt
white pepper
1 cup (8 fl oz/250 ml) light (single) cream
2 teaspoons chopped fresh dill or parsley
1 cup (6 oz/185 g) canned or fresh shelled clams
  (optional)

Serves 6

Cut the fish into 2-in (5 cm) pieces and place in a casserole. Add the wine, cover the pan and simmer gently for 6 minutes. Cut the asparagus into 1³/₄-in (4 cm) lengths and boil in lightly salted water for 4 minutes; drain. Boil the peas in lightly salted water until almost tender; drain. Add to the casserole with salt, pepper and the cream. Simmer gently for 3–4 minutes, then add the chopped herbs and clams and check the seasonings. Serve with boiled potatoes or rice.

Smoked Salmon, Avocado and Egg Crêpe Roulade

Crêpes
3 cups (12 oz/375 g) all-purpose (plain) flour
6 eggs
3¹/₄ cups (26 fl oz/810 ml) milk
butter

Smoked salmon filling
10 oz (315 g) smoked salmon
3 tablespoons sour cream
1 small onion, finely chopped
1 tablespoon chopped capers

Avocado filling
2 small avocados
2 teaspoons lemon juice
2 tablespoons sour cream

Egg filling
5 hard-boiled eggs
2 tablespoons chopped chives
¹/₄ cup (2 fl oz/60 ml) mayonnaise

Horseradish and lime sauce
³/₄ cup (6 fl oz/185 ml) sour cream
¹/₂ cup (4 fl oz/125 ml) mayonnaise
¹/₄ cup (2 fl oz/60 ml) lime juice
2 tablespoons chopped dill
2 tablespoons prepared horseradish

Serves 8

To make crêpes: place flour in food processor and process for 5 seconds. Add eggs and process until

Fish, asparagus and pea casserole

combined. Gradually add milk and process until batter is smooth. Heat frying-pan, add butter and coat pan completely with butter. Pour ¹/₂ cup (4 fl oz/125 ml) of the batter into pan, swirling it evenly around pan. Cook over moderately high heat until golden; turn crêpe over and cook on other side. Repeat this process with remaining batter.

For the fillings: combine smoked salmon, sour cream, onion and capers in a bowl and mix well. In another bowl, mash avocado flesh with lemon juice and sour cream. Chop eggs very finely, place in another bowl with chives and mayonnaise and mix well.

To assemble roulade: place 1 crêpe on a flat surface. Spread one-third of the salmon mixture evenly onto crêpe, then place another crêpe on top of the salmon mixture. Spread one-third of the avocado mixture onto crêpe, then cover with another crêpe. Spread one-third of the egg mixture on top, then roll up the crêpe securely to form a large roll. Repeat this process with the remaining crêpes and fillings to make 2 more complete rolls.

At serving time, preheat oven to 350°F (180°C). Place rolls on greased oven tray, cover with foil and bake for 10 minutes, or until warmed through.

Combine all sauce ingredients in bowl and mix well. Slice roulade, arrange the slices on serving plates and serve with sauce (photograph pages 204–205).

NOTE: Unfilled crêpes can be frozen.

Seafood in Saffron and Lemon Sauce with Salmon Roe

4 cups (1 qt/1 l) water
parsley sprigs
1 onion, chopped
2 saffron threads
2 garlic cloves
2 small fresh lobster medallions (slices of
    tail meat)
8 oz (250 g) shrimp, peeled
8 oysters
2 tablespoons salmon roe

Lemon sauce
1/3 cup (3 oz/90 g) butter
1/4 cup (2 fl oz/60 ml) lemon juice
4 egg yolks
1/2 cup (4 fl oz/125 ml) light (single) cream

1 tablespoon fresh chopped dill
2 tablespoons chopped chives

Serves 2

Preheat oven to 350°F (180°C).

Pour water into a large frying-pan; add parsley, onion, saffron and garlic. Bring to a boil and add lobster. Reduce heat and cook lobster for about 10 minutes, or until shell turns bright red and flesh is white. Add shrimp and cook for about 5 minutes, or until shrimp turn pink. Place seafood, covered, in oven to keep warm while making sauce.

For the lemon sauce: place butter and lemon juice in saucepan and stir until melted. Reduce heat to very low, add combined egg yolks and cream; whisk until sauce thickens. Do not allow to boil. Remove from heat, stir in dill and chives.

Arrange warm lobster, shrimp and oysters on serving plates, spoon on sauce and top with salmon roe.

When broiling foods, always bring food to room temperature before cooking. Always preheat the broiler so that the cut edges of the food seal, retaining the juices.

Seafood in saffron and lemon sauce with salmon roe

Crisp Fish Fingers with Tartar Sauce

Tartar sauce
2 hard-boiled eggs
1 raw egg yolk
salt
white pepper
1 cup (8 fl oz/250 ml) vegetable oil
1 tablespoon white wine vinegar
1 teaspoon finely chopped parsley
1 teaspoon finely chopped capers
1 teaspoon finely chopped dill pickle (gherkin)
1½ lb (750 g) fillets of thin white fish such as halibut, turbot or sole, or small fillets of whiting
1½ cups (6 oz/185 g) all-purpose (plain) flour
1 teaspoon salt
½ teaspoon white pepper
2 large eggs, beaten

2 cups (8 oz/250 g) fine dry bread crumbs
vegetable oil, for deep-frying

Serves 4 (or 8 as an appetizer)

For sauce: remove yolks from the hard-boiled eggs and press them through a sieve into a mixing bowl. Add the raw egg yolk and seasonings and beat until smooth. Slowly add the vegetable oil, whisking briskly, to make an emulsion in the same way as mayonnaise. From time to time add a few drops of the vinegar. When done, stir in the remaining ingredients. Spoon into a small serving dish.

Cut the fish diagonally across the fillets into pieces ¾ in (2 cm) wide. Mix flour, salt and pepper together. Dip each piece of fish into the seasoned flour, then into the beaten egg and finally into bread crumbs to coat evenly. Chill for 30 minutes. Heat the deep-frying oil and fry the fish, no more than 5–6 pieces at a time, until crisp and golden. Drain on a rack covered with paper towels and serve hot with the sauce and wedges of lemon.

Crisp fish fingers with tartar sauce

Red onion salad with avocado dressing (top, page 87); marinated whole trout with olives and chili (bottom)

Marinated Whole Trout with Olives and Chili

1/2 cup (4 fl oz/125 ml) olive oil
3/4 cup (6 fl oz/185 ml) coconut milk
1/4 cup (2 fl oz/60 ml) lime juice
2 hot red chilis, chopped
1/2 cup (3 oz/90 g) stuffed olives
1 onion, chopped
1/4 cup (1/4 oz/8 g) chopped mint leaves
2 limes, sliced
8 small trout, cleaned

Serves 8

Combine oil, coconut milk, lime juice, chilis, olives, onion and mint in a shallow dish; add lime slices and trout. Refrigerate for at least 4 hours.

When ready to barbecue, wrap each fish in foil with 2 tablespoons of marinade and a slice of lime. Barbecue fish for about 8 minutes on each side, or until fish is cooked through. To serve, arrange fish on serving platter and pour on marinade.

Steamed Whole Fish Chinese Style

2 1/2 lb (1.25 kg) whole fish, such as bream or
    snapper
2 tablespoons vegetable oil
2 dried Chinese black mushrooms, soaked in
    boiling water for 20 minutes
1/4 red bell pepper
1/2 stalk celery
2–3 large scallions (spring onions)
4 thin slices fresh ginger
2 tablespoons light soy sauce

Serves 4

Clean, rinse and thoroughly dry the fish and make several deep slashes diagonally across each side. Brush an oval heatproof plate with some of the oil, place the fish on the plate and set on a rack in a steamer.

Drain the mushrooms and trim off stems, then cut caps into fine shreds. Cut the bell pepper and celery into matchstick strips. Shred the scallions (spring onions) and ginger. Pile the shredded vegetables evenly on top of the fish and sprinkle on the soy sauce and the remaining oil.

Cover the steamer and bring the water to a boil. Reduce heat slightly to keep water simmering. Cook for about 12 minutes, then check the fish by inserting a small knife into the thickest part. Continue cooking until the fish is tender but still moist. Serve immediately on the same plate, with plain white rice (photograph page 108).

Insects are always the uninvited guests at an outdoor event. A picnic or boating trip, particularly, can turn into a nightmare if you are unprepared. Always take insect repellent sprays and balms with you. Check for gadgets that you can hang in the garden or trees to repel the irritating visitors; there are some slow-burning citronella varieties that release an odor that dissuades them (but not your guests), and various types of trap that will lure them away from guests.

Photograph following pages, "Family Supper," clockwise from front: bacon and asparagus salad (page 79); caramel–nut self-saucing pudding (page 218); apple and parsley salad with tomato dressing (page 84); turkey, leek and potato pie (page 138)

Poultry and Game

Historically, poultry and game have been strongly identified with luxury, feasting and celebration in much the same way as other meats. Now it's a different story. Aside from chicken, today quail, turkey, duck, rabbit, and others of this group are reasonably priced, widely available and sold in all kinds of cuts.

The chicken breast is tremendously versatile and relatively easy to cook. But the cheaper cuts—thighs, drumsticks and wings—are also useful. Their flavor is more intense than that of the breast meat, which perhaps balances their need for slightly more involved preparation methods. These items are particularly suited to buffets and picnics as they are compact and easily transportable and make good finger food.

The smaller birds such as quail or squab are impressive in appearance and flavor and are perfect food for entertaining. Broiled or roasted, stuffed or marinated, served hot or cold, these birds look splendid when brought to the table on a platter of vine leaves or wreathed in fresh herbs such as rosemary.

When time is not a problem, choose the larger poultry and game items that require slower cooking to show them off to their best advantage. A fine roast duck, turkey or chicken needs little adornment and is always well received.

A pot-roasted rabbit is a sumptuous treat on an early fall day when there's a slight chill in the air and you're enjoying those last few opportunities for outdoor entertaining.

Opposite: lettuce-wrapped chicken thighs in Thai sauce (page 133)

Baked Chicken Breasts with Apricots

6 boneless, skinless whole chicken breasts
1 can (14 oz/440 g) apricot halves, drained with
 1 cup (8 fl oz/250 ml) liquid reserved
6 slices Camembert cheese
salt
black pepper
1/2 cup (4 fl oz/125 ml) Sweet Chili and Garlic
 Sauce (see recipe, page 33)
1–2 teaspoons finely chopped parsley

Serves 6

Preheat oven to 350°F (180°C).
 Use a sharp knife to cut the chicken breasts horizontally almost in two, open out and place on a sheet of heavy plastic. Cover with another piece of plastic and pound to flatten slightly. Place 2 apricot halves and a slice of Camembert cheese on each breast, fold over to enclose and pinch the edges to seal.
 Arrange the breasts side by side in a buttered casserole just large enough to accommodate them. Sprinkle with salt and pepper, then pour on the reserved apricot juice and chili sauce. Bake for about 35 minutes, until the breasts are tender.

Baked chicken breasts with apricots (left); smoked chicken, egg and mushrooms in puff pastry roll (right)

Serve over the white rice, and sprinkle on the chopped parsley.

Smoked Chicken, Egg and Mushrooms in Puff Pastry Roll

8 oz (250 g) fresh mushrooms, finely chopped
2 tablespoons (1 oz/30 g) butter
6 eggs
1 1/4 lb (600 g) boneless smoked chicken meat
1/4 cup finely chopped parsley
salt
black pepper
1 large sheet puff pastry (about 20 x 16 in/50 x
 40 cm)
1–2 tablespoons Seasoned Bread Crumbs (see
 recipe, page 39)

Serves 6

Preheat oven to 400°F (200°C).
 Sauté the mushrooms in the butter until tender. Transfer to a colander to drain. Hard-boil

Pan-fried chicken breasts with tarragon cream sauce

5 of the eggs, cool under running cold water, then peel and cut in halves. Shred the smoked chicken.

Mix parsley into the drained mushrooms and season with salt and pepper. Spread along the center of the pastry sheet and top with the chicken. Press the egg halves into the chicken, regularly spaced. Fold the sides of pastry over the filling, pinch together and invert onto a greased baking sheet. Tuck the ends under to seal. Use a sharp knife to slash the pastry on the diagonal, making cuts about 1¼ in (3 cm) apart. Sprinkle with the bread crumbs. Bake for about 20 minutes until the pastry is puffed and golden. Slice to serve.

NOTE: The roll can be assembled in advance, using very well-drained mushrooms. Wrap in plastic wrap and chill until ready to bake.

Pan-fried Chicken Breasts with Tarragon Cream Sauce

6 boneless, skinless chicken breasts, each about
    5 oz (155 g)
salt
pepper
3 tablespoons (1½ oz/45 g) unsalted butter
1 tablespoon dried tarragon
¾ cup (6 fl oz/185 ml) light (single) cream

Serves 6

Season the chicken breasts with salt and pepper and sauté in the butter until cooked through and the surface is golden brown—about 6 minutes.

Stir the tarragon into the cream. Remove the chicken to warmed plates, pour the cream into the pan and cook gently for 2–3 minutes, spoon over the chicken and serve at once with rice or vegetables.

Grilled Chicken Breasts with Tarragon–Lemon Marinade

4 boneless, skinless chicken breasts, each about
    5 oz (155 g)
juice of 1 lemon
2 tablespoons vegetable oil
½ teaspoon white pepper
2 teaspoons dried tarragon
fresh tarragon sprigs
lemon slices

Serves 4

Place the chicken breasts in a glass dish. Mix the lemon juice, oil, pepper and dried tarragon together in a screw-top jar and shake vigorously to emulsify. Pour over the chicken and marinate for 20 minutes. Heat a barbecue grill or oven broiler and cook the chicken over moderate heat until just cooked through, turning once. Test by pressing the thickest part; it should feel firm. Transfer to warmed plates and serve with fried potatoes. Garnish with sprigs of fresh tarragon and lemon slices (photograph page 136).

NOTE: Chicken can be marinated several hours in advance, if necessary. Cover and refrigerate.

In the fresh air, where there is so much to distract the eye from the food, don't go overboard on garnishes. Keep the food presentation simple and stylish; lemon or lime slices, fresh herbs or a few unshelled shrimp.

Grilled squab marinated in garlic and ginger (left); bacon-wrapped barbecued chicken drumsticks with plum sauce (right)

Bacon-wrapped Barbecued Chicken Drumsticks with Plum Sauce

8 chicken drumsticks
¹/₂ teaspoon salt
¹/₂ teaspoon pepper
1 small garlic clove, mashed (optional)
8 rashers bacon
1 tablespoon vegetable oil
¹/₂ cup (4 oz/125 g) plum jam
1 tablespoon cider vinegar (or to taste)
1 tablespoon mild chili sauce (or to taste)

Serves 4

Rub the drumsticks with the salt, pepper and garlic, if used. Wrap a strip of bacon firmly around each drumstick, securing the ends with toothpicks. Brush with the vegetable oil and barbecue or broil until cooked through—about 12 minutes. Turn frequently and brush with additional oil as the drumsticks cook. To test for doneness, pierce

in the thickest part with a thin skewer. The juices that run out should be clear.

To make the sauce: heat jam, cider vinegar and chili sauce in a small pan or microwave oven and beat together. Arrange the hot drumsticks on a platter around a dish of the sauce for dipping.
NOTE: Drumsticks can be prepared in advance, wrapped in plastic wrap and refrigerated or frozen until needed. Sauce can be made several days in advance and refrigerated.

Grilled Squab Marinated in Garlic and Ginger

4 squab
3 tablespoons vegetable oil
1 tablespoon finely grated ginger
2 large garlic cloves, mashed
1¹/₂ teaspoons salt
¹/₂ teaspoon black pepper
1 medium onion, thinly sliced
1 small cucumber, thinly sliced

1 medium carrot, thinly sliced
2 teaspoons sugar
1¹/₂ tablespoons white wine vinegar

Serves 4

Rinse and thoroughly dry the squab, then cut in half down the backbone and press out flat. Rub with a little of the oil. Mix the ginger, garlic, ³/₄ teaspoon salt and the pepper together and rub evenly over the squab. Set aside for 1 hour.

Barbecue or broil, brushing occasionally with the remaining oil. Turn several times and cook until the surface is golden-brown and the meat feels firm when pressed. Place the vegetables in a dish. Mix remaining salt with the sugar and vinegar and pour over the vegetables. Knead with the fingers for a few minutes until softened. Arrange the squab on warmed plates and garnish the dish with the pickled vegetables.

NOTE: Vegetables can be marinated up to 2 days in advance and stored in a covered container in the refrigerator. Marinate the squab up to 1 day in advance, wrap in plastic wrap and refrigerate.

Rock Cornish Hen Smoked over Mesquite

2 cups mesquite wood chips, for smoking
4 rock Cornish hens
3 tablespoons (1¹/₂ oz/45 g) butter, softened
2 medium garlic cloves, mashed
¹/₂ teaspoon salt
¹/₂ teaspoon freshly ground black pepper
¹/₄ teaspoon cayenne pepper (optional)

Serves 4

Soak the mesquite overnight, or for at least several hours, then drain well. Cut the rock Cornish hens in half, rinse and dry well. Make a paste of the butter, garlic, salt, pepper and cayenne and spread over the hens. Add the wood chips to the barbecue and place the hens skin side down on the rack over the coals. Cover and cook for 15 minutes, turn and cook the other side until done, another 15–20 minutes. Brush with remaining butter from time to time to keep the hens moist. To test for doneness, insert a fine skewer into the thickest part of the meat. If no pink liquid runs off, the hen is done. Serve with salads and crusty bread.

Pot-roasted Rabbit

2 rabbits, each about 1¹/₂ lb (750 g)
salt
pepper
¹/₂ cup (2 oz/60 g) all-purpose (plain) flour
¹/₄ cup (2 fl oz/60 ml) olive or vegetable oil

Pot-roasted rabbit (back); rock Cornish hen smoked over mesquite (front)

1 medium onion
2 whole cloves
1 large carrot, cubed
12 oz (375 g) button mushrooms (champignons)
1 tablespoon tomato paste
1 cup (8 fl oz/250 ml) dry white wine
2 bay leaves
2 thyme sprigs
2 tablespoons dry gin (optional)

Serves 6

Preheat oven to 375°F (190°C).

Cut the rabbits into serving pieces and season with salt and pepper. Coat lightly with flour and brown in the oil. Transfer to a casserole and add the onion stuck with the cloves and the cubed carrot. Add 1 cup (8 fl oz/250 ml) water and place in the oven. Roast for 30 minutes, then add the mushrooms, tomato paste, wine, bay leaves and thyme. Return to the oven for another 45 minutes–1 hour to cook until tender. Add extra water if needed. Add the gin, if used, and check seasonings. Cook another 10–15 minutes. If you like, stir a little flour mixed with butter into the gravy to thicken. Serve in a casserole with a dish of boiled potatoes.

NOTE: This dish improves in flavor if cooked a day in advance; reheat in the microwave oven or in a moderate oven.

Crispy Chicken Wings with Mustard Cream Sauce

2 lb (1 kg) chicken wings
2 tablespoons Dijon mustard
2 tablespoons grainy mustard
1/2 cup (4 fl oz/125 ml) light (single) cream
2 tablespoons honey
1 1/2 teaspoons curry powder
salt
pepper

Serves 4–6

Preheat oven to 375°F (190°C).

Place the chicken wings in an ovenproof dish and bake for about 45 minutes, basting several times with the pan juices. Mix the remaining ingredients together and brush over the wings, return to the oven and bake for another 30 minutes. Serve over rice.

NOTE: The wings can be half-cooked in advance. Spread with the mustard cream sauce and refrigerate until ready to cook again.

Cheesy Chicken Pie

Filling
1 1/2 lb (750 g) boneless, skinless chicken breasts
1 medium onion, finely chopped
1 garlic clove, finely chopped
2 strips bacon, diced
1 package (8 oz/250 g) frozen spinach, thawed
1/2 teaspoon grated nutmeg
3/4 cup (6 fl oz/185 ml) light (single) cream
1/4 cup (2 fl oz/60 ml) water
2 tablespoons all-purpose (plain) flour
salt
pepper

Cheesy pie crust
3 cups (12 oz/375 g) self-rising flour
3 tablespoons (1 1/2 oz/45 g) butter
1/2 teaspoon salt
3/4 cup (3 oz/90 g) grated Cheddar cheese
2 teaspoons finely chopped parsley
1–1 1/4 cups (8–10 fl oz/250–300 ml) milk

Serves 4–6

Preheat oven to 350°F (180°C).

Cut the chicken into small cubes and set aside. In a nonstick sauté pan, lightly brown the onion, garlic and bacon. Remove and set aside. Fry the chicken cubes in the same pan. Return the onion mixture, add the spinach and cook for 2 minutes. Add nutmeg, cream and water and sprinkle on the flour. Cook, stirring, for 5 minutes. Add salt and pepper to taste. Remove from the heat and set aside.

To make the pie crust: sift the flour into a mixing bowl, add the butter cut into small cubes and use fingertips to rub it lightly into the flour to make fine crumbs. Add salt, cheese and pars-ley, then add enough milk to make a soft, but not sticky, dough. Transfer to a lightly floured board and press out to a thickness of 3/4 in (2 cm). Use a 1 1/3 in (4 cm) biscuit cutter to cut into rounds.

Transfer the chicken mixture to a deep pie dish or casserole. Arrange the biscuits over the top and brush them with a little of the remaining milk. Bake in oven for about 15 minutes until the top is well risen, golden and crusty. Serve at once.

NOTE: The chicken filling can be prepared a day or two in advance, but the crust must be made immediately before serving.

Lettuce-wrapped Chicken Thighs in Thai Sauce

6 coriander (cilantro) stems with roots
3 tablespoons fish sauce
1 tablespoon oyster sauce
2 garlic cloves
8 chicken thighs
1 head lettuce, leaves separated, washed and dried
8 oz (250 g) soba noodles, cooked and drained
1 bunch coriander (cilantro) sprigs, washed and dried
1 bunch mint sprigs, washed and dried
1 bunch chives

Thai sauce
2 cups (1 lb/500 g) sugar
1 cup (8 fl oz/250 ml) water
1 small red bell pepper
4 garlic cloves, peeled
3 tablespoons fish sauce
5 tablespoons (2 1/2 fl oz/75 ml) lemon juice
1 teaspoon salt
1 teaspoon Tabasco sauce

Serves 6

Place coriander (cilantro) stems, fish sauce, oyster sauce and garlic in a blender and process until smooth. Cover thighs with paste and refrigerate, covered, overnight.

Grill thighs skin side down for 5 minutes, then turn and cook until skin is crisp and chicken is done. Cool, then cut into strips 1/2 in (1 cm) wide. Arrange the lettuce leaves, chicken strips, soba noodles, coriander, mint sprigs and chives on a platter and cover.

For the sauce: bring sugar and water to a boil over high heat stirring until sugar is dissolved. Boil rapidly for 10 minutes. Remove and cool completely.

Remove stem from bell pepper and cut in half, retaining seeds. Place bell pepper, garlic and 1/2 cup (4 oz/125 g) sugar syrup in food processor and blend until smooth. Add fish sauce, lemon juice, salt and Tabasco sauce and process until blended.

To serve, wrap chicken, noodles, coriander and mint in a lettuce leaf, tie together with a chive, then dip into sauce and eat (photograph page 126).

Opposite: cheesy chicken pie (left); crispy chicken wings with mustard cream sauce (right)

When there's a chill in the air, make sure one course of the meal is robust and well-flavored—an Asian-influenced spicy chicken dish, a substantial soup, or a wickedly rich hot pudding.

Grilled Duck Breasts with Fig Sauce

2 plump ducks
1 small onion
1 small carrot
1 bay leaf
2 peppercorns
6 oz (185 g) dried figs
1 cup (8 fl oz/250 ml) dry sherry
1 small cinnamon stick
1 whole clove
salt
pepper
1 cup (8 fl oz/250 ml) orange juice
2 tablespoons (1 oz/30 g) unsalted butter, melted

Serves 4

Remove the breasts from the ducks. Place the neck, wings and backbones of the ducks in a saucepan to make a stock; wrap and chill the duck breasts. Freeze the remainder for another use. Add onion, carrot, bay leaf and peppercorns to the stockpot and pour in 4 cups (1 qt/1 l) water. Bring to a boil, reduce heat and simmer for 1 hour, skimming the surface occasionally.

Meanwhile, in a saucepan, soak the figs in sherry with the cinnamon stick and clove. Strain the stock into a smaller pan and boil to reduce to 1 cup (8 fl oz/250 ml). Remove the spices from the figs

A simple, impromptu picnic should, ideally, consist of food that can be eaten with the fingers: chicken legs, savory pies, cakes, rolls filled with a delicious mixture of fillings, fresh fruit, nuts and cheese.

and add the stock. Simmer gently until the figs are very tender, then purée in a blender or food processor, return to the saucepan and add the orange juice with salt and pepper to taste. Boil gently to make a very thick sauce.

Preheat oven to 425°F (220°C).

Season the duck breasts with salt and pepper. Brush with melted butter and cook under the broiler or on a barbecue grill for about 15 minutes, until cooked through. Turn several times during cooking to brown the surface evenly. Test if done by piercing with a fine skewer; if no pink liquid runs off, the breasts are done. (They can also be cooked in the oven. Melt butter and brown the breasts in a hot oven dish, turning once, then place in the oven and cook for about 25 minutes, or until done to taste.) Serve on warmed plates and coat with the sauce. Add steamed vegetables and serve at once.

NOTE: The sauce can be made in advance and refrigerated until needed.

Squab with Ricotta and Herbs

1 cup (8 oz/250 g) ricotta cheese
1/4 cup (2 oz/60 g) finely grated Fontina cheese
1/4 cup (2 oz/60 g) crumbled Gorgonzola cheese

Grilled duck breasts with fig sauce

6 slices mortadella, finely chopped
2 tablespoons chopped parsley
1 tablespoon chopped fresh marjoram
2 tablespoons chopped fresh sage
¼ cup (2 oz/60 g) butter, melted
6 1-lb (500 g) squab, washed and dried
¾ cup (6 fl oz /185 ml) olive oil
3 tablespoons fresh rosemary leaves
2 cups (16 fl oz/500 ml) dry white wine

Serves 6

Preheat oven to 425°F (220°C).

Combine the cheeses, mortadella, parsley, marjoram, sage and butter in a bowl and mix well. Using one-sixth of the filling, gently ease filling down and over squab breast, between the skin and the meat. Repeat this process with remaining filling and squab. Heat oil in a small roasting pan, add squab, scatter with rosemary and bake for 30 minutes. Reduce temperature to 350°F (180°C), add wine and bake for 20 minutes, or until tender. During cooking time, baste frequently with pan juices. At serving time, arrange squab on a platter and keep warm. Place roasting pan over high heat, bring to a boil, pour a little sauce over and around squab (photograph pages 74–75).

Chicken Thighs Stuffed with Leeks and Cream Cheese

5 tablespoons (2½ oz/75 g) butter
2 leeks, finely chopped
1 garlic clove, crushed
2 tablespoons chopped parsley
3 tablespoons chopped tarragon
¾ cup (6 oz/185 g) cream cheese, softened
¼ cup (1 oz/30 g) walnuts, chopped
6 chicken thighs
2 tablespoons oil
2 teaspoons dried rosemary

Serves 6

Preheat oven to 350°F (180°C).

Melt 1½ tablespoons (¾ oz/25 g) of the butter, add leeks and cook over low heat until leeks soften, add garlic and cook for an additional 1 minute. Place the leeks in a bowl with parsley, 1 tablespoon of the tarragon, cream cheese and walnuts and beat until combined. Place an equal amount of the cheese mixture under the skin of each chicken thigh, then smooth skin over filling.

Heat oil and remaining 3½ tablespoons (1¾ oz/50 g) butter in baking dish, add chicken and bake for about 30 minutes, or until chicken is golden brown and cooked through. During cooking time baste chicken frequently. After cooling, sprinkle chicken with the remaining tarragon and the rosemary (photograph pages 22–23).

Buffalo wings

Buffalo Wings

18 small chicken wings
6 cups (1½ qt/1.5 l) vegetable oil, for deep-frying
3 tablespoons (1½ oz/45 g) unsalted butter
⅔ cup (5 fl oz/155 ml) hot barbecue sauce
3 large stalks celery
½ cup (4 fl oz/125 ml) sour cream
3 oz (90 g) blue cheese, crumbled
¼ teaspoon coarsely cracked black pepper
1 scallion (spring onion), finely chopped
dash of lemon juice

Serves 6

Fry wings in hot oil until golden and crisp—about 14 minutes. Remove and drain well.

In a small pan, melt the butter, add the barbecue sauce and stir until smooth. Keep hot. Cut the celery into short sticks. Make a creamy sauce of the sour cream, mashed blue cheese, pepper, scallion and lemon juice and spoon into a small serving dish.

Pour barbecue sauce over chicken, brushing each one so it is thickly and evenly coated. Place the dip in the center of a wide serving dish and surround with the chicken. Decorate dish with the celery sticks or serve separately.

Cold Stuffed Boned Chicken

1 large chicken (about 3 lb/1.5 kg)
2 boneless chicken breasts (each about 4 oz/125 g)
1 thick slice cooked ham
1 small onion, very finely chopped
2 tablespoons finely chopped parsley
1 tablespoon finely chopped red bell pepper
2 tablespoons chopped stuffed olives
³/₄ teaspoon salt
¹/₂ teaspoon black pepper
¹/₂ teaspoon dried mixed herbs
1 large egg
2 tablespoons (1 oz/30 g) butter or 2 strips
  bacon

Serves 6–8

Preheat oven to 350°F (180°C).

Debone the chicken by using a small knife to work between carcass and meat beginning at the neck. Sever the wing and drumstick joints at the carcass. Pull the meat off the bones and reserve it. Freeze the bones and carcass for later use in stock or soup. Cut the chicken breasts, ham and reserved chicken leg meat into small cubes and chop to a smooth paste in a food processor. Add the onion, parsley, bell pepper, olives, salt, pepper, herbs and egg and process until well mixed but retaining texture. Stuff the chicken skin and sew up the openings or close with skewers. Rub the skin of the chicken with salt and pepper, and squeeze gently until the original shape of the chicken is regained. Place in a buttered oven dish just large enough to comfortably accommodate the chicken. Spread the butter over the top, or cover with the strips of bacon. Bake the chicken in oven for about 1 hour. Test with a fine skewer and if no pink liquid runs out, the chicken is done. Increase the oven heat, remove the bacon strips and cook for a few minutes to brown the top. Remove from the oven and allow to stand for 5–6 minutes before slicing to serve.

NOTE: The chicken can be fully prepared and re-

From left: cold stuffed boned chicken; rolled chicken breasts stuffed with mozzarella and prosciutto; grilled chicken breasts with tarragon–lemon marinade (page 129)

frigerated or frozen until needed. If frozen, thaw slowly before cooking.

Rolled Chicken Breasts Stuffed with Mozzarella and Prosciutto

4 boneless, skinless chicken breasts
1/2 teaspoon salt
1/4 teaspoon white pepper
1 tablespoon tomato paste
1 cup (4 oz/125 g) grated mozzarella cheese
4 large, paper-thin slices prosciutto
very small pinch dried thyme (optional)
1 1/2 cups (6 oz/185 g) all-purpose (plain) flour
2 eggs, beaten
1 1/2 cups (6 oz/185 g) fine dry bread crumbs
vegetable oil or a mixture of oil and butter, for
   shallow-frying

Serves 4

Place chicken breasts between 2 sheets of waxed paper and pound to flatten, without tearing. Season with salt and pepper and spread tomato paste over the inside of each breast. Sprinkle mozzarella over half of each breast and lay ham on top, folding in layers. Sprinkle on the herbs, if used. Fold the breasts in half and pinch around the edges to enclose the filling.

   Put the flour, eggs and bread crumbs in 3 separate shallow dishes. Dip chicken into flour, coating thinly and evenly, then dip into egg and allow to drain before placing in the crumbs. Place on a plate and refrigerate for 1–2 hours.

   Heat oil to moderate and fry chicken rolls until golden brown and just cooked through—about 5 minutes—turning once. Serve at once with buttered pasta and vegetables.

NOTE: The chicken rolls can be prepared several hours in advance, or the night before. Cover with plastic wrap and refrigerate.

Chicken Burger

1/2 cup (4 fl oz/125 ml) good-quality olive oil
1 eggplant (aubergine), very finely sliced
4 boneless, skinless chicken breasts, seasoned with
   salt and cayenne pepper
lettuce
1 cup Onion Confit (see recipe, page 37)
4 sandwich rolls, halved

Serves 4

Heat 3 tablespoons oil in a heavy-based pan. Add eggplant slices and cook until golden. Set aside to drain. Add 3 tablespoons oil to pan and cook chicken

breasts slowly until golden and tender.

   Brush bread rolls with olive oil. Place a lettuce leaf on base of each roll, top with chicken, eggplant and onion confit. Replace roll top and serve.

Chicken burger

Wine and Herb Marinade

This marinade is suitable for chicken, seafood and fish. This quantity is enough for 5 lb (2.5 kg) boneless chicken or fish, or about 6 2/3 cups (3 lb/1.5 kg) seafood.

1 1/2 cups (12 fl oz/375 ml) olive oil
1 cup (8 fl oz/250 ml) dry white wine
1/2 cup (4 fl oz/125 ml) dry vermouth
1/2 cup (4 fl oz/125 ml) lemon juice
2 garlic cloves
6 shallots, chopped
2 tablespoons lemon thyme, crumbled
several parsley sprigs
2 tablespoons chopped dill
1 lemon, sliced

Makes 4 cups (1 qt/1 l)

Combine all ingredients in a bowl. Place chicken, seafood or fish in a shallow bowl; pour on the marinade. Marinate, covered, for several hours or in the refrigerator overnight. Brush with marinade during cooking.

Stuffed turkey breast roll

Don't try too hard. There are no points to be won for planning a complicated menu that leaves you anxious at every turn of preparation. Particularly when catering for a crowd, stick with your favorite, tried and trusted recipes. Leave experimentation for occasions when you have only two or three people to cook for, and when time is on your side.

Stuffed Turkey Breast Roll

1 small boneless turkey breast, about 3 lb (1.5 kg)
1 cup (6 oz/185 g) green peas
1 lb (500 g) pork or spicy pork sausages
1 small onion, finely chopped
1 rasher bacon, finely diced
2 teaspoons butter or vegetable oil
2 tablespoons finely chopped red bell pepper or
*   canned pimiento*
1 teaspoon dried mixed herbs
1 teaspoon chopped parsley
1/4 teaspoon ground sage
salt
black pepper

Serves 6–8

Preheat oven to 375°F (190°C).

Place the turkey breast skin-side down on a worktop and trim the thicker parts of meat, transferring them to areas where the meat is thinner, to give an even thickness of meat. The spread breast should be approximately 14 x 11 in (35 x 28 cm) in size.

Boil the peas in lightly salted water and drain well. Slit open the sausages to extract the meat and place in a mixing bowl. Sauté the onion and bacon in butter until lightly colored; add the bell pepper and fry briefly. (Canned pimiento does not require cooking.) Mix with the pork, peas and herbs and season generously with salt and pepper. Spread over the turkey breast and roll up. Use fine clean string to tie the roll at 3/4 in (2 cm) intervals. Rub the surface with butter or oil; sprinkle with salt and pepper. Place, seam side down, in a baking dish just large enough to hold the turkey. Place in oven and roast for about 1 hour. Test with a meat thermometer after 45 minutes, and cook for the

required extra time, if needed. Remove from the oven and let stand for 10 minutes. Cut into thick slices to serve hot with vegetables, or allow to cool completely and slice thinly to serve cold with a salad. NOTE: The dish can be assembled in advance, wrapped in aluminum foil and refrigerated for up to 1 day before cooking. The uncooked roll can be frozen. Place in the oven and cook for about 1½ hours.

Turkey, Leek and Potato Pie

2¼ cups (9 oz/280 g) all-purpose (plain) flour,
*   sifted*
½ cup (4 oz/125 g) butter, cut into pieces
³/4 cup (6 fl oz/185 ml) sour cream

Filling
¼ cup (2 oz/60 g) plus 2 tablespoons butter
3 leeks, chopped
4 oz (125 g) mushrooms
2 potatoes, cooked and cubed
3 tablespoons all-purpose (plain) flour
1 cup (8 fl oz/250 ml) chicken stock
¼ cup (2 fl oz/60 ml) dry white wine
½ cup (4 fl oz/125 ml) heavy (double) cream
2 tablespoons chopped parsley
2 egg yolks, lightly beaten
1 lb (500 g) smoked turkey, cooked and chopped
1 whole egg, lightly beaten

Serves 6

Preheat oven to 350°F (180°C).

For the pastry: place flour into a large bowl, rub in butter until mixture resembles coarse bread crumbs. Stir in sour cream and mix to a soft dough. Turn onto floured surface and knead lightly. Cover and refrigerate for 30 minutes.

For filling: melt ¼ cup (2 oz/60 g) butter, add

leeks and cook over low heat for 5 minutes, or until softened. Add mushrooms and cook for another few minutes or until softened. Using a slotted spoon, remove leeks and mushrooms from pan, drain on paper towels and set aside. Add potatoes to pan and cook until lightly golden; remove from pan. Set aside with leeks and mushrooms.

Melt remaining butter in the same pan, add flour and cook, stirring, for 1 minute. Gradually add stock and cook, stirring, until sauce boils and thickens. Add the wine, bring to a boil, stirring. Reduce heat, add cream and stir until sauce boils and thickens. Remove from heat. Add leeks, mushrooms, potatoes, parsley and egg yolks, mix well, allow to cool.

Roll out two-thirds of the pastry and line the bottom and sides of a greased 8-in (20 cm) deep pie dish. Prick base and sides with fork and bake in oven for 25 minutes, or until lightly golden brown. Remove from oven; set aside to cool. Fill pie shell with alternate layers of turkey and sauce mixture. Roll out remaining pastry to fit top of pie. Set in place, crimp edges and trim pastry, then make slits in top of pie to allow steam to escape. Brush top of pastry with beaten egg and bake in oven for 20 minutes, or until golden brown (photograph pages 124–25).

Quails Roasted in Grape Leaves

12 large fresh or salted grape vine leaves
12 plump quails
2 tablespoons (1 oz/30 g) butter, softened
2 small garlic cloves
³/₄ teaspoon salt
¹/₃ teaspoon black pepper
2 tablespoons cognac (optional)

Serves 6

Preheat oven to 375°F (190°C).

Soak salted vine leaves in cold water for 20 minutes, or blanch fresh leaves in boiling water. Drain well. Rinse and dry quails. Make a paste of the butter, garlic, salt and pepper and spread over the breasts of quail. Place a grape leaf over each quail and truss the birds to hold the leaf in place. Place in an oven dish and roast for about 30 minutes. Remove to a serving plate. Deglaze the oven dish with the cognac, if you like, and scrape up the pan juices. Pour on quails and serve at once.

NOTE: The quail can be trussed and kept in the refrigerator, well wrapped in plastic, for up to 1 day before cooking.

Photograph following pages, "Garden Barbecue for Twenty," clockwise from front: sausages marinated in beer (on barbecue, page 147); avocado and mushroom salad (page 80); cheese and scallion bread (page 190); olive and herb bread (page 190); wild berry and apricot trifle (page 209); festive coleslaw (page 84); curried mango rice salad (page 80)

Quails roasted in grape leaves

Meat

For centuries meat has been the food of celebration. Today, the ever-popular roast, be it pork, beef, veal or lamb, has become a favorite dish for outdoor entertaining as the kettle barbecue has enabled it to be cooked out-of-doors.

The prime cuts of meat are ideal for roasting, broiling and quick frying. These methods develop the flavor of the meat while preserving its natural juiciness. Cooked long and slow with a dash of wine or beer, the less expensive cuts will also mellow into very tender, succulent dishes.

Enhancing the natural qualities of meat is a simple process. Marinades add a variety of interesting flavors as well as tenderize the meat. They can transform the humble chop or sausage into something distinctly out of the ordinary. Unless you want to impart only the mildest of flavors, the longer the marinating time the better. The combinations of oils, vinegars, spices and fresh herbs that can be employed in marinades are endless.

Contrary to the belief that sauces are complicated, they often require minimal skills and preparation time. After pan-frying, for example, just pour off any excess fat and deglaze the pan with water, stock or wine, stirring the crusty pan juices to create the easiest sauce of all. Try adding lemon juice to a pan in which veal has been cooked, or cream for a beef dish.

Savory butters and many delicious sauces can be prepared ahead of time. Add them at the last minute, just before serving, to enhance anything from a modest hamburger to char-grilled prime-cut steaks or skewers of marinated lamb.

Meat's versatility, as the following recipes show, offers a wealth of possibilities to the busy, innovative cook.

Opposite: broiled beef kebabs with minted coconut chutney (page 150)

Herb and Lime Butter

This butter is suitable to serve with meat, fish and poultry.

1 cup (8 oz/250 g) butter, softened
1 tablespoon grated lime zest
2 tablespoons lime juice
1 garlic clove, crushed
2 shallots, chopped
2 tablespoons chopped parsley
2 tablespoons chopped chives
1 tablespoon chopped tarragon

Makes 1¼ cups (10 oz/315 g)

Place butter in bowl of food processor with lime zest and juice, garlic and herbs, and process until combined. Spoon butter into a serving dish and refrigerate until firm.

Mustard and Horseradish Butter

This butter is suitable to serve with red meats.

1 cup (8 oz/250 g) butter, softened
1 garlic clove, crushed
2 tablespoons grainy mustard
1 tablespoon prepared horseradish
2 tablespoons chopped chives
1 tablespoon chopped fresh rosemary

Makes 1¼ cups (10 oz/315 g)

Place butter in the bowl of a food processor with garlic, mustard and horseradish and process until combined. Transfer to a bowl, stir in chives and rosemary. Spoon the butter into serving dish and refrigerate until firm.

Chili–Ginger Butter

This butter is suitable to serve with meat, fish or poultry.

1 cup (8 oz/250 g) butter, softened
1 garlic clove, crushed
2 teaspoons chili oil
1 teaspoon chopped fresh chili
1 tablespoon grated ginger
2 teaspoons paprika
1 tablespoon tomato paste

Makes 1¼ cups (10 oz/315 g)

Place all of the ingredients in the bowl of a food processor and process until combined. Spoon the butter into a serving dish and refrigerate until firm.

Marinated steaks with herb and lime butter (left); sausages marinated in beer (front, page 147)

Dress up ham or beef from the local delicatessen with this quick and delicious uncooked chutney. Cut a mango into small cubes, add some minced garlic and finely chopped fresh ginger, a little chopped fresh chili to taste and coriander leaves. Bind with coconut cream.

Red Wine and Mustard Marinade

This marinade is suitable for red meat and game. This quantity of marinade is enough for 20 medium-size pieces of meat.

2½ cups (20 fl oz/625 ml) dry red wine
2 cups (16 fl oz/500 ml) olive oil
½ cup (4 fl oz/125 ml) port
¼ cup (2 fl oz/60 ml) balsamic vinegar
¼ cup (2 fl oz/60 ml) Dijon mustard
2 onions, sliced
2 garlic cloves
2 bay leaves, crumbled
several parsley sprigs
2 tablespoons brown sugar
several black peppercorns

Makes 6 cups (1½ qt/1.5 l)

Combine all the ingredients in a bowl. Place meat in a shallow bowl; pour on marinade. Marinate, covered, for several hours or in the refrigerator overnight. Occasionally brush with the marinade during cooking.

Spicy Marinade

This marinade has an Asian flavor and is most suited to meat or chicken. This quantity is enough for 20 medium-size pieces of meat or chicken.

1 cup (8 fl oz/250 ml) soy sauce
1 cup (8 fl oz/250 ml) plum sauce
1 cup (8 fl oz/250 ml) safflower oil

Marinated barbecued leg of lamb

146

¹/₄ cup (2 fl oz/60 ml) oyster sauce
¹/₄ cup (2 fl oz/60 ml) lemon juice
1 tablespoon sesame oil
1 tablespoon grated fresh ginger
1 tablespoon chopped lemon grass
2 teaspoons chili oil
1 teaspoon five-spice powder
1 teaspoon ground coriander
2 garlic cloves
1 small chili, finely chopped

Makes 4 cups (1 qt/1 l)

Combine all ingredients in a bowl. Place meat or chicken in a shallow bowl and pour on the marinade. Marinate, covered, for several hours or in the refrigerator overnight. Brush meat or chicken with marinade during cooking.

Sausages Marinated in Beer

This quantity of marinade is enough for 20 sausages.

4 cups (1 qt/1 l) beer
1 cup (8 fl oz/250 ml) olive or safflower oil
1 cup (8 fl oz/250 ml) tomato sauce
¹/₄ cup (2 fl oz/60 ml) Worcestershire sauce
¹/₂ cup (4 fl oz/125 ml) Dijon mustard
2 onions, chopped
2 garlic cloves, peeled
black peppercorns

Makes 6 cups (1¹/₂ qt/1.5 l)

Combine all ingredients in a bowl. Place sausages in a shallow bowl and pour on marinade. Prick sausages. Marinate, covered, for several hours or in refrigerator overnight. Brush with marinade during cooking (photograph pages 144–45).

Marinated Barbecued Leg of Lamb

1 leg of lamb, about 6 lb (3 kg)
4–6 garlic cloves, slivered

Marinade
2 tablespoons red wine vinegar
2 cups (16 fl oz/500 ml) dry white or red wine
1 teaspoon black peppercorns
4 bay leaves
1 teaspoon juniper berries
2 parsley sprigs
1 medium onion, chopped
1 small carrot, chopped
1 teaspoon salt
3 tablespoons vegetable oil or melted butter
cracked black pepper

Serves 6

Trim excess fat from the lamb, then slit open the length of the bone and use a small sharp knife to trim around the bone until it can be completely removed. Pierce the leg with the point of a knife and insert the garlic slivers evenly over the whole piece.

Mix the marinade in a large bowl and add the lamb. Cover with plastic wrap and place in the refrigerator, or in a cool place, for 24 hours, turning several times.

Drain well. Pat the surface of the lamb with paper towels to dry and rub with the oil or melted butter, then season with the pepper. Brush the barbecue grill with oil and cook the lamb over moderate charcoals or heat until the surface is well crisped and the meat just cooked through—45 minutes to 1 hour. Turn several times during cooking, basting each time with additional oil or butter. Remove from the heat and let stand for 5–6 minutes. Slice to serve with salads or potatoes baked in foil.

If picnics are your preferred style of entertaining, always have an "emergency kit" of essentials ready to add to the hamper just before you set off. This could include a corkscrew, bottle opener, can opener, box of matches, small salt and pepper shakers, insect repellent, aspirin, adhesive bandages and a ball of string. They may be mundane items, but you'll be lost without them.

Cut the chicken crosswise into 6 pieces and rub with oil, then sprinkle with lemon pepper.

When the beef has been marinated, thread all the meats alternately on oiled metal skewers, adding a bay leaf, mushroom and tomato to each. Brush the kebabs with melted butter and cook on a barbecue grill, turning frequently, until done.

Spiced Beef and Egg Roll

1 large sheet frozen puff pastry
4 eggs
6 spinach leaves (optional)
1 medium onion, finely chopped
2 tablespoons olive oil or clarified butter
1 large, very ripe tomato, finely chopped
1$\frac{1}{2}$ lb (750 g) finely ground (minced) beef or lamb
1 garlic clove, crushed
1 tablespoon finely chopped parsley
1 teaspoon chopped basil
1 teaspoon salt
$\frac{1}{2}$ teaspoon ground black pepper
$\frac{1}{2}$ teaspoon paprika
$\frac{1}{4}$ cup (1$\frac{1}{2}$ oz/45 g) finely chopped stuffed green olives
2 tablespoons all-purpose (plain) flour

Serves 4

Preheat oven to 400°F (200°C).

Set the pastry aside to thaw.

Meanwhile, hard-boil 3 of the eggs and cool under running cold water. Blanch the spinach leaves and drain. Sauté the onion in the oil until soft and lightly colored, add the tomato and cook gently to a pulp—about 7 minutes. Add the beef and garlic and cook, stirring, until the meat changes color. Add the herbs, spices and olives, sprinkle on the flour and mix in evenly. Cook for 2 minutes, stirring.

Cut a piece of pastry 12 in (30 cm) long and the width of the roll. Spread half the meat mixture along the center. Peel the eggs and cut in halves. Arrange end to end on the meat filling and cover with the remaining meat. Fold the sides of the pastry over the filling, bringing them together in the center. Pinch to seal, and pinch the ends to seal as well. Place, seam side down, on a greased and floured baking sheet, and make regularly spaced slashes diagonally across the top. Beat the remaining egg and brush over the pastry to glaze. Bake in the preheated oven for about 20 minutes, until the top is golden.

NOTE: You can prepare the filling in advance and freeze, thaw and assemble as above. Or you could even prepare the roll completely—dust lightly with flour and wrap tightly with plastic wrap before freezing. After thawing, remove plastic wrap and bake in a moderate oven for about 45 minutes.

Barbecued meat kebabs

Barbecued Meat Kebabs

12 oz (375 g) lean tender beef (tenderloin, filet or rump)
salt
black pepper
2 tablespoons light soy sauce
2 teaspoons sugar
1 tablespoon dry sherry or brandy
6 baby lamb chops, bone trimmed
1 garlic clove, mashed
3 spicy sausages
1 large boneless, skinless chicken breast
2 tablespoons olive or vegetable oil
lemon pepper
6 small bay leaves
6 button mushrooms (champignons)
6 large cherry tomatoes
2 tablespoons melted butter or oil

Serves 6

Cut the beef into 1-in (2.5 cm) cubes. In a shallow bowl, mix the salt and pepper, soy sauce, sugar and sherry. Add the beef cubes and marinate for 20 minutes. Rub the lamb cutlets with garlic and set aside. Cut the sausages in halves and set aside.

Spiced Meatballs

1¹/₄ lb (625 g) finely ground (minced) beef or lamb
1 medium onion, grated and drained
2 garlic cloves, mashed
1¹/₂ teaspoons dried mint
1 teaspoon salt
¹/₂ teaspoon black pepper
1¹/₂ teaspoons ground cumin
¹/₂ teaspoon ground allspice
1 egg, well beaten
vegetable oil or clarified butter

Accompaniments
thinly sliced onion
tomato coulis
natural yogurt
sprigs of mint

Serves 4

In a bowl, mix the ground meat with onion, garlic, herbs, and spices. Add the egg and blend thoroughly with the hands, kneading to a smooth consistency. Form into 2-in (5 cm) long croquette shapes. Insert a metal skewer lengthwise through the ovals, placing 3 on each for main course servings, 2 for appetizers. Brush with oil and broil, turning frequently, until cooked through and crisp on the surface.

Separate the onion into rings (if you like, marinate for a few minutes in a mixture of vinegar, sugar, and salt). To make the tomato coulis, cut very red tomatoes in halves and squeeze out the seeds; dice the flesh very finely and season lightly with salt and pepper. Serve meatballs on a platter with the accompaniments.

NOTE: The meatballs can be made in advance on wooden skewers, wrapped tightly in plastic wrap and frozen. Thaw for 30 minutes and remove plastic wrap before cooking.

Spiced meatballs (left);
spiced beef and egg roll
(right)

149

Broiled Beef Kebabs with Minted Coconut Chutney

1 lb (500 g) lean tender beef (tenderloin, filet or
    rump)
1 small onion, grated
1–2 garlic cloves, mashed
1 piece (about 1/2 in/1 cm) fresh ginger, grated
2 tablespoons vegetable oil
1 tablespoon dark soy sauce
1/4 teaspoon salt
1/2 teaspoon black pepper
4–6 large scallions (spring onions)

Minted coconut chutney
1 cup (1 1/2 oz/45 g) loosely packed fresh mint
    leaves
1 medium onion, quartered
1/2 cup (1 oz/30 g) flaked unsweetened
    (desiccated) coconut
1/4 teaspoon black mustard seeds (optional)
1/4 cup (2 fl oz/60 ml) white wine vinegar
2–3 tablespoons sugar
salt to taste

Serves 6

Trim the meat and cut into 1-in (2.5 cm) cubes.
Place in a dish. Mix together the onion, garlic,
ginger, oil, soy sauce, salt, and pepper. Brush over
the meat and cover with plastic wrap. Set aside for
40 minutes.

Cut scallions into 1 1/4-in (3 cm) lengths. Thread
the meat onto oiled metal skewers, alternating
with scallions. Brush with additional oil or butter
and broil, turning frequently until done.

To make the chutney: in a food processor, chop
the mint leaves finely and remove. Chop the onion
to a smooth paste, add remaining ingredients and
process until well mixed. Spoon into a small serving dish.

Serve the kebabs on a bed of saffron rice with
the chutney on the side (photograph page 142).
NOTE: Kebabs can be marinated and threaded onto
bamboo skewers several hours in advance, or the
night before. Wrap tightly with plastic wrap and
refrigerate. Chutney can be made up to 3 days in
advance.

Beef Stroganoff in a Puff Pastry Hat

2 lb (1 kg) beef filet or rump steak
salt
pepper
1 tablespoon all-purpose (plain) flour
2 medium onions, thinly sliced
4 tablespoons (2 oz/60 g) butter
8 oz (250 g) fresh button mushrooms
    (champignons), sliced
1 tablespoon tomato paste
1/2 cup (4 fl oz/125 ml) sour cream

1 sheet (8 oz/250 g) frozen puff pastry, thawed
1 egg, beaten

Serves 6

Preheat oven to 400°F (200°C).

Cut the beef into narrow strips and season
with salt and pepper. Sprinkle flour over meat.
Fry onions in half the butter until golden. Add
mushrooms and fry to soften. Remove and set
aside. Fry beef strips in the same pan with the
remaining butter. Return onions and mushrooms
to the pan, add salt and pepper, tomato paste
and sour cream. Transfer to a large, deep pie
dish and smooth the surface.

Roll out the pastry to fit the dish, allowing a
1/2-in (1 cm) border. Place the pastry over the pie
and trim around the edges. Remove the pastry.
Cut the trimmings into narrow strips. Moisten the
edge of the dish and stick the pastry strips around
the edge. Moisten the top and position the pastry
top over this, pressing around the edges to seal.
Brush with beaten egg and make a steam vent in
the center of the pastry. Bake until the pastry is
golden brown—about 20 minutes.
NOTE: To prepare and cook the stroganoff in advance, place the meat mixture in the pie dish and
cover with plastic wrap. Chill until needed. Warm
through in a microwave, then cover with pastry
and continue as above.

This dish can be completely prepared and frozen.
Remove from the freezer 1 hour before cooking and
bake for about 30 minutes.

Filet of Beef with Red Wine and Pear

1 lb (500 g) beef filet, trimmed
2 tablespoons walnut oil
1 cup (8 fl oz/250 ml) dry red wine
1 tablespoon grainy mustard
1/2 onion, chopped
1 small carrot, peeled and chopped
1 tablespoon red currant jelly
1 pear, peeled
1 tablespoon brown sugar
1/4 cup (2 oz/60 g) crumbled blue cheese

Serves 2

Preheat oven to 350°F (180°C).

Tie beef with string to secure the shape. Heat
oil in a baking dish, add meat and cook in oven for
20 minutes for rare beef—25–30 minutes for medium
and 35 minutes for well done. While the beef is
cooking, pour the wine into the saucepan; add the
mustard, onion, carrot, and red currant jelly. Bring
to a boil, reduce heat; add pear and simmer for
about 15 minutes, or until pear is tender.

At serving time, remove pear from wine, cut in
half and place in oven to keep warm. Bring the
wine back to a boil and boil rapidly for 3 minutes.
Reduce heat, add the brown sugar and stir until
dissolved. Remove onion and carrot from sauce.

Music sets the tone for a party but you do not need it for every occasion. It's a must at large, outdoor informal buffet parties—lunch or dinner—and a pleasant backdrop for drinks on the patio prior to a formal dinner. It is not necessary once guests are seated unless you are creating a partic- ularly romantic setting for just two people.

Slice the beef and arrange on a serving plate with pear halves. Spoon sauce onto the meat and pears, garnish with crumbled cheese (photograph pages 184–85).

Marinated Peppercorn and Mustard Beef with Horseradish Mayonnaise

2 filets of beef tenderloin (each about 3 lb/1.5 kg)
2 cups (16 fl oz/500 ml) dry red wine
$^{1}/_{2}$ cup (4 fl oz/125 ml) vegetable oil
2 garlic cloves, crushed
2 bay leaves
1 onion, chopped
cracked black peppercorns

Horseradish mayonnaise
$^{1}/_{4}$ cup (2 oz/60 g) butter, melted

$^{3}/_{4}$ cup (6 fl oz/185 ml) mayonnaise
2 tablespoons sour cream
2 tablespoons prepared horseradish
1 tablespoon Dijon mustard
2 tablespoons white wine vinegar
$^{1}/_{2}$ cup ($^{1}/_{2}$ oz/15 g) chopped chives

Serves 8

Preheat oven to 350°F (180°C).

Tie the beef with string and place in a shallow dish. Add red wine, oil, garlic, bay leaves, and onion; leave to marinate for several hours. Pour off 2 cups (16 fl oz/500 ml) of the marinade and discard. Place beef in the oven with remaining marinade and bake for about 1$^{1}/_{4}$ hours or until cooked as desired. Allow to cool to room temperature, remove string and roll meat in cracked peppercorns.

Combine all mayonnaise ingredients and mix well. At serving time, slice beef and serve with mayonnaise (photograph pages 40–41).

Beef stroganoff in a puff pastry hat

Beef and Asparagus Rolls with Blue Cheese Sauce

8 boneless, thin beef or veal cutlets (about 1¼ lb/ 625 g)
salt
pepper
8 asparagus spears
8 thin slices cooked ham or prosciutto
1 tablespoon olive oil

Blue cheese sauce
2 tablespoons (1 oz/30 g) butter
1½ tablespoons all-purpose (plain) flour
¼ cup (2 fl oz/60 ml) dry white wine
1 cup (8 fl oz/250 ml) milk
¼ cup (1 oz/30 g) grated Cheddar cheese
¾ cup (3 oz/90 g) blue cheese
salt
pepper

Serves 4

Preheat broiler.

Place the steaks on a worktop, sprinkle with salt and pepper, cover with plastic wrap and pound to thin and tenderize. Trim the asparagus to even lengths and parboil in lightly salted water for 3 minutes; drain and cool under cold running water. Drain again. Place a slice of ham and a spear of asparagus on each steak and roll up. Secure with toothpicks, and brush with the oil. Cook under the broiler, turning frequently, until the meat is done to taste.

Meanwhile, make the cheese sauce by melting the butter in a small pan. Add the flour and cook briefly, then stir in the wine and milk and boil, stirring continuously, until thickened. Add cheeses and seasonings and cook until the cheeses melt and the sauce is creamy. Arrange the rolls on a platter and pour on the sauce or serve separately.

Quick-sautéed Liver with Oregano

1¼ lb (625 g) lamb liver, thinly sliced
1 cup (4 oz/125 g) all-purpose (plain) flour
salt
black pepper
4 tablespoons (2 fl oz/60 ml) olive or vegetable oil
2 teaspoons chopped fresh oregano
1 tablespoon brandy
½ cup (4 fl oz/125 ml) veal stock
oregano sprigs
shredded orange zest

Serves 4

Dry liver on absorbent paper. Season the flour

Quick-sautéed liver with oregano (top); beef and asparagus rolls with blue cheese sauce (bottom)

with salt and pepper and coat each slice of liver thinly and evenly. Heat half the oil in a heavy pan over moderately high heat. Cook the liver, several slices at a time, very quickly, until the surface is well seared and the liver is tender and slightly underdone. Keep warm while the remaining liver is cooked, adding more oil as needed. Arrange on a warmed serving plate and scatter on the oregano. Deglaze the pan with the brandy, add the stock and boil briskly to reduce. Season to taste. Pour over the liver, garnish with oregano and zest and serve at once.

Baked Glazed Ham with Raisins

2 lb (1 kg) cooked ham
1 cup (8 fl oz/250 ml) dry white wine
1 cup (8 fl oz/250 ml) water
1 cup (6 oz/185 g) raisins
2 tablespoons (1 oz/30 g) butter
2 tablespoons brandy

Serves 6

Preheat oven to 350°F (180°C).

Remove rind from the ham and score the surface if the fat is reasonably thick. Place the ham in a casserole and pour on the wine and water, then arrange the raisins and butter around the meat. Pour on the brandy and place in the oven to bake for about 40 minutes, basting frequently with the pan liquids. When the surface is crisp and golden, remove and let stand for 10 minutes before slicing. Serve hot or cold.

NOTE: The ham can be cooked in advance and reheated to serve hot. Cover with aluminum foil and warm for 20–25 minutes in a moderate oven, or wrap in plastic wrap and microwave for about 4 minutes.

Baked glazed ham with raisins

Roast Pork Fillet with Mustard Crust and Apple and Apricot Confit

$^1\!/_2$ cup (1$^1\!/_2$ oz/45 g) dried apricots
1$^1\!/_2$ cups (12 fl oz/375 ml) warm water
2 pork tenderloins (fillets) (each about 1$^1\!/_2$ lb/750 g)
2 garlic cloves
$^1\!/_2$ teaspoon salt
$^1\!/_2$ teaspoon black pepper
3 tablespoons Dijon mustard
1 teaspoon dried basil
2 tablespoons (1 oz/30 g) butter, softened
1 green apple, peeled and cored
2 tablespoons sweet sherry
3 tablespoons sugar
1 tablespoon white wine vinegar

Roast pork fillet with mustard crust and apple and apricot confit

Serves 4

Preheat oven to 375°F (190°C).

Soak the apricots in the warm water for 30 minutes. Trim the pork and place in a flat dish. Mash the garlic with the salt and pepper, then stir in the mustard, basil and butter. Beat to a smooth cream. Spread over the pork and set aside for 20 minutes.

Drain the apricots, reserving the liquid. Finely chop the apricots and apple and simmer in a pan with the sherry, sugar, and vinegar until the fruit is very soft. The confit should be quite thick but not dry, so add as much of the reserved soaking liquid as needed.

Place the pork in a roasting pan and roast for about 25 minutes, or until done to taste. Remove and slice, arrange on a warmed platter and serve with the confit.

Roast Pork with Glazed Pears

1 pork roast (loin or leg) (about 6 lb/3 kg)
coarse salt
6 small firm pears, peeled
2 cups (16 fl oz/500 ml) semisweet white wine
³/₄ cup (6 oz/185 g) sugar
salt
pepper
butter
all-purpose (plain) flour

Serves 6

Preheat oven to 425°F (220°C).

Score the rind of the pork and place roast in a strainer over a large bowl. Pour on boiling water—this causes the skin to contract, making it more crispy. Dry and rub with coarse salt. Place on a rack in a roasting pan, cook for 30 minutes, turning once, then reduce heat to 350°F (180°C) and cook for an additional 2–2¹/₄ hours, until roast is done.

Simmer pears separately with the wine, 2 cups (16 fl oz/500 ml) water and ¹/₄ cup (2 oz/60 g) of the sugar. When just tender, remove pears and drain on paper towels; reduce liquid.

Remove the roast, add the reduced liquid to the pan juices and boil to make a gravy. Thicken with butter and flour kneaded together and add salt and pepper. Place the roast on a large platter and set aside to settle for 15–20 minutes before carving. Simmer the remaining ¹/₂ cup sugar with 2 tablespoons water in a small pan until it turns to a golden toffee. Working quickly, dip the pears one by one into the toffee, spooning it evenly over the tops. Arrange around the roast and serve at once with the gravy in a jug.

Roast pork with glazed pears

Marinated Honeyed Pork Spareribs

1 cup (8 fl oz/250 ml) plum sauce
1 cup (8 fl oz/250 ml) barbecue sauce
1 cup (8 fl oz/250 ml) sweet sherry
1 cup (8 fl oz/250 ml) olive or safflower oil
$^1/_2$ cup (4 fl oz/125 ml) honey
1 teaspoon ground cumin
1 teaspoon ground cardamom
1 teaspoon ground turmeric
4 lb (2 kg) pork spareribs

Serves 8

Combine all ingredients, except ribs, in a large shallow dish. Add the ribs and baste with marinade. Allow to marinate in refrigerator overnight, brushing frequently with marinade. Barbecue ribs for about 40 minutes, basting frequently with marinade and turning during cooking.

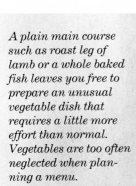

A plain main course such as roast leg of lamb or a whole baked fish leaves you free to prepare an unusual vegetable dish that requires a little more effort than normal. Vegetables are too often neglected when planning a menu.

Corn-on-the-cob with sweet butter (left, page 175); marinated honeyed pork spareribs (right)

Glazed Ham and Mango

oil or melted butter
4 thick ham steaks
1¹/₂ tablespoons brown sugar
2 tablespoons (1 oz/30 g) butter, softened
salt
black pepper
2 fresh medium-size mangoes

Serves 4

Cut 4 pieces of aluminum foil, each 12 in (30 cm) square. Brush with oil or melted butter. Place a steak on each sheet. Make a paste with the brown sugar, butter, salt, and pepper and spread thickly over one side of each steak. Peel and thickly slice the mangoes and spread slices evenly over each steak, using ¹/₂ mango for each. Wrap foil around the parcels, and fold edges together to seal.

Broil or barbecue for about 6 minutes, or place on a baking sheet and bake in a hot oven—375°F (190°C)—for 15 minutes.

Pork Chops with Tangy Chutney

4 large pork chops
¹/₂ teaspoon salt
¹/₃ teaspoon black pepper
3 tablespoons fruit chutney
1 teaspoon vindaloo paste or other hot curry sauce
2–3 tablespoons vegetable oil

Serves 4

Trim excess fat from pork chops and season them with the salt and pepper. Make a paste with the chutney and vindaloo and brush over both sides of each chop. Set the remainder aside.

Grill over moderately hot charcoals, turning frequently and brushing with oil. When the chops are almost done, thickly spread the remaining chutney over one side and continue to cook on the other side until done. Serve with white rice and a cucumber salad.

Glazed ham and mango (left); pork chops with tangy chutney (right)

Racks of lamb with Oriental crust

Racks of Lamb with Oriental Crust

4 small racks of lamb, each containing 3–4 chops
1 medium onion
2 garlic cloves
1 piece (about 1/2 in/1 cm) fresh ginger
2 slices white bread, crusts removed
salt
pepper
1 teaspoon powdered lemon grass
2 tablespoons ground coriander
1 tablespoon vegetable oil
2 tablespoons light soy sauce
2 teaspoons dry sherry

Serves 4

Preheat oven to 375°F (190°C).

Set the racks on a dish. Chop the onion, garlic, ginger, and bread in a food processor and add the remaining ingredients, mixing to a smooth paste. Spread the seasoning on the lamb and set aside for 30 minutes. Place on a rack in a roasting pan and roast for 35 minutes, or until the lamb is done to taste.

NOTE: The crust can be prepared at least one day in advance. Spread over the lamb and wrap in plastic wrap. Refrigerate until needed.

Broiled Lamb Chops with Ratatouille Sauce

3 garlic cloves, mashed
18 small lamb loin chops, well trimmed
salt
black pepper

Ratatouille sauce
1 medium onion
1 medium eggplant (aubergine)
2 medium zucchinis (courgettes)
4 medium ripe tomatoes
1/4 cup (2 fl oz/60 ml) olive oil
1 garlic clove
1 bay leaf
pinch of dried mixed herbs or Provençal herbs
melted butter or olive oil
sprigs of rosemary or other herbs

Serves 6

Rub some of the garlic over the cutlets, then season lightly with salt and pepper. Set aside.

Cut the vegetables into small cubes. In a heavy pan, heat the oil. Cook the onion for 2–3 minutes over moderate heat, then add the eggplant and zucchini and stir over medium heat for 3–4 minutes. Add garlic, tomatoes, bay leaf, dried herbs, and season with salt and pepper; mix well. Cover tightly and cook over very low heat until the vegetables are so tender they start breaking up—about 1 hour. Check seasoning.

Brush the cutlets with melted butter or oil and broil until crisp on the surface and pink and tender inside. Arrange on a serving platter and cover with the sauce. Garnish with sprigs of rosemary or other fresh herbs. Serve at once (photograph pages 10–11).

Barbecued Boned Stuffed Leg of Lamb

1 leg of lamb (about 5 lb/2.5 kg)
salt
black pepper
6 oz (185 g) ground (minced) pork
6 oz (185 g) ground (minced) veal
4 oz (125 g) cooked ham, finely ground (minced)
4 oz (125 g) chicken livers or pâté, minced
1 small onion, finely chopped
2 tablespoons (1 oz/30 g) butter
3 oz (90 g) fresh button mushrooms
    (champignons), finely chopped
1 teaspoon dried mixed Provençal or Italian
    herbs
10 small rosemary sprigs
2 garlic cloves, slivered

Serves 6

Debone the lamb by cutting the length of the bone on the thinnest side where the bone is close to the surface. Use a small sharp knife to work around the bone until it can be removed. Season the inside surface with salt and pepper.

Mix together the ground meats, ham and chicken livers. Sauté the onion in the butter until softened and lightly colored, add the mushrooms and cook for 2–3 minutes. Add the herbs, season with salt and pepper and mix with the meats. Knead the stuffing to mix thoroughly. Spread over the inside of the leg and fold the meat around the stuffing, forming it into its original shape. Tie at close intervals with kitchen string. Rub with salt and pepper, pierce in several places with a sharp knife and insert in each hole a small sprig of rosemary and a sliver of garlic. Roast in a kettle barbecue for about 1$\frac{1}{2}$ hours, or until cooked through. Remove and allow to settle for 10 minutes before slicing to serve.

NOTE: The filling can be prepared in advance, the leg deboned, filled, rolled, and tied. The uncooked, stuffed, and prepared leg can be frozen. Defrost slowly before use.

Barbecued boned stuffed leg of lamb

Pork Spareribs with Red Currant Sauce

1 large onion, finely chopped
2 garlic cloves, crushed
³/₄ cup (8 oz/250 g) red currant jelly
¹/₄ cup (3 fl oz/90 ml) honey
¹/₄ cup (2 fl oz/60 ml) soy sauce
¹/₄ cup (2 fl oz/60 ml) white wine vinegar
¹/₂–1 teaspoon chili sauce to taste
black pepper to taste
2 lb (1 kg) pork spareribs

Serves 4

Combine onion, garlic, jelly, honey, soy sauce and vinegar in a large bowl. Stir in the chili sauce and black pepper. Add spareribs and stir well to coat with marinade. Cover the dish and leave overnight in the refrigerator—or for at least 30 minutes so the meat can absorb the flavors.

Remove spareribs from bowl (reserving marinade). Place ribs in a single layer in a baking dish and bake in oven at 425°F (220°C) for 30 minutes.

Pour off the excess fat from the dish. Spoon on the sauce and bake for 1 hour at 375°F (190°C), turning the ribs occasionally and basting with the sauce. (If necessary, the sauce may be thinned during cooking with a little stock or orange juice.)

Peach-glazed Veal

3 lb (1.5 kg) leg or loin of veal
1 teaspoon (³/₄ oz/20 g) butter, softened
paprika to taste
2 tablespoons honey
¹/₂ cup (4 fl oz/125 ml) puréed peaches
1 tablespoon soy sauce
1 tablespoon cornstarch (cornflour)
¹/₂ cup (4 fl oz/125 ml) water
1 fresh peach, halved, for garnish
sprigs of watercress, for garnish

Serves 4

Preheat the oven to 350°F (180°C).

Place veal on a rack in a roasting dish; brush with the butter and bake for 15 minutes.

Meanwhile, combine honey, peaches and soy sauce. After 15 minutes, brush the veal with this honey mixture and continue cooking for another 75 minutes, basting the meat from time to time with the combined pan juices and glaze.

Remove the veal from the pan, cover with aluminum foil and allow to stand for 15 minutes.

Stir the cornstarch into the water and add to the pan juices. Cook on the stove over medium heat, stirring constantly, until the sauce comes to a boil and thickens.

Slice veal and pour a little sauce on top. Garnish with peach halves and watercress and serve.

Peach-glazed veal (left); pork spareribs with red currant sauce (right)

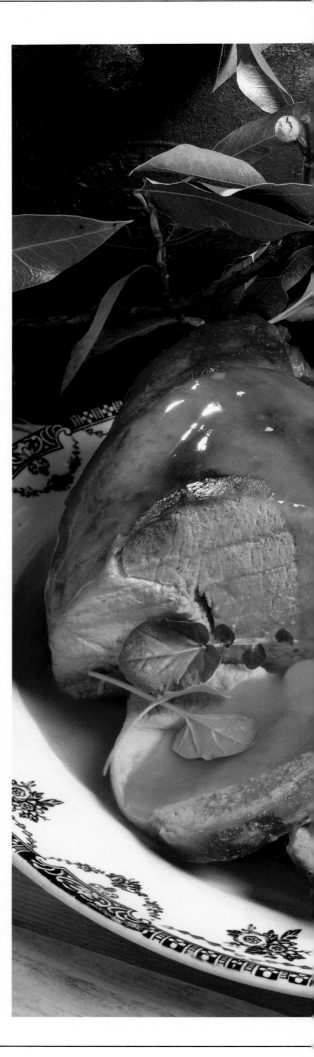

Veal, Ham and Salami Layered Pie

6 thin veal scaloppine (cutlets) (about
    1 lb/500 g)
4 eggs
1 large or 2 medium red bell peppers, sliced
1 large onion, sliced
2 tablespoons olive oil
2 large tomatoes, sliced
2 large sheets prepared puff pastry
6 oz (185 g) cooked ham, shredded
2 tablespoons chopped parsley
salt
pepper
4 oz (125 g) spicy salami, thinly sliced

Serves 6

Preheat oven to 375°F (190°C).

Place the veal between 2 sheets of plastic wrap and pound until very thin. Hard-boil 3 of the eggs and lightly beat the other, set aside. Sauté the bell peppers and onion in the oil until softened.

Place 1 sheet of pastry on a lightly greased baking sheet, and cut into a large circle. Arrange the veal over the pastry leaving a 1-in (2.5 cm) border. Cover with the shredded ham, then the sautéed onion and bell peppers, chopped parsley, salt and pepper, salami, sliced eggs and tomatoes. Season lightly. Moisten the edge of the pastry with cold water, then place the other sheet of pastry over the top and trim to fit the base pastry. Pinch the edges together and use a fork to decorate. Brush with the beaten egg. Bake for about 45 minutes, until the pastry is well browned and the filling cooked. Let stand for about 5 minutes before cutting into wedges.

NOTE: If assembling the pie ahead of time, slice the tomatoes and drain on paper towels before use to remove excess moisture before using.

When going on a picnic, place food in airtight containers. Don't put perishable foodstuffs in the trunk of your car if any chemicals or strong-smelling items are stored there. Store raw foods, such as steaks for the barbecue, away from cooked ones, such as quiche, to avoid cross-contamination.

Veal, ham and salami layered pie

Hamburger Deluxe

1¹/₄ lb (600 g) lean ground (minced) beef
1 small onion, very finely chopped
1 small garlic clove, very finely chopped
1 tablespoon finely chopped parsley
1 tablespoon very finely chopped red bell pepper
1 tablespoon barbecue sauce
¹/₂ teaspoon ground oregano
¹/₄ teaspoon ground sage
salt
black pepper
1 egg
3 tablespoons olive or vegetable oil
4 strips bacon
4 large hamburger buns
1¹/₂ tablespoons mayonnaise
3 large lettuce leaves, shredded
1 large red tomato, sliced
4 very thin slices fresh or canned pineapple

1 medium onion, thinly sliced
1 large dill pickle, thinly sliced
8 thin slices cheese
barbecue sauce and hot mustard

Serves 4

In a bowl mix the beef with chopped onion, garlic, parsley, and bell pepper; add the sauce, herbs and seasonings, and egg and mix well. Form into 4 patties. Heat a pan or griddle and add the oil. Cook the patties over moderate heat until well browned on the surface and just cooked through. Remove. Fry the bacon until crisp. Cut in halves.

To assemble the burgers, split the buns in halves and toast the cut surfaces. Spread the base of the buns with the mayonnaise and add a little of the lettuce. Top with a pattie and then arrange the other ingredients on top, adding sauces to taste. Position the top of the bun and insert a toothpick to hold. Serve at once.

Hamburger deluxe

Photograph following pages, "Supper for Unexpected Guests," clockwise from front: pear salad with walnuts and blue cheese (page 79); tagliatelle with lemon and parsley (page 97); mocha zabaglione (page 222); artichoke hearts with bacon (page 168)

Vegetables

Contrasting the different flavors, textures and colors of vegetables affords plenty of scope for experimentation. Platters of raw or lightly steamed snow peas, mushrooms, baby carrots, florets of cauliflower and red and white radishes served with dips make beautiful centerpieces on an outdoor table setting. Eggplants (aubergines), bell peppers and squash are ideal "containers" in which to bake a wide variety of fillings.

Take a good look at the wealth of produce at your grocery store. Compared to many foods, vegetables are an inexpensive staple, satisfying many of the body's nutritional requirements. Health and diet are important, of course, and for this reason stir-frying and steaming should play an important part in your culinary repertoire. Overcook vegetables and you will cook the life out of them. Their precious nutrients, bright colors and firmness will be lost.

Stir-frying is well suited to entertaining as the process is rapid (because food is cooked over high heat), uses minimum oil and is visually appetizing. The vegetables are sliced into small, even-size pieces which hastens the cooking process. If steaming is your preferred technique, remember that the liquid remaining after cooking can be used as stock in soup dishes or in sauces.

A vast number of traditional vegetable recipes can be used for entertaining, such as baked eggplant, ratatouille, braised peas and rice, potato gnocchi and vegetable pies—all colorful and full of flavor. And, as far as the easy-going informality of outdoor entertaining is concerned, they're the kinds of items that are wholly appropriate.

Opposite: gado gado (left, page 182); cauliflower gratin (right, page 173)

Artichoke Hearts with Bacon

¹/₃ cup (3 oz/90 g) butter
2 leeks, washed, dried and sliced (or 2 onions, peeled and sliced)
2 tablespoons chopped capers
2 tablespoons chopped anchovies
1 lb (500 g) canned artichoke hearts, drained
¹/₂ cup (4 fl oz/125 ml) dry white wine
1 garlic clove, crushed
1 cup (8 fl oz/250 ml) light (single) cream
2 teaspoons cornstarch (cornflour)
1 tablespoon olive or safflower oil
6 strips bacon

Artichoke hearts with bacon (front); mocha zabaglione (back, page 222)

2 tablespoons chopped fresh dill (or 2 teaspoons dried dill)
1 tablespoon chopped parsley

Serves 6

Melt butter in a frying-pan; add leeks and cook over low heat for 5 minutes, or until leeks soften. Add capers, anchovies, drained artichokes, wine and garlic. Bring to a boil, reduce heat and simmer for 3 minutes. Add combined cream and cornstarch and stir until sauce boils and thickens; remove from heat. Heat oil in frying pan, fry bacon until crisp, then roughly chop. Add bacon to artichokes with dill and parsley and stir over low heat until heated through.

Asparagus with Olive Oil and Parmesan

2 bunches (1½ lb/750 g) asparagus
⅓ cup (3 fl oz/90 ml) olive oil
6 oz (185 g) Parmesan cheese, shaved
freshly ground pepper

Serves 4

Steam asparagus until tender. Place on a large platter, drizzle with olive oil and sprinkle with Parmesan and pepper. Serve with extra Parmesan, pepper and olive oil (photograph page 15).

Broccoli with Lemon and Herbs

1 lb (500 g) broccoli
½ cup (4 oz/125 g) butter
2 tablespoons lemon juice
2 tablespoons chopped fresh herbs (parsley, oregano, thyme, basil)
salt
freshly ground pepper

Serves 6

Cut broccoli into pieces. Steam until tender. Melt butter; add lemon juice and chopped fresh herbs. Season to taste. Pour butter mixture over broccoli, toss and serve immediately.

Peas with Ham and Onions

8 scallions (spring onions) or baby onions
4 garlic cloves
8 oz (250 g) sugar snap peas
8 oz (250 g) snow peas
1 tablespoon olive oil
2 slices cooked ham, chopped

Serves 4

Place scallions and garlic in cold water. Bring to a boil and boil gently for 1 minute. Drain and remove skins. Chop garlic into pieces. Bring a pot of water to a boil, add sugar snap peas, cook for 30 seconds, add snow peas and cook for another 30 seconds. Drain.

Heat oil in a frying-pan. Add ham, scallions and garlic. Sauté for 2 minutes. Toss peas, ham, garlic and scallions together and serve immediately.

Broccoli with lemon and herbs (left); peas with ham and onions (right)

Stuffed bell peppers; stuffed mushrooms

Stuffed Mushrooms

8 large, open-capped mushrooms
    (champignons)
1¼ cups (5 oz/155 g) dry bread crumbs
½ cup (2½ oz/75 g) chopped olives
5 anchovy fillets
2 tablespoons capers
2 tablespoons chopped parsley
1 tablespoon chopped basil
⅓ cup (1½ oz/45 g) finely chopped walnuts
⅓ cup (3 fl oz/90 ml) olive oil
salt and pepper

Serves 4

Preheat oven to 375°F (190°C).
  Remove mushroom stems. Mix remaining ingredients together thoroughly. Stuff mushrooms with mixture and bake in oven for 25 minutes.

Stuffed Chili Peppers

10 medium (poblano banana) chilis
2 tablespoons olive or safflower oil
2 onions, chopped
2 garlic cloves, crushed
1 teaspoon chili powder
3 tomatoes, peeled and chopped
2 tablespoons tomato paste
¼ cup (2 fl oz/60 ml) dry white wine
¼ cup (2 fl oz/60 ml) water
2½ cups (1 lb/500 g) cooked and shredded chicken
½ cup (2 oz/60 g) stuffed olives, chopped
¼ cup (1½ oz/45 g) pine nuts
½ cup (3 oz/90 g) raisins, chopped

Tomato sauce

2 tablespoons olive or safflower oil
1 onion, chopped
1 garlic clove, crushed
6 tomatoes, peeled and chopped
1 cup (8 fl oz/250 ml) chicken stock
2 tablespoons tomato paste

Batter

4 eggs, separated
¼ cup (1 oz/30 g) all-purpose (plain) flour
oil, for deep-frying

Serves 10

Cut tops off chilis. Remove seeds and any hard core inside.
  Heat oil in a saucepan, add onions and cook over moderate heat until softened. Add garlic and chili powder and cook for 1 minute. Add the tomatoes and cook, stirring, for 5 minutes or until slightly softened. Add tomato paste, wine and water and stir until combined. Bring to a boil, reduce heat, add chicken and simmer until mixture becomes thick. Stir in olives, pine nuts and

Stuffed Bell Peppers

¼ cup (2 oz/60 g) butter
2 small red onions, chopped
2 garlic cloves
11 oz (345 g) spicy sausage meat or skinned,
    spicy sausages
4 oz (125 g) cooked bulgur (cracked wheat)
1 tablespoon chopped parsley
10 cherry tomatoes, quartered
salt and pepper
4 medium-size red bell peppers
olive oil

Serves 4

Preheat oven to 375°F (190°C).
  Melt butter in a frying-pan and add onions and garlic. Fry gently until onions begin to brown. Add sausage meat and fry gently for 5 minutes. In a bowl, mix together bulgur, parsley and tomatoes. Add sausage meat mixture; season with salt and pepper.
  Halve bell peppers and discard seeds. Fill the peppers with stuffing and place in a shallow baking dish. Drizzle with a little olive oil and bake for 30 minutes.

raisins. Fill chilis with mixture.

For sauce: heat the oil in a saucepan, add onion and cook over low heat until softened. Add garlic and tomatoes and cook, stirring, for 5 minutes. Add chicken stock and tomato paste; bring to a boil. Reduce heat and simmer for 10 minutes. Place tomato sauce in a blender or food processor and purée. Return puréed sauce to saucepan to reheat at serving time.

To make batter, beat egg whites until soft peaks form; fold in lightly beaten egg yolks and flour. Coat chilis in additional flour, then dip in batter. Deep-fry chilis until golden-brown on all sides. Remove from oil and drain on paper towels. To serve, arrange chilis on serving plates, reheat sauce, then spoon sauce over and around chilis.

Stuffed chili peppers (bottom); Mexican rice (top, page 102)

171

Eggplant Parmigiana

1 large garlic clove, finely chopped
3 tablespoons olive oil
2 cans (each 14 oz/425 g) tomatoes, or 10 oz
   (300 g) very ripe tomatoes, peeled
2 tablespoons tomato paste
salt
pepper
1 tablespoon chopped fresh oregano
1 tablespoon chopped fresh parsley
4 eggplants (aubergines)
¹/₄ cup (1 oz/30 g) all-purpose (plain) flour
¹/₂ cup (4 fl oz/125 ml) olive oil
6 oz (185 g) mozzarella cheese
¹/₄ cup (1 oz/30 g) freshly grated Parmesan cheese

Serves 8

In a large frying-pan, cook garlic in oil until tender and aromatic. Add tomatoes, tomato paste, salt, pepper and herbs. Bring to a boil and simmer for about 1 hour, or until sauce is thick and reduced by half. Meanwhile cut eggplants into thin slices. Sprinkle with salt and allow to drain for 1 hour.

Preheat oven to 400°F (200°C). Pat eggplants dry and dust with flour. Heat ¹/₄ cup (2 fl oz/60 ml) oil in frying-pan and fry slices over moderately high heat until lightly browned on both sides. Add more oil as necessary. Cut mozzarella into thin slices. Cover bottom of an oiled gratin dish with a thin layer of tomato sauce and add a layer of eggplant and one of mozzarella. Spoon on more sauce, add another layer of eggplant and mozzarella and sprinkle with Parmesan. Repeat. Bake in oven for 30 minutes.

Potato Gnocchi with Uncooked Tomato Sauce

1 lb (500 g) potatoes
1³/₄ cups (6¹/₂ oz/200 g) all-purpose (plain) flour
1 teaspoon salt
1 teaspoon ground nutmeg
melted butter

Tomato sauce

8 medium tomatoes, peeled and seeded
4 garlic cloves, finely chopped
³/₄ cup (³/₄ oz/20 g) loosely packed basil leaves
¹/₂ cup (4 fl oz/125 ml) olive oil
salt and pepper

Serves 4

Steam potatoes until cooked but firm; peel. Spread flour on a board and sprinkle with ¹/₂ teaspoon of the salt and the nutmeg. When potatoes are cool, mash without adding any butter or milk. Place potato in a mound in the center of the flour and start incorporating the flour with your hands, little by little, until all but ¹/₂ cup flour is incorporated. Begin to knead the flour and potato mixture, incorporating the last ¹/₂ cup of flour. Knead for 5

minutes. Divide the mixture into 3 pieces, roll each piece into a roll ¹/₂ in (1 cm) in diameter. Cut each roll into 1 in (2.5 cm) pieces, pressing each individual gnocchi with the tines of a fork.

Heat a large amount of water with the remaining ¹/₂ teaspoon of salt in a large saucepan. When boiling, add gnocchi, one by one. Gently stir with a wooden spoon. After gnocchi come to the surface, allow them to cook for 1 minute more. Remove with a slotted spoon to a dish containing warmed, melted butter. When all are cooked, combine with tomato sauce and serve.

Balance a menu so that it is not too rich and doesn't feature the same ingredient such as cheese or fish in two different courses.

172

To make the tomato sauce: chop tomatoes into small pieces, place in a bowl with garlic. Tear basil leaves into small pieces, and add to tomato mixture. Stir in olive oil, mix well. Refrigerate for 2 hours. Season with salt and pepper and toss with gnocchi while gnocchi are still warm.

Cauliflower Gratin

1¹/₂ lb (750 g) large florets cauliflower
1 cup (8 oz/250 g) cottage cheese
¹/₂ cup (4 fl oz/125 ml) milk
¹/₄ cup (2 fl oz/60 ml) light sour cream
¹/₄ cup (1 oz/30 g) freshly grated Parmesan cheese
¹/₄ cup (¹/₄ oz/8 g) tightly packed basil leaves
1 garlic clove

Serves 6

Boil cauliflower in salted water for about 5 minutes, or until tender. Drain. Place remaining ingredients in the bowl of food processor and blend until smooth. Heat gently until just warm and pour over hot cauliflower (photograph page 166).

Potato gnocchi with uncooked tomato sauce (left); eggplant parmigiana (right)

Baked potatoes with (clockwise from front): smoked salmon and sour cream filling, gorgonzola and pistachio filling, chili filling, avocado and bacon filling, and pesto and mayonnaise filling; potato and parsnip chips (bottom right)

Potato Chips

3 large potatoes
peanut oil, for frying
salt

Serves 6

Peel potatoes and slice very thinly using a sharp knife. Place in a bowl of cold water for 20 minutes.

Fill a pan to one-third full with oil and heat to 375°F (190°C).

Drain the potatoes and pat until dry. Deep fry in batches in a single layer for 1–2 minutes. Remove to drain; sprinkle with salt and serve.

NOTE: Potato chips can be kept in an airtight container for up to 2 days.

Parsnip Chips

3 large parsnips
peanut oil, for frying
salt

Serves 6

Peel parsnips and slice very thinly using a sharp knife. Place in a bowl of cold water for 20 minutes.

Fill a pan with oil to one-third of its volume and heat to 340°F (170°C).

Drain the parsnips and pat until dry. Cook in batches in a single layer for 3–4 minutes. Remove to drain; sprinkle with salt and serve.

NOTE: Parsnip chips can be kept in an airtight container for up to 2 days.

Corn-on-the-Cob with Sweet Butter

1 cup (8 oz/250 g) butter, softened
2 tablespoons grated orange zest
1/4 teaspoon ground nutmeg
1/4 teaspoon ground cinnamon
1/4 teaspoon ground cardamom
8 ears corn-on-the-cob with husks
oil, for brushing husks

Serves 8

Place the butter in a food processor with the orange zest, nutmeg, cinnamon and cardamom and process until combined. Refrigerate until ready to use.

Remove and reserve dark green outer husks from corn. Peel away light green inner husks, leaving them attached to base of cobs. Remove silk, replace husks to cover cobs and tie with reserved leaves. Soak corn in water for 30 minutes. Place corn on barbecue for about 30 minutes, turning frequently and brushing with oil. Serve corn with butter (photograph page 156).

Crisp Potato Cakes

3 potatoes, peeled and cut into fine julienne strips
1 egg yolk
1 tablespoon all-purpose (plain) flour
oil, for frying

Serves 2

Combine potatoes, egg yolk and flour in bowl and mix well. Divide potato mixture into 4 parts and shape into rounds. Fry rounds in hot oil, pressing down with spatula to maintain round shape, until potato is golden-brown on both sides. Drain on paper towels (photograph pages 184–85).

Stuffed Baked Potatoes

8 medium potatoes

Serves 4

Preheat oven to 350°F (180°C).

Scrub potatoes and pierce with a fork. Cook for 45 minutes. Remove from oven and cut open before stuffing with your choice of filling. Serve hot with the following fillings.

Chili Filling

2 tablespoons olive oil
1 small onion, chopped
1 garlic clove
1 can (10 oz/315 g) red kidney beans
2 teaspoons dried oregano
1 tablespoon ground cumin
1/2 teaspoon chili powder, or to taste
1/2 cup (4 fl oz/125 ml) tomato sauce
2 tablespoons tomato paste
2 teaspoons Worcestershire sauce

Heat oil in pan. Add onion and garlic and cook for 2 minutes. Add kidney beans and the other ingredients. Cook for 5 minutes and serve.

Pesto and Mayonnaise Filling

1/2 cup (4 fl oz/125 g) Basil Pesto (see recipe,
page 28)
2 tablespoons Mayonnaise (see recipe, page 30)

Combine ingredients and serve.

Gorgonzola and Pistachio Filling

6 1/2 oz (200 g) Gorgonzola or other blue cheese
1/3 cup (3 fl oz/90 ml) light (single) cream
1/2 cup (2 oz/60 g) pistachio nuts, shelled

Place cheese in a food processor. Process for 20 seconds. Pour in cream in a steady stream. Process until combined. Serve with pistachios.

Smoked Salmon and Sour Cream Filling

3 slices smoked salmon
1 cup (8 fl oz/250 ml) sour cream
juice of 1 lime
salt
pepper

Cut salmon into thin strips. Combine other ingredients. Stir in salmon and serve.

Avocado and Bacon Filling

1 avocado
juice of 1/2 lemon
1/4 cup (2 fl oz/60 ml) sour cream
2 strips bacon
2 scallions (spring onions), chopped
2 tablespoons olive oil
salt
pepper

Peel avocado, mash flesh and combine with lemon juice and sour cream. Fry bacon and scallions in oil. Combine avocado and bacon mixture, season with salt and pepper and serve.

Simple touches can turn cooked vegetables into something special when you're in a hurry. Try adding garlic salt, grainy mustard, lemon juice or a dash of tarragon wine vinegar to melted butter and pouring it over lightly steamed vegetables. Or, sprinkle them with chopped hard-boiled egg, slivered toasted almonds, crumbled bacon or toasted sesame seeds.

Eggs Florentine

Eggs Florentine

1 package (8 oz/250 g) frozen chopped spinach
1¹/₂ tablespoons butter
1¹/₂ tablespoons all-purpose (plain) flour
1 cup (8 fl oz/250 ml) milk
salt
black pepper
freshly grated nutmeg
¹/₄ cup (1 oz/30 g) grated Parmesan cheese
4 large eggs

Serves 4

Place the spinach in a small saucepan and cover tightly. Cook over low heat for about 8 minutes, removing the lid for the final 3 minutes to evaporate the liquids. Drain. In another pan melt the butter, stir in the flour, then add the milk and whisk constantly to make a béchamel (white) sauce. Stir continually as it thickens. Season to taste with salt, pepper and nutmeg, then stir in the well-drained spinach and the cheese. Set aside, keeping warm.

Poach the eggs until the whites are set but the yolks are still soft. To serve, spoon a mound of creamed spinach in the center of each plate and make a well in the center. Remove the eggs with a slotted spoon and place one on each bed of spin-

ach. Serve at once, with buttered toast.

NOTE: The béchamel sauce can be made up to 1 day in advance and kept in the refrigerator. Place a piece of plastic wrap or waxed paper directly on the surface of the sauce to prevent a skin from forming.

Squash Fritters with Coriander Pesto

1 lb (500 g) butternut squash sliced ¹/₂ in (1 cm)
  thick
¹/₂ cup (2 oz/60 g) all-purpose (plain) flour
1 teaspoon baking powder
1 egg
1 tablespoon olive oil
²/₃ cup (5 fl oz/155 ml) water
oil, for deep-frying
Coriander Pesto (see recipe, page 29)

Serves 4

Remove skin and seeds from squash. Pat slices dry. Combine flour and baking powder in a bowl; beat in egg, olive oil and water, adding extra water if batter is too thick. Dip squash slices in the batter and fry in oil until golden.

Opposite: squash fritters
with coriander pesto

Braised Scallions

1 tablespoon butter
2 tablespoons dry white wine
4 scallions (spring onions), washed and
    trimmed
1 tablespoon chopped parsley

Serves 2

Melt the butter in a pan, add wine and bring to a boil. Reduce heat, add scallions and simmer for about 5 minutes, or until tender. Remove from heat and stir in the parsley (photograph pages 184–85).

Baked Tomatoes with Thyme

8 medium tomatoes
2 tablespoons olive oil
2 tablespoons coarse salt
6 thyme sprigs

Baked tomatoes with thyme

Serves 4

Preheat oven to 300°F (150°C).
    Cut off the stem ends of tomatoes and wipe each with a little of the olive oil. Place on a baking sheet and bake for 10 minutes. Sprinkle with salt and sprigs of thyme. Bake for another 5 minutes.

Marinated Beets

4 beets (beetroot)
2 tablespoons grated orange zest
2 scallions (spring onions), finely chopped
2 tablespoons chopped tarragon
2 tablespoons orange juice
2 tablespoons olive or safflower oil
pinch of nutmeg

Serves 8

Cook the beets in a pot of boiling water for about 30 minutes, or until tender. Rinse under cold water and peel away the skin. Dry on paper towels. Cut in half and place in a bowl. Combine the remaining ingredients and add to beets. Allow to stand for at least 1 hour. Serve as an accompaniment to chicken, meat or fish (photograph pages 106–107).

Pickled Cucumber

1 large cucumber, peeled and thinly sliced
salt
1/2 cup (4 fl oz/125 ml) white wine vinegar
1 tablespoon sugar
2 tablespoons chopped dill

Serves 8

Place cucumber in strainer, sprinkle with salt and let stand for several hours. Rinse under cold running water and dry on paper towels. Place cucumber in a bowl with vinegar, sugar and dill. Refrigerate for several hours before serving. At serving time, pour off almost all the liquid. Serve as an accompaniment to chicken, meat or fish (photograph pages 106–107).

Marinated Red Onions

1 teaspoon chili oil
1/4 cup (2 fl oz/60 ml) olive oil
3 tablespoons white wine vinegar
1 teaspoon sugar
3 red (Spanish) onions, quartered

Serves 8

Place oils, vinegar and sugar in bowl and whisk until combined. Add onions; stir until coated. Refrigerate until ready to serve. Serve as an accompaniment to chicken, meat or fish (photograph pages 106–107).

Asian Stir-fry

1 bunch asparagus, sliced diagonally
6¹/₂ oz (200 g) baby squash, quartered
1 tablespoon vegetable oil
2 teaspoons sesame oil
2 tablespoons grated fresh ginger
2 garlic cloves, finely chopped
6¹/₂ oz (200 g) button mushrooms
    (champignons), cut in half
6¹/₂ oz (200 g) sugar snap peas
6¹/₂ oz (200 g) snow peas

4 oz (125 g) soybean shoots
6¹/₂ oz (200 g) snow pea sprouts
1 tablespoon soy sauce
freshly ground black pepper

Serves 4

Blanch asparagus and squash in boiling water.
Refresh under cold water and drain. Heat oils in
a large pan or wok. Add ginger and garlic, cook
for 30 seconds, then add other vegetables in order
given, tossing continuously for 4–5 minutes. Season with soy sauce and pepper and serve.

Asian stir-fry

179

Vegetable Terrine with Tomato Coulis

Tomato layer

1/4 cup (2 oz/60 g) unsalted butter
2 yellow onions, finely chopped
4 medium tomatoes, peeled, seeded and chopped
2 garlic cloves, finely chopped
2 tablespoons chopped basil
3 tablespoons tomato paste
1 teaspoon chili powder
salt
pepper
1 whole egg
1 egg yolk

Leek layer

1/3 cup (3 oz/90 g) unsalted butter
3 leeks, thinly sliced
2 garlic cloves, finely chopped
1/2 cup (1/2 oz/15 g) chopped parsley
salt
pepper
1 whole egg
1 egg yolk

To assemble

12 large cabbage leaves, blanched and refreshed
*   in cold water*
1 bunch asparagus, blanched and refreshed in
*   cold water*
2 red bell peppers, roasted, skinned and seeded
6 yellow squash, thinly sliced, blanched and
*   refreshed in cold water*

Tomato coulis

5 medium tomatoes, peeled and seeded
2 tablespoons red wine vinegar
dash of Tabasco sauce
1/2 teaspoon chili powder (optional)
salt
pepper
1/3 cup (3 fl oz/90 ml) olive oil

Serves 6

Keep a supply of vol-au-vent shells in the freezer (either baked or uncooked). They take little time to defrost or cook and look impressive when filled with lightly steamed vegetables, seafood in a quickly made cream sauce, or pieces of steamed chicken in a lemon-flavored mayonnaise. Also keep a supply of rolls (a variety of shapes and textures) and pita bread. Sliced bread and pita bread can be thawed quickly, with care, under the broiler.

For tomato layer: melt butter in a large heavy-based pan. Add onions, cover and cook over low heat for 20 minutes. Drain tomatoes and add to onions. Cook, stirring often, for 20 minutes. Add garlic, basil, tomato paste, chili powder, salt and pepper, and cook for 15 minutes, or until mixture is very thick. Cool to room temperature. Using a whisk, beat egg and egg yolk into tomato mixture. Cover and refrigerate until very cool. (This can be done up to a day ahead.)

For leek layer: melt butter in a heavy-based pan, add leeks, cover and cook over low heat for 30 minutes. Do not let leeks brown. Add garlic, parsley, salt and pepper and cook, uncovered, for another 10 minutes. Cool to room temperature. Beat egg and yolk together in a small bowl. Stir into leek mixture. Cover and refrigerate until very cool. (This can be done up to a day ahead.)

To assemble: preheat oven to 375°F (190°C). Drain all vegetables and pat dry. Lightly butter a 9 x 5 x 3 in (23 x 12 x 7.5 cm) terrine or loaf pan. Trim heavy ribs from cabbage leaves. Line the pan with the leaves, overlapping them and allowing tops to hang over the edge of the pan. Reserve 2 or 3 for the top. Restir cooled leek and tomato mixtures. Smooth half the tomato mixture on the bottom of the pan. Layer the asparagus on top,

*Vegetable terrine with
tomato coulis*

then smooth over all the leek mixture. Layer the roasted bell peppers on top; cover with rest of tomato mixture. Place the squash on top. Fold overhanging cabbage leaves over the top, tucking excess down sides of the pan.

Wrap pan in aluminum foil and place in a large baking pan. Pour boiling water around the edges to reach halfway up the sides. Set on center rack of oven and bake for 2 hours, or until center is firm to touch. Remove from water and unwrap

foil. Cool for 15 minutes. Set a weight on top and cool completely. Then remove weight, cover and refrigerate. To unmold, dip pan briefly in hot water and run a thin knife around the sides; then invert. Serve with tomato coulis.

For tomato coulis: place all ingredients, except oil, in bowl of a food processor. Process thoroughly. Add oil in a slow, steady stream and process until completely combined. Refrigerate. Adjust seasoning just before serving.

Mushrooms with Fried Polenta

Polenta
4 cups (1 qt/1 l) cold water
$^1/_2$ teaspoon salt
1$^1/_2$ cups (8 oz/250 g) cornmeal
$^1/_4$ cup (2 fl oz/60 ml) extra-virgin olive oil

Mushrooms
2 tablespoons (1 oz/30 g) butter
1 small onion, chopped
1 garlic clove
2 cans (each 14 oz/425 g) tomatoes
2 teaspoons red wine vinegar
salt
pepper
$^1/_3$ cup (3 fl oz /90 ml) olive oil
1 lb (500 g) small button mushrooms
   (champignons)
2 small eggplants (aubergines), thinly sliced
2 red bell peppers, roasted, peeled and cut in strips
basil, for garnish

Serves 4

Mushrooms with fried polenta

To make polenta: bring the water to a boil in a large pot. Add salt. Pour in cornmeal in a slow, steady stream, stirring constantly with a wooden spoon in one direction to prevent lumps from forming. Stir slowly without stopping for 30 minutes. Leave polenta on the heat for another 2 minutes without stirring. Shake the pot a little and remove polenta to a baking dish and spread out evenly about $^1/_2$ in (1 cm) thick. Cool. When completely cool, cut into rectangles about 2 x 1 in (5 x 2.5 cm). Heat extra-virgin olive oil in a pan. When hot, add polenta and cook pieces, turning, until golden. Remove and drain. Sprinkle with salt and serve with mushrooms.

To prepare the mushrooms: heat butter in a large heavy-based saucepan. Add onion and cook for 4 minutes. Add garlic and cook for 1 minute. Add tomatoes and vinegar and simmer for 30 minutes. Season with salt and plenty of freshly ground black pepper.

Heat $^1/_4$ cup (2 fl oz/60 ml) oil in a large frying-pan. Add mushrooms and cook until tender—about 3 minutes. Remove from pan and set aside to drain. Add remaining oil and gently fry eggplant. Remove from pan and drain. Heat tomato sauce to a simmer. Add mushrooms, eggplant and bell peppers. Stir together gently. Serve immediately, garnished with basil. Serve with polenta.

Gado Gado

Peanut sauce
$^1/_4$ cup (2 fl oz/60 ml) vegetable oil
2 garlic cloves, finely chopped
1$^1/_2$ cups (6 oz/185 g) finely crushed peanuts
2 tablespoons curry powder
$^1/_4$ cup fruit chutney
2 small chilis, finely chopped
$^1/_4$ cup (2 fl oz/60 ml) lemon juice
2 tablespoons soy sauce
1$^1/_4$ cups (10 fl oz/315 ml) coconut cream
1 cup (8 fl oz/250 ml) water

Vegetables
1 lb (500 g) broccoli, cut into small florets
2 carrots, peeled and cut in thick julienne strips
12 small new potatoes
6$^1/_2$ oz (200 g) bean sprouts
6 oz (185 g) sugar snap peas

Serves 6

To make peanut sauce: place oil in a saucepan over moderate heat. Add the garlic and crushed nuts and cook, stirring, for 2 minutes. Add curry powder, chutney and chilis and cook for another 2 minutes. Add lemon juice, soy sauce, coconut cream and water and cook, slowly, for 30 minutes, stirring occasionally to prevent sticking and burning. If necessary, thin with extra water or coconut cream. Meanwhile, prepare the vegetables: cook broccoli and carrots in separate pans of salted water. Simmer potatoes over moderate heat for 10–12 minutes, or until tender.

Arrange all vegetables on a platter. Top with the warm peanut sauce and serve immediately (photograph page 166).

Creamed vegetables in curry-flavored crêpes

Creamed Vegetables in Curry-flavored Crêpes

Crêpe batter

1¼ cups (5 oz/155 g) all-purpose (plain) flour
¼ teaspoon salt
1 teaspoon mild curry powder
½ teaspoon white pepper
1½ cups (12 fl oz/375 ml) milk
1 tablespoon vegetable oil
1 large egg

Tomato salsa

2 large very red tomatoes, very finely chopped
1 small onion, very finely chopped
1 small garlic clove, very finely chopped
1 tablespoon chopped basil
1 teaspoon red wine vinegar
salt
pepper

Creamed vegetable filling

4 cups finely chopped vegetables (broccoli,
    onions, cauliflower, peas, green beans,
    potatoes, carrots)
2½ tablespoons butter
2½ tablespoons all-purpose (plain) flour
2 cups (16 fl oz/500 ml) milk
salt
pepper
½ cup (4 fl oz/125 ml) sour cream
½ cup (2 oz/60 g) grated Cheddar cheese
1 tablespoon finely chopped parsley
1½ teaspoons chopped basil

Serves 6

To make crêpes: sift flour, salt, curry powder and pepper into a bowl and make a well in the center. Add the milk, oil and egg and beat until smooth. Set aside for 20 minutes. Rub an omelet or crêpe pan with a ball of paper towel dipped in melted butter or oil. Pour in a thin layer of the batter. Cook until golden underneath, then turn and cook the other side. Cook all of the crêpes in this way, stacking together when done.

For salsa: mix ingredients together, adding salt and pepper to taste.

For filling: parboil the vegetables in lightly salted water. Drain thoroughly. Melt the butter in a large saucepan and stir in the flour. Add milk with salt and pepper to taste and stir until thickened. Stir in sour cream, cheese, parsley, basil and vegetables. Fill crêpes. Serve with the tomato salsa.

NOTE: Both the crêpes and filling can be made up to 2 days in advance. Stack crêpes with waxed paper or plastic wrap in between. Store filling in a sealed plastic container. Microwave on MEDIUM or reheat in a warm oven.

Baby new potatoes need little adornment to taste their best. Don't peel them; a wipe with a damp cloth is sufficient. Wrap in foil with a little butter and fresh mint or tarragon, and bake in the oven or in the embers of a barbecue.

Photograph following pages, "Romantic Dinner for Two," clockwise from front: seafood in saffron and lemon sauce with salmon roe (page 120); filet of beef with red wine and pear (page 150); braised scallions (page 178); crisp potato cakes (page 175); individual chocolate truffle cakes (page 202)

Breads, Cakes and Biscuits

In England during the 1830s, when lunch was taken rather early and dinner rather late, "afternoon tea" was introduced at five o'clock. It quickly became an institution among the upper classes. Subsequently the entire British nation took it to heart, with the early colonists bringing the tradition with them to the USA.

Around this charming little interlude the British wove their customary web of social etiquette. Downstairs, cooks conjured the lightest biscuits (scones), mere wisps of sponge cake and slivers of shortbread. Winter saw the arrival of toast and English muffins, crumpets and buns.

Afternoon tea offers a delightful excuse for a social gathering, especially when eaten out-of-doors at a table beneath the trees where sunlight and the scent of flowers can play their part. Tried and trusted recipes, handed down from great-grandmother, are the traditional dishes to serve.

Bread-based recipes are particularly suitable for afternoon tea: bruschetta (garlic toast) topped with sun-dried tomatoes and fresh, melted Italian cheese; bread rings flavored with fresh herbs; fried bread boxes filled with salad greens; stir-fried vegetables or seafood in a creamy sauce.

There's much more to bread than a sandwich, and you'll find some pleasant surprises in the next few pages.

Opposite: chocolate hazelnut torte (page 203)

Let cheese come to room temperature before serving. On a very sunny day offer several small portions of cheese on a platter. It is better to return to the kitchen for fresh supplies than to serve too great a quantity that the heat will turn into an unpleasant mess.

Pizza

4 cups (1 lb/500 g) all-purpose (plain) flour
1 envelope (¹/₄ oz/8 g) active dried yeast
³/₄ teaspoon salt
1 tablespoon olive oil
¹/₃ cup (3 fl oz/90 ml) Fresh Tomato Sauce (see
    recipe, page 32)
8 oz (250 g) spicy salami, thinly sliced
2 strips bacon, cooked and crumbled
6 fresh button mushrooms (champignons),
    thinly sliced
1 medium red bell pepper, thinly sliced
1 small onion, very finely chopped
18 black olives
1¹/₃ teaspoons dried mixed or Italian herbs
³/₄ cup (3 oz/90 g) grated mozzarella cheese

Makes 2 14-in (35 cm) pizzas

Sift the flour into a mixing bowl and stir in the yeast and salt. Add enough tepid water to make a soft dough. Remove to a lightly floured board and knead for about 10 minutes, until the dough is smooth and elastic. Place in a clean oiled bowl and cover with a piece of oiled plastic wrap. Set in a warm place to rise until doubled in size—about 40 minutes.

Knead again lightly, divide in half and roll out to fit 2 14-in (35 cm) pizza pans. Press the dough evenly into the pans and prick evenly all over with a fork. Set aside for at least 25 minutes.

Preheat oven to 400°F (200°C).

For filling: brush dough with the olive oil, then spread on the tomato sauce. Arrange the ingredients evenly over the pizza, covering with the cheese. Place in the oven and bake until the crust is golden and the cheese is melted. Cut into wedges and serve at once.

Schiacciata

Fragrant freshly baked bread makes a superb accompaniment to any meal. Schiacciata is quick to make and can be imbued with different flavors. Try sprinkling on chopped garlic and salt, fresh rosemary, cracked pepper or grated cheese.

1 envelope (¹/₄ oz/8 g) active dried yeast
¹/₃ cup (3 fl oz/90 ml) tepid water
4 cups (1 lb/500 g) unbleached bread flour or all-
    purpose (plain) flour
2 tablespoons olive oil
2 teaspoons coarse salt
2 teaspoons finely chopped garlic
1¹/₂ teaspoons dried or fresh rosemary

Serves 6

Sprinkle the yeast over the water and whisk with a fork until bubbles appear, then set aside in a warm place for 10 minutes. Sift the flour into a mixing bowl and make a depression in the center. Pour in the yeast mixture, cover with flour and stir in. Add enough room temperature water to make a soft, but not sticky, dough. Remove to a lightly floured board and knead for 10 minutes. Shape it into a ball and place in an oiled bowl. Cover with a cloth or piece of oiled plastic and set aside in a warm part of the kitchen to rise for about 45 minutes.

Preheat oven to 450°F (230°C).

Knead again briefly, then roll out on a lightly floured surface to a thickness of about ³/₄ in (2 cm) and transfer to a floured baking sheet. Brush with the olive oil. Make indentations all over the surface of the bread with the thumb; sprinkle on the salt, garlic and rosemary. Bake until crisp and golden. Serve hot.

Folded Pizza Bread with Garlic and Camembert

¹/₂ cup (4 fl oz/125 ml) tepid water
1 envelope (¹/₄ oz/8 g) active dried yeast
4 cups (1 lb/500 g) bread flour or unbleached all-
*   purpose (plain) flour*
1 tablespoon olive oil
3–4 teaspoons finely chopped garlic
4 oz (125 g) ripe Camembert cheese
salt
black pepper
1 teaspoon dried Provençal-style mixed herbs

Serves 6

Sprinkle the yeast over the water and whisk with a fork to dissolve. Set aside for 10 minutes. Sift the flour into a bowl and make a well in the center. Pour in the yeast and cover with flour, then add enough tepid water to make a soft dough. Transfer to a lightly floured board and knead until the dough is smooth and elastic—at least 10 minutes—then shape into a ball. Place in an oiled dish and cover with a piece of oiled plastic wrap. Set aside in a warm place until doubled in size.

Preheat oven to 425°F (220°C).

Punch down the dough and knead gently and briefly. Divide into halves and roll out into rounds about ¹/₂ in (1 cm) thick. Brush the dough with the olive oil, leaving an un-oiled border of ³/₄ in (2 cm). Sprinkle on chopped garlic. Slice the Camembert and arrange evenly over half of each piece. Sprinkle on salt, pepper and herbs. Fold the dough over and pinch the edges to seal. Place on a floured baking sheet and bake until golden brown—about 15 minutes.

Folded pizza bread with garlic and Camembert (left and front); schiacciata (rear)

189

Olive and Herb Bread

2 onions, chopped
1 tablespoon olive oil
1 cup (6 oz/185 g) chopped, pitted black olives
2 tablespoons dried rosemary
1/2 cup (1/2 oz/15 g) chopped parsley
2 garlic cloves, crushed
1 cup (8 oz/250 g) butter, softened
2 large white or whole wheat cottage loaves

Serves 20

Preheat oven to 350°F (180°C).

Cook the onions in heated oil until tender. Transfer to a bowl. Add olives, rosemary, parsley, garlic and butter and mix well. Slice bread, cutting almost to the base (do not cut completely through). Spread with olive mixture, wrap in foil and bake in oven (or on barbecue) for about 10 minutes, or until heated through (photograph pages 140–41).

Cheese and Scallion Bread

Olive oil and caraway seed loaf (rear); herbed bread ring (front)

1 cup (8 oz/250 g) butter, softened
6 scallions (spring onions), chopped
2 garlic cloves, crushed
1 1/2 cups (6 oz/185 g) grated Cheddar cheese
2 teaspoons paprika
1/2 cup (4 fl oz/125 ml) mayonnaise
2 long, thin loaves French bread

Serves 20

Preheat oven to 350°F (180°C).

Beat the butter in a bowl. Add the scallions, garlic, cheese, paprika and mayonnaise and mix well. Slice the bread, cutting almost to base (but do not cut completely through). Spread each slice with cheese mixture. Wrap each loaf in foil and then bake in oven (or on barbecue) for about 10 minutes, or until heated through (photograph pages 140–41).

Olive Oil and Caraway Seed Loaf

2 cups (8 oz/250 g) all-purpose (plain) flour
1 1/4 teaspoons baking powder
1 cup (7 oz/220 g) white sugar
2–3 teaspoons caraway seeds
grated zest of 1 lemon
1 cup (8 fl oz/250 ml) olive oil
1/2 cup (4 fl oz/125 ml) milk
3 eggs, separated

Serves 6

Preheat oven to 350°F (180°C). Grease and flour a medium-size cake pan or loaf pan; set aside.

Sift the flour and baking powder into a mixing bowl. Stir in the sugar, caraway seeds and lemon zest. Add the oil, milk and egg yolks and beat

until smooth. Whisk the egg whites to stiff peaks and fold them in.

Spoon into the prepared pan and smooth the surface. Bake for about 50 minutes, or until the cake comes away from the sides of the pan and is firm and dry on the surface. Invert onto a wire rack and leave to cool. Slice and serve warm.

Herbed Bread Ring

4 cups (1 lb/500 g) bread flour or all-purpose (plain) flour
1/2 teaspoon sugar
1 teaspoon salt
1 envelope (1/4 oz/8 g) active dried yeast
1 cup (8 fl oz/250 ml) tepid water (or half water, half milk)
2 teaspoons vegetable oil or melted butter
1 tablespoon finely chopped fresh herbs (parsley, marjoram, thyme)
1/2 teaspoon dried mixed herbs
1/4 teaspoon dried oregano

Serves 4–6

Sift flour into a bowl and add sugar, salt and yeast. Mix well. Add water and oil and work to a smooth dough. If it seems dry, add extra water or milk. Knead on a lightly floured board for 2 minutes, then sprinkle on herbs and continue to knead for 10 minutes to make a smooth and elastic dough. Form into a ball and place in an oiled bowl. Cover with a piece of oiled plastic wrap and set in a warm place to rise until doubled in size—about 45 minutes.

Knead again lightly and cut in halves. Knead each piece again briefly and form into thick strands. Pinch the 2 pieces together at one end and twist around each other, then form into a ring and pinch the ends together. Place on a nonstick baking sheet and brush the top with warm water. Set aside to rise for another 35–40 minutes. Preheat oven to 425°F (220°C). Bake the bread in oven for about 20 minutes, or until the loaf is well browned on top and makes a hollow sound when tapped on the bottom. Serve warm.

NOTE: This bread can be baked ahead of time and served cold, or wrapped in aluminum foil and reheated in a moderate oven. You can substitute chopped chives and finely grated Parmesan for the herbs.

Cheese and Chive Scones

1 1/2 cups (6 oz/185 g) self-rising flour
1/2 teaspoon salt
1 tablespoon (1/2 oz/15 g) margarine
3/4 cup (3 oz/90 g) finely grated Cheddar cheese
2 tablespoons finely snipped chives
3/4 cup (6 fl oz/185 ml) milk
extra milk, for glazing

Makes 12

Cheese and chive scones

Preheat oven to 400°F (200°C). Grease and flour a baking sheet. Sift flour and salt into a bowl. Rub in the margarine with the fingertips to make fine crumbs, then add cheese, chives and three-quarters of the milk to make a soft dough. Add remaining milk only if needed. Turn onto a lightly floured surface. Press out the dough with the fingertips until 3/4 in (2 cm) thick. Cut into rounds with a floured biscuit cutter and place on the baking sheet. Brush the tops with milk and bake for about 10 minutes, until well colored and cooked through.

Blueberry Muffins

2 cups (8 oz/250 g) self-rising flour
1/2 cup (4 oz/125 g) superfine sugar
1 egg
1 cup (8 fl oz/250 ml) milk
1/4 cup (2 oz/60 g) butter, melted
1 tablespoon grated orange zest
3/4 cup (6 oz/185 g) blueberries

Makes 12

Preheat oven to 400°F (200°C). Grease 12 3-in (8 cm) muffin cups.

Place flour and sugar in bowl. Stir until combined. In another bowl beat egg and stir in milk and butter. Add to dry ingredients with orange zest and blueberries. Mix lightly and quickly; do not overbeat. Spoon mixture into prepared cups, filling each two-thirds full. Bake for 20 minutes, or until firm to touch (photograph pages 204–205).

Quick Pita Bread Pizza

*2 large white pita bread pockets (about 8 in/
    20 cm in diameter)*
*¹/₄ cup (2 fl oz/60 ml) store-bought pasta sauce or
    Fresh Tomato Sauce (see recipe, page 32)*
6 thick slices spicy salami, shredded
*2 thick slices cooked ham, finely diced or ground
    (minced)*
2 tablespoons sliced, stuffed green olives
3 tablespoons diced green bell pepper
*3 tablespoons drained and crushed or finely
    diced canned pineapple*
*¹/₂ cup (2 oz/60 g) grated mozzarella or other
    melting cheese*
*2 teaspoons dried Italian or Provençal mixed
    herbs*

Serves 2–4

*Quick pita bread pizza
(front); anchovy toast
(rear)*

Place the pita breads on a baking sheet and spread
with the pasta sauce. Mix the salami and ham together and spread evenly over. Top with the
remaining ingredients, scattering the cheese on top.
Heat under a hot broiler until the cheese melts—
about 4 minutes. Serve immediately.

Anchovy Toasts

*In Spain this is served as a snack with apéritifs. Try it
with a lightly chilled fino sherry.*

*4 slices country-style bread, cut ¹/₂ in (1 cm) thick
olive oil
1 large, very ripe tomato
48 oil-packed anchovy fillets*

Serves 4

Lightly toast the bread, then brush with olive oil.
Cut the tomato in half and rub over one surface
of the bread to coat with the tomato juice and
pulp. Arrange 12 drained anchovy fillets diagonally on each piece of toast. Cut in halves and
serve at once.

Fried Bread Boxes

Decorative edible food containers can be cut from a loaf of day-old bread and deep-fried in olive or vegetable oil. Fill them with pâté, sautéed seafood, hot vegetables, meat or vegetables in mornay sauce or small meat or fish balls. Instead of adding croûtons to your Caesar salad, serve it in a fried bread box.

Small boxes
Use a small square loaf at least 1, but preferably 2 days old. Remove crusts and cut bread into 2½-in (6 cm) cubes. Using a small, sharp knife with a thin blade, cut a ½-in (1 cm) layer from the top, then cut away the center of each cube to make a square box.

In a deep fryer, heat 4 in (10 cm) of vegetable oil (or a mixture of olive and vegetable oil) until hot. Test by frying a small cube of bread—it should immediately cast a froth of small bubbles. Fry the boxes and their lids no more than 2 at a time, until well colored, turning several times. Do not overbrown as they will turn slightly darker as they cool.

Drain well on a rack covered with a double thickness of paper towels.

Large boxes
Preheat oven to 350°F (180°C).

Use round, country-style loaves of coarse-textured bread. Use a thin, sharp knife to pare away the crust. Remove the top and cut out the center of the loaf (it can be used for bread crumbs, croûtons or smaller boxes). Fry in very hot oil until the surface is golden. Drain and place on baking sheet. Bake in the oven until it feels firm and dryish.

NOTE: If the bread is not old enough to feel dry to the touch, place in a warm oven for about 1 hour before frying.

When the bread boxes are cool they can be stored for up to 1 week in an airtight container.

They can also be frozen if packed in a plastic freezer container.

Bread and butter cucumbers (left, recipe page 52); fried bread boxes (center, back and front)

*Corn bread (left);
pumpkin bread (right)*

For speedy sandwiches with a difference, slice a crusty baguette lengthwise, or use one of the soft round rolls, and fill with cottage cheese or ricotta spiced with chopped anchovy fillets and fresh herbs. Try cold pork with pickled walnuts; goat cheese and slices of fennel; or smoked salmon with lime juice and thick yogurt.

Corn Bread

Traditional corn bread is always made in a cast-iron frying-pan. Add a cup of chopped pork cracklings for extra crunch, or stir in a dash of maple syrup to sweeten.

2 cups (10 oz/315 g) yellow cornmeal
$^{1}/_{2}$ cup (2 oz/60 g) all-purpose (plain) flour
$^{1}/_{2}$ teaspoon baking powder
1 teaspoon salt
$1^{3}/_{4}$ cups (14 fl oz/430 ml) buttermilk
1 large egg, lightly beaten
$^{1}/_{3}$ cup (3 fl oz/90 ml) bacon drippings or
    butter
melted butter

Serves 4–6

Preheat oven to 425°F (220°C).

In a bowl, combine the cornmeal, the flour, baking powder and salt. Add the buttermilk, lightly beaten egg and half the drippings. Mix well. Heat the remaining drippings in a large cast-iron frying-pan. Pour in the batter and place in the oven. Bake for another 10 minutes, then brush the surface with melted butter and bake for a further 10 minutes, until golden. Serve warm, cut into squares.

Pumpkin Bread

$1^{1}/_{2}$ cups (8 oz/250 g) mashed cooked pumpkin
1 large egg, lightly beaten
$^{3}/_{4}$ cup (6 fl oz/185 ml) milk
4 cups (1 lb/500 g) self-rising flour
1 teaspoon salt
3 tablespoons ($1^{1}/_{2}$ oz/45 g) butter or margarine
1 teaspoon dried mixed herbs
milk and all-purpose (plain) flour or cornmeal,
   for coating

Serves 6

Preheat oven to 425°F (220°C). Grease and flour a baking sheet.

Mash pumpkin until smooth; mix with the egg and milk. In a bowl, sift the flour and salt, rub in the butter with the fingertips until the mixture resembles fine crumbs, add herbs, then stir in the pumpkin mixture. Knead lightly to a smooth dough.

Form the dough into a mounded, round shape and place on the prepared baking sheet. Score the top from center outwards to make 8 wedge shapes. Brush with milk and dust with flour. Bake for about 25 minutes, then reduce heat to 350°F (180°C) and cook for another 10–15 minutes, until the loaf sounds hollow when tapped on the underside. Serve hot.

Muesli–Apricot Squares with Yogurt Topping

1 cup (6 oz/185 g) untoasted muesli
1 cup (4 oz/125 g) self-rising flour
1 cup (5 oz/155 g) rolled oats
⅔ cup (2 oz/60 g) unsweetened flaked (desiccated) coconut
1 cup (4 oz/125 g) finely chopped dried apricots
½ cup (3 oz/90 g) packed dark brown sugar
¾ cup (6 oz/185 g) butter
2 tablespoons dark corn syrup or golden syrup
1 large egg, lightly beaten

Yogurt topping
2 tablespoons plain (natural) yogurt
1½ cups (8 oz/250 g) confectioners' (icing) sugar

Makes 12–16 pieces

Preheat oven to 350°F (180°C). Lightly grease a 10-in (25 cm) square cake pan.

In a large bowl combine the muesli, flour, oats and coconut. Add the apricots and dark brown sugar and stir in evenly. Melt together the butter and corn syrup in a small pan. Pour over the dry ingredients, add the lightly beaten egg and mix well. Press into the prepared pan. Bake for 25–30 minutes. Allow to cool in the pan.

Beat together the yogurt and confectioners' sugar until smooth. Spread over the muesli mixture and cut into squares. Store in an airtight container.

Chocolate–Coconut Brownies

⅔ cup (5 oz/155 g) butter
1 cup (5 oz/155 g) soft brown sugar
1 cup (3 oz/90 g) unsweetened flaked (desiccated) coconut
⅔ cup (1 oz/30 g) shredded coconut
⅔ cup (2½ oz/75 g) unsweetened cocoa powder
1 cup (4 oz/125 g) self-rising flour

Chocolate frosting
2 tablespoons (1 oz/30 g) unsalted butter, softened
3 tablespoons unsweetened cocoa powder
1½ cups (8 oz/250 g) confectioners' (icing) sugar, sifted
milk

Makes about 18 pieces

Preheat oven to 350°F (180°C). Line an 8-in (20 cm) square cake pan with parchment or waxed paper and butter the paper.

Cream butter and brown sugar, then stir in all of the dry ingredients. Press into the prepared pan and bake for about 25 minutes. It will still feel soft while hot but will grow firm as it cools. Cool in pan.

For frosting: cream the butter and cocoa, then add sifted confectioners' sugar and enough milk to make a thick frosting. Spread evenly over the brownies and cut into squares.

Chocolate–coconut brownies (top); muesli–apricot squares with yogurt topping (bottom)

Strawberry–hazelnut shortcake

Strawberry–Hazelnut Shortcake

1 cup (5 oz/155 g) hazelnuts
¹/₂ cup (4 oz/125 g) unsalted butter, at room temperature
¹/₂ cup (4 oz/125 g) white (granulated) sugar
1¹/₄ cups (5 oz/155 g) all-purpose (plain) flour

Filling

1³/₄ cups (14 fl oz/440 ml) heavy (double) cream
¹/₂ cup (3 oz/90 g) confectioners' (icing) sugar
2 tablespoons Cointreau
1¹/₂ cups (12 oz/375 g) strawberries

Serves 8

Preheat oven to 375°F (190°C).

Spread the hazelnuts on a baking sheet and roast in the oven for about 20 minutes, or until well colored. Remove and tip out onto a rough cloth. Rub the nuts with the cloth to remove the skins, then allow to cool for a few minutes before grinding in a food processor or nut grinder.

Cream together the butter and granulated sugar, then add the flour and nuts to make a dough. Divide into 3 equal portions. Place an 8-in (20 cm) pastry (flan) ring on a large baking sheet and press one portion of the dough evenly into it. Remove the ring and reposition. Press out the second and third portions of dough in the same way. Chill for 30 minutes, then cook for about 10 minutes, or until lightly golden and firm. Remove and immediately cut each one into 8 wedges; allow to cool.

To make the filling: whip the cream to soft peaks, sweetening with 2 tablespoons of the confectioners' sugar and the Cointreau.

Position the 8 wedges of one shortcake so that they form a ring. Spread this layer with cream and cover with sliced strawberries, positioning them so as not to overlap the edges. Top with 8 wedges from the second shortcake and cover again with cream and strawberries, reserving enough to garnish the top. Top with the 8 wedges of the third shortcake. Pipe a rosette of cream at the rim of each and decorate with strawberries.

Place the remaining confectioners' sugar in a fine sieve and dust the top of the cake. Serve within 30 minutes of preparation.

NOTE: Try this with fresh raspberries, adding Framboise liqueur to the whipped cream. It is best assembled just before serving.

Apple and Poppy Seed Cake

1 cup (8 oz/250 g) unsalted butter
1¹/₂ cups (8 oz/250 g) firmly packed brown sugar
3 eggs
3 cups (12 oz/375 g) all-purpose (plain) flour
1 tablespoon baking powder
¹/₂ cup (4 fl oz/125 ml) milk
¹/₄ cup (1 oz/30 g) poppy seeds
1 tablespoon grated orange zest
1 tablespoon grated lemon zest
3 apples, peeled, cored and sliced

Serves 6–8

Preheat oven to 350°F (180°C). Grease and line a loaf pan 5 x 8 in (12 x 20 cm). Cream the butter and sugar until light and fluffy. Add the eggs, one at a time, beating with an electric mixer between each addition. Sift the flour with the baking powder and stir it into the butter mixture alternately with the milk. Fold in poppy seeds, zests and slices of 2 apples.

Spoon the batter into the pan; top with the remaining apple slices overlapping in rows. With the back of the spoon, push the apples into the mixture until they are just buried. Bake for 1¹/₂ hours, or until a skewer inserted comes out clean. Check the cake after 1 hour and, if becoming too brown, cover loosely with foil. Leave cake in pan for 15 minutes, or until cooled.

NOTE: Suitable for freezing.

If you like to add whole fresh strawberries to fruit juices or sparkling wine, wash them very briefly by dipping them in and out of chilled water. Dry immediately—leaving water on the fruit for prolonged periods makes the skin soggy and dilutes the sweetness and flavor. Remove the stem ends after washing to prevent water getting inside. Add fruit to the juice or wine just before serving.

Apple and poppy seed cake

Chocolate chip bundt cake

Chocolate Chip Bundt Cake

1 cup (8 oz/250 g) butter or margarine, softened
1 cup (8 oz/250 g) superfine (caster) sugar
4 medium eggs, beaten
1¼ cups (5 oz/155 g) self-rising flour
½ cup (2 oz/60 g) unsweetened cocoa powder

Chocolate topping
5 oz (155 g) bittersweet or semisweet (dark
*   cooking) chocolate*
3 tablespoons butter
maraschino cherries

Serves 8

Preheat oven to 350°F (180°C). Grease a 9-in (23 cm) ring or bundt pan and line the bottom with greased parchment (baking) paper. Cream together the butter and sugar until very light and smooth. Slowly incorporate the eggs; then fold in the flour and the cocoa, mixing until thoroughly blended. Spoon into the cake pan.

Bake for about 50 minutes, or until the cake comes away from the sides of the pan and feels firm on top. Test the center by piercing with a thin skewer—it should come out dry. Cool in the pan for a few minutes, then turn out onto a wire rack to cool.

For topping: slowly melt the chocolate in a small saucepan over simmering water or in a microwave oven. Stir in the butter. Pour over the top of the cake, allowing it to flow down the sides. Decorate with cherries.

Melting Moments

1 cup (8 oz/250 g) butter
⅓ cup (2 oz/60 g) confectioners' (icing) sugar
½ cup (2 oz/60 g) cornstarch (cornflour)
1½ cups (6 oz/185 g) all-purpose (plain) flour

Chocolate cream frosting
2 oz (60 g) bittersweet or semisweet (dark)
*   chocolate*
¼ cup (2 oz/60 g) butter
½ cup (3 oz/90 g) confectioners' (icing) sugar

Makes 30 double cookies

Preheat oven to 350°F (180°C).

In a bowl, cream butter and sugar until the mixture is light and fluffy. Sift the cornstarch and flour together over the mixture and stir in lightly with a metal spoon. Transfer to a pastry bag fitted with a star tube. Lightly grease a baking sheet and squeeze the dough in rosettes on the sheet. Bake for about 12 minutes until pale golden and dry to the touch. Leave to cool.

To make the frosting: melt the chocolate. Beat with butter and sugar to a smooth cream. Spread the flat side of half the cookies with the cream, pressing unfrosted ones on top.

Pine Nut Cookies

1 cup (4 oz/125 g) pine nuts
1½ cups (6 oz/185 g) all-purpose (plain) flour
¾ cup (4 oz/125 g) confectioners' (icing) sugar
½ teaspoon ground cinnamon
½ cup (4 oz/125 g) unsalted butter
1 teaspoon grated lemon zest
1 egg yolk
2 oz (60 g) bittersweet or semisweet (dark) chocolate

Makes 36

Preheat oven to 375°F (190°C).

Spread the pine nuts on a baking sheet and roast until golden—about 12 minutes—(or microwave on HIGH for 3–4 minutes, stirring after each minute). Cool, then grind finely. Combine flour, sugar and cinnamon. Rub in the butter with the fingertips until the mixture resembles fine crumbs; then stir in the nuts, lemon zest and egg yolk, mixing well. Knead lightly, then roll out on a lightly floured board ⅛ in (3 mm) thick and use a fluted cutter to cut into 2-in (5 cm) rounds.

Transfer to a greased baking sheet and bake for 10–15 minutes, until golden. Leave to cool.

Melt the chocolate over simmering water or in a microwave oven. Dip one side of each cookie into the chocolate and refrigerate to set.

Pine nut cookies (left); melting moments (right)

Polvorones

½ cup (4 oz/125 g) butter
½ cup (4 oz/125 g) lard
½ cup (4 oz/125 g) sugar
2 large egg yolks
1 large orange
2 cups (8 oz/250 g) all-purpose (plain) flour
*2 cups (8 oz/250 g) finely ground
    almonds*

Makes about 36

Preheat oven to 400°F (200°C).

In a bowl, beat the butter, lard and sugar to a smooth light cream. Add the egg yolks separately, beating well after each. Very finely grate the orange peel and add to the batter with the juice of the orange, then fold in the flour and the almonds.

The dough should be quite crumbly.

On a floured surface, roll out the dough ¾ in (2 cm) thick. Cut out 1¼-in (3 cm) circles. Place on a greased baking sheet and bake for about 15 minutes, until cooked but still golden. They will still feel soft but will grow firm as they cool. Store in an airtight container.

Poppy Seed Roll

*½ oz (15 g) fresh yeast, or ½ teaspoon active
    dried yeast*
¼ cup (2 oz/60 g) plus ½ teaspoon white sugar
½ cup (4 fl oz/125 ml) milk
*2½ cups (10 oz/315 g) all-purpose (plain)
    flour*

*Polvorones (left); poppy
seed roll (right)*

¹/₄ cup (2 oz/60 g) butter
1 egg
pinch of salt
3 cups (12 oz/375 g) poppy seeds
¹/₂ cup (4 oz/125 g) honey or sugar
2 tablespoons (1 oz/30 g) golden raisins
   (sultanas)
¹/₄ cup (1 oz/30 g) chopped walnuts
1 tablespoon confectioners' (icing) sugar
   (optional)

Serves 8

In a small bowl, cream the yeast and the ¹/₂ teaspoon of sugar with a little tepid water. Heat the milk to lukewarm, add yeast and half the flour and work to a soft dough; cover and set aside for 30 minutes.

Melt the butter in a small pan or in the microwave oven and add to the dough with the remaining sugar, the egg, the salt and the remaining flour, work to a soft, nonsticky dough. Knead for 10 minutes, then place in an oiled bowl. Cover and set aside until doubled in size—about 45 minutes.

Meanwhile, pour poppy seeds into a bowl, cover with boiling water and set aside for 40 minutes.

Knead the dough again lightly, then roll out to a thickness of ¹/₄ in (0.5 cm). Drain the poppy seeds, pressing out the water, then grind to a smooth paste in a food processor. Add the honey, raisins and nuts and spread evenly over the pastry. Roll up, divide in two, pinch the ends down to seal contents, then place on a greased baking sheet and set aside for 30 minutes. Preheat the oven to 350°F (180°C). Bake for 20–30 minutes. Dust with confectioners' sugar before serving warm or cold.

Keep an eye on the weather. Special clips are available to hold down the edges of tablecloths on windy days. A garden umbrella is a must in hot weather to shield guests from the glare.

Panettone fruit basket

Panettone Fruit Basket

2 lb (1 kg) Italian panettone bread
4 oz (125 g) bittersweet or semisweet chocolate
1 tablespoon (^{1}/$_2$ oz/15 g) unsalted butter
4–6 cups cubed fresh fruit
^{1}/$_2$ cup (3 fl oz/90 ml) Cointreau or other
    liqueur
confectioners' (icing) sugar (optional)

Serves 6

Cut around the top of a panettone, leaving a border of 1^1/$_2$ in (4 cm). Cut deeply downwards to
remove the center of the bread. Lift out and trim
the cavity to make it smooth on the inside.

Melt the chocolate in a microwave oven or over
simmering water and stir in the butter. Use a
pastry brush to spread the mixture over the inside of the panettone, then set aside to firm up.

In the meantime, soak the fruit in the liqueur.
Use a slotted spoon to fill the panettone with the
fruit. Dust heavily with confectioners' sugar and
serve with whipped cream.

Individual Chocolate Truffle Cakes

1^1/$_2$ tablespoons (^{3}/$_4$ oz/20 g) butter
1 teaspoon raspberry jam
1^1/$_3$ tablespoons white sugar
2 small eggs, separated
1^1/$_3$ oz (45 g) bittersweet or semisweet
    chocolate, melted and cooled
^{1}/$_4$ cup (1 oz/30 g) ground hazelnuts
2 tablespoons all-purpose (plain) flour

Truffles
4 oz (125 g) bittersweet or semisweet chocolate,
    chopped
2 tablespoons heavy (double) cream
2 teaspoons coffee liqueur
^{1}/$_4$ cup (2 oz/60 g) unsalted butter
^{1}/$_4$ cup (1^1/$_3$ oz/45 g) packed brown sugar

Chocolate bands
6^1/$_3$ oz (200 g) bittersweet or semisweet
    chocolate, melted

Serves 2

Preheat the oven to 350°F (180°C). Grease 2 straight-sided ³/₄-cup (6 fl oz/185 ml) metal molds.

Beat butter, jam and granulated sugar in a bowl until light and creamy. Add egg yolks and beat until combined. Transfer mixture to a larger bowl and stir in the cooled chocolate, hazelnuts and flour. Beat egg whites in a small bowl until soft peaks form; fold into chocolate mixture.

Spoon cake mixture into prepared molds and bake for 20 minutes, or until cakes are firm. Let stand for 5 minutes before turning cakes out onto a wire rack. Allow to cool completely.

For truffles: place chocolate, cream and liqueur in top of a double boiler over simmering water until chocolate melts. Melt butter in pan; add brown sugar and stir until sugar dissolves. Add to chocolate mixture. Refrigerate until mixture is firm enough to roll. Roll, heaping teaspoonfuls of mixture into balls. Refrigerate.

For chocolate bands: cut 2 pieces of parchment (baking) or waxed paper 14 in (35 cm) long and 2 in (5 cm) higher than cakes. Oil paper, spread chocolate evenly onto paper and refrigerate until firm. Remove the chocolate from the refrigerator and allow to become pliable. Using scissors, cut one edge of chocolate straight to go around bases of cakes. Wrap one piece of chocolate around each cake and gently mold edge of chocolate into cakes, so chocolate is secure and the cake is fully encased in chocolate. Arrange truffles on top of the cakes.

Chocolate Hazelnut Torte

1¹/₂ cups (6¹/₃ oz/200 g) hazelnuts
8 oz (250 g) bittersweet or semisweet chocolate
6 large egg whites
¹/₃ teaspoon salt
¹/₃ cup (5 oz/155 g) superfine (caster) sugar
9 oz (250 g) pitted dates, finely chopped

Serves 10

Preheat oven to 350°F (180°C). Line a 9-in (23 cm) springform pan with foil and grease the foil.

Place hazelnuts and chocolate in the bowl of a food processor and process until fine. Beat together egg whites and salt until stiff peaks form. Gradually add sugar and continue beating until mixture resembles a meringue. Stir in one-third of the chocolate-hazelnut mixture and one-third of the dates. Fold in remaining ingredients. Pour into the prepared pan. Bake in oven for 45 minutes. Switch oven off and allow cake to cool in the oven with the door ajar. When completely cool, unmold, wrap and refrigerate overnight. Serve with thick heavy (double) cream and fresh berries (photograph page 186).

Individual chocolate truffle cake

Photograph following pages, "Weekend Brunch," clockwise from front: cream cheese blintzes with strawberry glaze (page 212); smoked salmon, avocado and egg crêpe roulade (page 119); blueberry muffins (page 191); peaches and berries in toffee syrup (page 211); herbed soufflé omelet (page 67)

Desserts

Although people might not go to the trouble of making desserts on a day-to-day basis, a sumptuous finale is essential when entertaining. Nostalgic childhood favorites such as chocolate cakes, deep-dish apple pies and cookies are among the much-loved classics. Fresh air sharpens the appetite and, if you've chosen to serve a light main course, your guests will have no difficulty finding room for these sweet temptations. When a lighter ending to a substantial meal is called for, there are many simple ways to prepare the fresh fruits of the season, enjoyed as much for their refreshing flavor as for the vibrant colors they add to a beautiful setting. Also, you could try making your own cheeses using ricotta or cottage cheese as a base mixed with fresh herbs, fruit, spices or nuts.

Many people think that preparing elaborate desserts is beyond their capabilities. If this is your feeling, don't overlook the ready-made products that can simplify the job. There are good-quality, ready-to-roll frozen pastry doughs available. A package of filo pastry is a particularly good stand-by for both sweet and savory foods. A plain pound cake bought at the supermarket can be transformed swiftly into something special. Slice it and soak the pieces in liqueur. Then, top with fresh fruit and a glaze made with one of the jams or preserves you're certain to have in your pantry, and you have an instant and delicious dessert.

Always draw on whatever resources you can to streamline the process of entertaining. In making good food, the word "difficult" need never cross your mind.

Cherry clafoutis (page 208)

Cherry Clafoutis

²/₃ cup (2¹/₃ oz/75 g) all-purpose (plain) flour
2 tablespoons sugar
3 eggs
¹/₄ teaspoon salt
1³/₄ cups (14 fl oz/430 ml) milk
1 tablespoon (¹/₂ oz/15 g) butter
1³/₄ cups (10 oz/315 g) pitted cherries (fresh
    or canned)

Serves 6

Preheat oven to 350°F (180°C).

    Sift the flour into a mixing bowl. Mix in sugar, eggs and salt and stir until smooth. Gradually add the milk and stir until mixture resembles a smooth batter. Grease a 10-in (25 cm) round baking dish with some of the butter. Spread cherries over the base. Pour on the batter and dot with the rest of the butter. Bake on the center rack of the oven for 40 minutes, or until set in the middle and browned. Serve warm or at room temperature (photograph page 206).

NOTE: Any fruit in season can be substituted for the cherries.

Summer Berry Pudding

1 loaf day-old white bread, crusts removed (about
    15 slices)
1¹/₂ cups (12 oz/375 g) raspberries
1 cup (8 oz/250 g) red currants
1¹/₂ cups (12 oz/375 g) blackberries
1¹/₂ cups (12 oz/375 g) blueberries
³/₄ cup (6 oz/185 g) strawberries, sliced
³/₄ cup (6 oz/185 g) superfine (caster) sugar

Serves 8

Line a medium-size bowl with the bread, reserving enough to make a lid. Combine raspberries, red currants, blackberries and sugar in a saucepan. Cook over moderate heat until the juice starts to run—about 8 minutes. Remove from heat and add strawberries. Pour into the bread-lined bowl and cover top with reserved pieces of bread. Lay a piece of plastic wrap over the top and place a plate over this. Weight down the plate with two cans or a heavy weight. Refrigerate for at least 24 hours. Turn out onto a plate and serve with heavy (double) cream.

Summer berry pudding

Wild Berry and Apricot Trifle

6 oz (185 g) strawberry or raspberry gelatin crystals
2 small store-bought or homemade sponge or
*   yellow cakes*
1¼ cups (13 fl oz/410 ml) strawberry jam
1½ cups (375 ml/12 fl oz) sweet sherry
1 cup (8 oz/250 g) strawberries, hulled and halved
2 cups (16 oz/500 g) blueberries
2 cups (16 oz/500 g) raspberries
8 oz (250 g) fresh apricot halves
4 cups (1 qt/1 l) milk
½ cup cornstarch (cornflour)
⅔ cup (5 oz/150 g) white (granulated) sugar
pinch of salt
6 eggs, lightly beaten
2 teaspoons vanilla extract (essence)
whipped cream, for decoration

Serves 20

Make gelatin according to directions on package. Refrigerate until set, then chop roughly. Cut cake into slices, spread with jam, sprinkle with sherry and set aside. Place berries and apricots in bowl and toss until combined. In saucepan, scald 3 cups (24 fl oz/750 ml) of the milk. Mix remaining milk with the cornstarch. When milk is hot, stir in sugar and salt until dissolved. Add cornstarch mixture and stir well. Cook this custard over low heat, stirring constantly, until mixture boils and thickens. Add some of the custard to the eggs to warm them. Add the eggs to the custard and cook, stirring, for 3 minutes, until the eggs are cooked and the custard coats a spoon. Pour custard into bowl, whisk in vanilla. Place a sheet of plastic wrap on custard to prevent skin from forming and chill.

To assemble trifle, arrange half the cake slices over the base of a very large serving dish (or two large dishes), top with half the custard, then half the gelatin and half the berries and apricots. Repeat these layers, finishing with a layer of fruit. Refrigerate overnight. At serving time, decorate trifle with whipped cream.

NOTE: This dessert is best made 1 day in advance.

Wild berry and apricot trifle

Strawberry Tortoni

Tortoni can be made in individual dishes or glasses or can be molded in foil-lined terrine molds. They are best served the day they are made. About 15 minutes before serving, remove from the freezer to the refrigerator to allow them to soften. Any berries can be used instead of strawberries.

3 cups (24 fl oz/750 ml) heavy (double) cream
1⅓ cups (12 oz/375 g) strawberries, roughly
    chopped
¾ cup (3 oz/90 g) toasted slivered almonds
9 amaretti cookies, crushed
⅓ cup (3 fl oz/90 ml) brandy
3 egg whites
¾ cup (6 oz/185 g) superfine (caster) sugar
½ teaspoon baking powder

Serves 6

Whip the cream and set aside. Mix the strawberries, almonds and crushed amaretti in a bowl with brandy. Set aside for 10 minutes. Beat egg whites until stiff and soft peaks form. Slowly add the superfine sugar and baking powder, and beat until shiny. Fold egg white and strawberry mixture into the cream, working it in lightly but thoroughly. Pour into the desired mold or individual serving dishes and freeze, covered, for 4–5 hours (depending on the size of the dish).

Mille-feuille

3 sheets frozen puff pastry, thawed
1 cup (8 oz/250 g) raspberries
2 tablespoons superfine (caster) sugar
1 tablespoon vodka or white rum
3 mangoes
1½ cups (12 fl oz/375 ml) heavy (double) cream
2 tablespoons Framboise liqueur
⅓ cup (2 oz/60 g) confectioners' (icing) sugar,
    for sprinkling

Serves 6

Preheat oven to 350°F (180°C).
    Cut 12 4-in (10 cm) circles out of the pastry. Make 4 cross-shaped incisions in each, using the point of a knife. Bake in oven for 15 minutes, or until golden. Remove from oven and allow to cool slightly before splitting each circle into 2 flat disks of pastry.
    For raspberry sauce: place raspberries, superfine sugar and vodka in the bowl of a food processor. Process to a smooth purée. Strain through a double layer of dampened cheesecloth. Refrigerate until ready to use.
    Peel mangoes and slice into strips and divide them into 6 equal portions. Whip cream. Stir in, very gently, the Framboise liqueur. Arrange each plate with layers of pastry, cream, then mango. Finish with a pastry layer and sprinkle generously with confectioners' sugar. Serve immediately with raspberry sauce.

Mille-feuille

Peaches and Berries in Toffee Syrup

8 peaches
2 cups (14 oz/440 g) sugar
1 cup (8 oz/250 g) raspberries
1 cup (8 oz/250 g) blackberries

Serves 8

Place peaches in a bowl of boiling water for a few minutes or until softened. Remove from water and peel away skin. Place 2 cups (16 fl oz/500 ml) water and sugar in saucepan and stir over low heat, without boiling, until sugar dissolves. Bring to a boil, without stirring, and boil rapidly until syrup turns pale golden brown. Remove saucepan from heat. Add 1 cup (8 fl oz/250 ml) water and stir over moderate heat until toffee melts; remove from heat.
    Place peaches in a bowl, pour on the syrup and allow to cool. At serving time, arrange peaches in a bowl with berries, and spoon the syrup on top (photograph pages 204–205).

Opposite: strawberry tortoni

Rhubarb Crumble

2 bunches rhubarb, cut into ³/₄-in (2 cm) slices
4 apples, peeled and thinly sliced
¹/₂ cup (3 oz/90 g) packed brown sugar
2 tablespoons all-purpose (plain) flour
1 teaspoon ground cinnamon
¹/₂ teaspoon ground nutmeg

Topping
³/₄ cup (4 oz/125 g) rolled oats
1 cup (6 oz/185 g) packed brown sugar
¹/₄ cup (2 oz/60 g) butter, melted

Serves 6

Preheat oven to 350°F (180°C).

Place rhubarb and apples in a bowl. Combine sugar, flour, cinnamon and nutmeg, then mix with the fruit. Place in a greased casserole dish. To make the topping: combine the oats, sugar and butter; sprinkle over the fruit mixture. Bake in oven for 30 minutes, or until browned.

Cream Cheese Blintzes with Strawberry Glaze

1 cup (4 oz/125 g) all-purpose (plain) flour
2 teaspoons superfine (caster) sugar
1 egg, lightly beaten
³/₄ cup (6 fl oz/185 ml) sour cream
1 cup (8 fl oz/250 ml) milk
¹/₄ cup (2 oz/60 g) unsalted butter

Use the broiler for simple desserts, ideal on a hot day when you're in a hurry to get outdoors with your guests. Cover blackberries or blueberries with whipped cream, sprinkle with sugar and brown quickly under a very hot broiler.

Rhubarb crumble

Cream cheese filling
³/₄ cup (4 oz/125 g) golden raisins (sultanas)
¹/₄ cup (2 fl oz/60 ml) brandy
¹/₂ cup (4 oz/125 g) cottage cheese
1 cup (8 oz/250 g) cream cheese, at room temperature
¹/₄ cup (2 oz/60 g) unsalted butter, at room temperature
¹/₄ cup (2 oz/60 g) white (granulated) sugar
2 teaspoons grated lemon zest (rind)
2 tablespoons sour cream
1 egg yolk
unsalted butter, for cooking

Strawberry glaze
³/₄ cup (8 oz/250 g) strawberry jam
2 tablespoons brandy
2 tablespoons water

Serves 8

Sift the flour and superfine sugar in a bowl. Add egg and mix well. Gradually add combined sour cream and milk and beat with a wooden spoon until batter is smooth; let stand 1 hour. Heat pancake pan, grease well with unsalted butter. From a small jug, pour ¹/₄ cup (2 fl oz/60 ml) mixture into pan, swirling batter evenly around pan. Cook over moderate heat until lightly golden. Toss pancake and cook on other side for a few minutes. Repeat with remaining batter. (Makes about 10 pancakes.)

To make the filling: place golden raisins in saucepan with brandy and bring to a boil. Reduce heat and simmer for 2 minutes. Remove from heat. Let stand 30 minutes. Beat together cheeses, butter and sugar until creamy. Add lemon zest, sour cream and egg yolk and mix well. Drain golden raisins and add to cream mixture. Place about ¹/₄ cup (2 fl oz/60 ml) cream mixture in center of pancake; fold pancake over filling to form parcel. Refrigerate for 2 hours before frying. Heat butter in pan. Fry blintzes until golden-brown on both sides.

To make the glaze: place jam, brandy and water in saucepan and stir until boiling, then pass through a fine sieve.

To serve, arrange blintzes on serving plate, spoon on glaze. If desired, decorate with raspberries (photograph pages 204–205).
NOTE: Blintzes with filling may be made 1 day in advance and can be frozen.

Old-fashioned High Apple Pie

3 cups (12 oz/375 g) all-purpose (plain) flour
³/₄ cup (6 oz/185 g) butter, chilled, chopped in pieces
4 tablespoons (2 fl oz/60 ml) very cold water

Filling
12 Granny Smith apples, peeled and thinly sliced
juice of ¹/₂ lemon
²/₃ cup (5 oz/155 g) packed brown sugar
2 tablespoons all-purpose (plain) flour

¹/₂ *teaspoon ground cinnamon*
¹/₂ *teaspoon ground nutmeg*
¹/₄ *teaspoon ground cloves*
2 tablespoons (1 oz/30 g) butter
¹/₄ *cup (2 fl oz/60 ml) heavy (double) cream*

Serves 8–10

Preheat oven to 325°F (160°C).

Process flour in food processor for 10 seconds, add butter, and process until mixture resembles bread crumbs. Add water, 1 tablespoon at a time. Process until pastry forms a ball. Remove and knead until smooth and elastic. Roll out two-thirds of the pastry to fit a pie dish 9 in (23 cm) wide, and 1³/₄ in (4 cm) deep. Leave edges hanging over. Roll out remaining third to comfortably fit across pie dish with ¹/₂-in (1 cm) overlap. Set aside.

Mix apples, lemon juice, sugar, flour and spices in a large bowl. Heap into pie shell. Dot with butter and drizzle with cream. Wet edges of pastry with milk; place crust on top. Crimp edges firmly. Trim and make a fluted edge. Prick top crust to allow steam to escape. Bake in oven for 40–45 minutes, until crust is golden and apples are cooked.

Old-fashioned high apple pie

Mexican Flan

³/₄ cup (6 oz/185 g) white (granulated) sugar
³/₄ cup (6 fl oz/185 ml) water
6 eggs
1 teaspoon vanilla extract (essence)
¹/₄ cup (2 oz/60 g) superfine (caster) sugar
1¹/₄ cups (10 fl oz/315 ml) milk
1¹/₂ cups (12 fl oz/375 ml) light (single) cream

Serves 5

Preheat oven to 350°F (180°C).

Combine granulated sugar and water in a saucepan. Stir over low heat, stirring until sugar dissolves. Bring to a boil and boil rapidly, without stirring, for about 5 minutes, or until golden brown.

Pour mixture into an 8-in (20 cm) round cake pan.

Beat together eggs, vanilla and superfine sugar until sugar is dissolved. Combine milk and cream in a saucepan, bring to a boil, remove from heat and allow bubbles to subside. Gradually whisk cream mixture into eggs. Strain. Place prepared dish in larger pan, pour custard into caramel-lined cake pan. Pour enough water into pan to reach halfway up sides of cake pan. Bake in oven for about 25 minutes, or until custard is just set. Remove dish from water, cool to room temperature, and refrigerate overnight. To serve, turn custard out onto a serving plate. Serve with whipped cream.

NOTE: This dessert is best made 1 day in advance; keep covered in refrigerator.

Mexican flan

Pumpkin Pie

1 cup (4 oz/125 g) all-purpose (plain) flour
$^1/_2$ cup (2 oz/60 g) self-rising flour
$^1/_4$ teaspoon ground nutmeg
$^1/_4$ teaspoon ground allspice
2 tablespoons brown sugar
$^1/_4$ cup (2 oz/60 g) butter, chopped
2 egg yolks, lightly beaten
about 2 tablespoons water
$1^1/_2$ cups (12 oz/375 g) cooked, mashed pumpkin
3 eggs
$^1/_4$ cup (2 fl oz/60 ml) honey
$^3/_4$ cup (6 fl oz/185 ml) light (single) cream
1 teaspoon ground ginger

Serves 8

Preheat oven to 350°F (180°C).

Sift flours into a bowl, stir in nutmeg, allspice and sugar. Rub in butter until mixture resembles fine bread crumbs. Add egg yolks and water and mix until pastry forms a firm dough. (You may need to add a little more water.) Turn dough onto lightly floured surface and knead gently.

Roll out pastry onto lightly floured board to cover bottom and sides of a 9-in (23 cm) pie plate. Crimp edges with fork. Line pie shell with foil, fill with beans or pie weights and bake for about 12 minutes or until lightly golden brown. Remove from oven, remove foil and weights and allow to cool.

Combine pumpkin, eggs, honey, cream and ginger in bowl, beat until smooth and spoon into prepared shell. Bake for 30 minutes, or until filling is set. Remove from oven and allow to cool.

Pumpkin pie

Citrus Roulade

Lemon curd
1/2 cup (4 oz/125 g) unsalted butter
2/3 cup (6 fl oz/185 ml) lemon juice
1 1/4 cups (10 oz/315 g) sugar
3 whole eggs
3 egg yolks

Cake
4 eggs
1/2 cup (4 oz/125 g) sugar
3/4 cup (3 oz/90 g) all-purpose (plain) flour, sifted
1/2 teaspoon baking powder
1 teaspoon grated lemon zest
1 teaspoon vanilla extract (essence)

Garnish
1/2 cup (3 oz/90 g) confectioners' (icing) sugar
1 cup (8 fl oz/250 ml) heavy (double) cream, whipped
2 cups (1 lb/500 g) blueberries

Serves 8

To make lemon curd: combine butter, lemon juice and sugar in a double boiler over simmering water; stir until butter melts and sugar dissolves. Whisk together the whole eggs and egg yolks in a bowl. Slowly add one-quarter of hot lemon mixture while whisking, then add the rest in a steady stream. Return to double boiler and cook, stirring, until thick. Cover and refrigerate for 12 hours.

For cake: preheat oven to 350°F (180°C). Line a jelly roll pan with parchment (baking) paper and butter the paper. In the top of a double boiler, whisk together the eggs and sugar until blended. Set over simmering water and heat, stirring, until warm to touch. Remove from heat and beat with electric mixer until doubled in volume and pale yellow in color. Fold in flour, baking powder, lemon zest and vanilla. Pour into prepared pan and bake for 13–15 minutes or until springy to touch. Run a knife around the edge of the cake and invert onto a damp tea towel. Roll up starting with short edge. Do not roll up tea towel.

To assemble: unroll cake, spread with lemon curd, re-roll cake and place, seam side down, on a plate. Cover the top and sides with sifted confectioners' sugar. Serve with whipped cream and berries.

Zuccotto

round sponge cake (9 in/23 cm in diameter)
2 tablespoons brandy
2 tablespoons coffee liqueur
1 1/2 cups (12 fl oz/375 ml) heavy (double) cream
1/2 cup (3 oz/90 g) confectioners' (icing) sugar
1/2 cup (2 oz/60 g) chopped toasted almonds
3/4 cup (3 oz/90 g) chopped roasted hazelnuts
2 oz (60 g) bittersweet or semisweet chocolate, chopped
3 oz (90 g) bittersweet or semisweet chocolate, melted
sifted cocoa and confectioners' (icing) sugar, for dusting

Serves 6

Cut cake in slices 1/2 in (1 cm) thick at widest end. Cut each slice diagonally, making 2 triangular sections. Combine brandy and coffee liqueur; brush 1 side of each piece of cake with mixture. Line a 5-cup (1 1/4 qt/1.25 l) mold with dampened cheesecloth, making sure cheesecloth overhangs top of the basin. Place unbrushed side of cake against cheesecloth to completely line basin. Fill any gaps with pieces of cake. Trim edges of cake level with basin. Leftover cake will cover top when filled.

Place cream and confectioners' sugar in a bowl and beat until soft peaks form; fold in nuts. Divide mixture in half, fold chopped chocolate into one half and melted chocolate into the other. Spoon the white cream mixture evenly over the entire cake surface, leaving a cavity in the center. Spoon the chocolate mixture into the cavity. Arrange remaining cake on top to completely cover surface. Cover mold and refrigerate overnight.

Turn out on serving plate and dust with cocoa and confectioners' sugar (photograph pages 74–75). NOTE: Suitable for freezing.

Cheesecake with Blueberry Sauce

8 oz (250 g) sweet cookies
1/2 cup (4 oz/125 g) unsalted butter, melted
2 cups (1 lb/500 g) cream cheese
2 cups (1 lb/500 g) ricotta cheese
1 cup (7 oz/220 g) sugar
4 large eggs
2 tablespoons lime juice
2 teaspoons grated lime zest
3 tablespoons all-purpose (plain) flour
3 tablespoons cornstarch (cornflour)
2 cups (16 fl oz/500 ml) light sour cream

Blueberry sauce
1 cup (8 oz/250 g) blueberries
3 tablespoons sugar
2 tablespoons vodka or other white spirit

Serves 10

Preheat oven to 300°F (150°C).

Place cookies in the bowl of a food processor and process to crumbs. Add melted butter and mix with cookie crumbs. Line the base and sides of a 9-in (23 cm) springform pan with crumb mixture. Refrigerate until ready to use.

Beat cream cheese, ricotta and sugar until smooth. Beat in eggs, one at a time. Stir in lime juice and zest. Stir in combined sifted flours, then fold in sour cream. Pour into crust-lined pan.

Bake on center rack of oven for 1 hour, or until firm in the center. Cool in oven for 15 minutes (with oven door open). Remove and cool. Refrigerate at least 2 hours. Serve with blueberry sauce.

For blueberry sauce: place blueberries, sugar and vodka in blender. Blend until smooth. Let stand 10–15 minutes before straining and serving. Best served cold.

Opposite: cheesecake with blueberry sauce (back); citrus roulade (front)

Use your microwave as often as possible to cut down on time spent on basic chores. To remove the skins of hazelnuts, for example, brown them and then place in a single layer of paper towels and microwave on HIGH for 30 seconds. Rub off the skins with a clean tea towel, and microwave the nuts until just golden.

Caramel–Nut Self-saucing Pudding

$^3/_4$ cup (3 oz/90 g) self-rising flour
$^1/_4$ cup (1 oz/30 g) packaged ground
    hazelnuts
$1^2/_3$ cups (13 fl oz/400 ml) condensed milk
1 tablespoon butter
1 teaspoon vanilla extract (essence)
$^1/_2$ cup (4 fl oz/125 ml) milk
1 cup (6 oz/185 g) firmly packed
    brown sugar
$1^3/_4$ cups (14 fl oz/430 ml) boiling water

Serves 6

Preheat oven to 350°F (180°C).

    Grease an 8-cup (2 qt/2 l) baking dish. Sift flour into bowl, stir in hazelnuts. Place condensed milk in saucepan and stir over moderate heat for 10 minutes, or until thickened and slightly golden brown. Stir in butter, vanilla and milk until butter is melted. Let cool slightly. Pour milk mixture into flour and mix well. Pour batter into prepared dish. Sift brown sugar over top of pudding mixture. Carefully pour boiling water evenly over top of pudding. Bake in oven for about 35 minutes, or until firm. Let stand for 5 minutes before serving.

Caramel–nut self-saucing pudding

Tiramisu

Exceptionally easy and delicious!

5 eggs, separated
$^1/_4$ cup (2 oz/60 g) sugar
2 cups (1 lb/500 g) mascarpone cheese
$^1/_4$ cup (2 fl oz/60 ml) dark rum
24 ladyfingers (savoiardi biscuits/sponge fingers)
$^3/_4$ cup (6 fl oz/180 ml) very strong black coffee
$^1/_2$ cup (2 oz/60 g) unsweetened cocoa powder

Serves 6–8

Whisk egg yolks and sugar until pale and thick. Fold in mascarpone and rum. Beat egg whites until soft peaks form. Stir one-third of whites into mascarpone mixture. Fold in remaining egg whites. Brush each ladyfinger with coffee. Line the base of a dish with 12 of the ladyfingers. Gently spread mascarpone mixture over ladyfingers. Sprinkle with half the cocoa powder. Repeat, finishing with the remaining cocoa. Refrigerate overnight. Serve with fresh raspberries.

Chocolate Dessert Cake

1 cup (8 fl oz/250 ml) boiling water
6 oz (185 g) unsweetened (dark cooking) chocolate
½ cup (4 oz/125 g) butter
1 teaspoon vanilla extract (essence)
1 cup (8 oz/250 g) superfine (caster) sugar
2 eggs, separated
½ cup (4 fl oz/125 ml) sour cream
1 teaspoon baking soda (bicarbonate of soda)
1⅓ cups (5½ oz/170 g) all-purpose (plain) flour
1 teaspoon baking powder
⅔ cup (2½ oz/75 g) ground almonds
8 oz (250 g) bittersweet or semisweet chocolate
2 tablespoons brandy
1 orange, thinly sliced
⅓ cup (3 fl oz/90 ml) orange-flavored liqueur

Serves 8

Preheat oven to 350°F (180°C).

Grease and line a 9-in (23 cm) round cake pan with parchment (baking) paper. In a mixing bowl, pour the boiling water over the unsweetened chocolate and butter. Let stand until melted. Stir in vanilla and sugar, then whisk in egg yolks, one at a time, blending well after each addition. Mix in sour cream and baking soda. Sift flour and baking powder together. Add to batter, along with ground almonds. Mix thoroughly. Beat egg whites until stiff, but not dry. Stir one-third of egg whites into batter. Fold in remaining egg whites. Pour into prepared pan and bake on center rack for 55 minutes. Cool in pan for 15 minutes.

For chocolate sauce: melt bittersweet chocolate in the bowl of a double boiler and stir in brandy.

Marinate the orange for at least 2 hours in liqueur.

To serve, spread cake with chocolate sauce and decorate with marinated orange slices and heavy (double) cream. If desired, serve with fresh, light (single) cream and brandy-soaked fruits or berries.

Tiramisu (back); chocolate dessert cake (front)

Port wine gelatin mold

Raisins soaked in brandy until plump are delicious when sprinkled over poached apples or pears. You can also add them to cooked spinach with a few pine nuts, or even mix them with stem ginger and butter and spread over salmon steaks before broiling.

Port Wine Gelatin Mold

2¹/₂ cups (20 fl oz/600 ml) water
¹/₂ cup (4 oz/125 g) sugar
2 tablespoons red currant jelly
2 tablespoons unflavored gelatin
10 fl oz (300 ml) port wine

Serves 8

Place water, sugar and red currant jelly in a saucepan. Stir over low heat until sugar and jelly dissolve.

Dissolve gelatin in 2 tablespoons of cold water over hot water. Add gelatin to jelly mixture. Stir in port. Pour into a large decorative mold and refrigerate until set.

Pear and Raspberry Pie

¹/₃ cup (3 oz/90 g) unsalted butter
¹/₄ cup (2 oz/60 g) white (granulated) sugar
1 egg, lightly beaten
1¹/₄ cups (5 oz/155 g) all-purpose (plain) flour
¹/₄ cup (1¹/₄ oz /35 g) self-rising flour
7 pears
1 cup (8 oz/250 g) raspberries
7 egg yolks
¹/₂ cup (6 oz/185 g) superfine (caster) sugar
1 cup (8 fl oz/250 ml) light (single) cream
2 teaspoons vanilla extract (essence)
cinnamon sugar
confectioners' (icing) sugar, for dusting

Serves 8

Preheat oven to 350°F (180°C).

Beat butter and granulated sugar until creamy, add egg gradually, beating well. Add flours and mix until combined. Turn pastry onto lightly floured surface and knead lightly until smooth. Refrigerate until firm.

Roll out pastry to line a 9-in (23 cm) deep pie dish. Peel, core and slice 6 of the pears. Arrange pears in pastry shell, leaving space in center for remaining pear. Cut base of remaining pear flat, peel pear, and place in space. Sprinkle on raspberries. Beat egg yolks and sugar together until light and fluffy. Add cream and vanilla and beat until combined. Pour mixture evenly into pastry. Sprinkle cinnamon sugar on top. Bake for about 1 hour, or until firm to touch. Allow to cool completely. Dust with confectioners' sugar.

Mustard and Port Cheese

2 cups (8 oz/250 g) grated Cheddar cheese
1 cup (8 oz/250 g) unsalted butter, chopped
¹/₂ cup (4 oz/125 g) grainy mustard
¹/₄ cup (2 fl oz/60 ml) port wine
2 tablespoons fennel seeds

Makes 3³/₄ cups (1¹/₄ lb/625 g)

Place cheese, butter, mustard and port in the bowl of a food processor and process until combined. Transfer mixture to a bowl and refrigerate until firm enough to roll. Shape mixture into a log shape and wrap cheese in plastic wrap. Using your hands, roll cheese into a neat log. Refrigerate until firm. Remove plastic from cheese and roll cheese in fennel seeds (photograph pages 226–27).

Pear and raspberry pie

Herb and Garlic Cheese

1½ cups (12 oz/375 g) grated Cheddar cheese
1½ cups (12 oz/375 g) ricotta cheese
1½ cups (12 oz/375 g) cream cheese, chopped
3 garlic cloves, crushed
1 cup (1 oz/30 g) chopped chives
½ cup (½ oz/15 g) chopped parsley
2 tablespoons chopped sage
2 tablespoons poppy seeds

Makes 6 cups (2½ lb/1.25 kg)

Place cheeses and garlic in the bowl of a food processor and process until combined. Transfer cheese mixture to a bowl, add herbs and mix well. Shape mixture into a ball. Refrigerate until firm, then press poppy seeds onto cheese (photograph pages 226–27).

Pesto Cheese

¾ cup (3 oz/90 g) toasted pine nuts
1½ cups (1½ oz/45 g) basil leaves, washed and dried
2 garlic cloves, crushed
¼ cup (2 fl oz/60 ml) olive oil
1½ cups (12 oz/375 g) chopped feta cheese
¼ cup (60 g/2 oz) grated Parmesan cheese
4 mozzarella cheeses, chopped
1 cup (8 oz/250 g) ricotta cheese
¾ cup (6 oz/185 g) unsalted butter, chopped
2 tablespoons sour cream

Makes 6 cups (2½ lb/1.25 kg)

Place ½ cup (2 oz/60 g) pine nuts in bowl of food processor with basil and garlic and process until puréed. Add oil, cheeses, butter, and sour cream and process until combined. Line a bowl with dampened cheesecloth and spoon mixture into bowl. Refrigerate until firm. At serving time, turn the cheese out, remove cheesecloth and sprinkle remaining pine nuts on top (photograph pages 226–27).

Date and Pistachio Cheese

2 cups (8 oz/250 g) shelled pistachios
1½ cups (12 oz/375 g) cream cheese, chopped
¾ cup (6 oz/185 g) unsalted butter
¾ cup (6 oz/185 g) ricotta cheese
2 tablespoons honey
2 tablespoons brandy
1 cup (6 oz/185 g) chopped dates

Makes 6 cups (2½ lb/1.25 kg)

Place pistachios in the bowl of a food processor and process until finely chopped. Remove nuts from processor and reserve ½ cup (2 oz/60 g) for pressing onto finished cheese. Place cream cheese, butter, ricotta, honey and brandy in bowl of food processor and process until combined. Transfer mixture to a bowl, add pistachios and dates; mix well. Line an 8-in (20 cm) loaf pan with plastic wrap and press mixture evenly into tin. Refrigerate until firm. Turn cheese out onto serving board, remove plastic wrap and press on reserved pistachio nuts (photograph pages 226–27).

Marinated Fruits

½ cup (4 oz/125 g) sugar
1 cup (8 fl oz/250 ml) water
¼ cup (2 fl oz/60 ml) Grand Marnier
¼ cup (2 fl oz/60 ml) almond liqueur
1 cantaloupe (rockmelon), cut into wedges and rind removed
1 cup (8 oz/250 g) raspberries
1 cup (8 oz/250 g) strawberries
1 cup (8 oz/250 g) blueberries

Serves 8

Place sugar and water in saucepan and stir over low heat until sugar dissolves. Bring to a boil, reduce heat, and simmer for 5 minutes. Allow to cool; add liqueurs. Arrange cantaloupe wedges in base of serving dish and spoon berries over the melon. Pour syrup gently over fruit (photograph page 8).

Mocha Zabaglione

8 egg yolks
½ cup (4 oz/125 g) sugar
2 tablespoons unsweetened cocoa powder
¼ cup (2 fl oz/60 ml) Marsala
¼ cup (2 fl oz/60 ml) coffee liqueur
½ cup (4 fl oz/125 ml) sweet white wine

Serves 6

Place egg yolks, sugar and cocoa in the top of a double boiler and beat with an electric mixer until combined. Place pan over simmering water. Add Marsala and coffee liqueur and beat until combined and creamy. Add wine and continue to beat for about 10 minutes, or until thick and creamy. Remove from heat and stir vigorously with a wooden spoon. Pour into glasses and dust the top with additional cocoa. Serve immediately (photograph page 168).
NOTE: This dessert can be served with fresh fruit or ladyfingers (sponge fingers/savoiardi biscuits).

Lemon Sorbet

2 cups (16 fl oz/500 ml) water
1 cup (8 oz/250 g) superfine (caster) sugar
1 cup (8 fl oz/250 ml) lemon juice
finely grated zest of 1 lemon
1 egg white

Serves 4–6

Serving ice cream outdoors on a sunny day? Chill the bowl you are going to serve it in for an hour or two in the refrigerator. Place the ice cream in the bowl and return it to the refrigerator just before you sit down for your main course. This takes away the teeth-tingling icy edge that you experience if ice cream is served straight from the freezer.

Make a syrup with water and sugar. Add lemon juice and zest. Pour mixture into a rectangular pan 13 x 9 in (33 x 23 cm), and freeze until partially set—about 1 hour. Remove mixture to bowl of food processor, add egg white and process until combined. Return to pan, cover and freeze.

NOTE: For easier serving, remove sorbets from freezer 30 minutes before serving.

Strawberry Sorbet

2 cups (1 lb/500 g) strawberries
2 cups (16 fl oz/500 ml) water
1/2 cup (4 oz/125 g) superfine (caster) sugar
1 tablespoon lemon juice
2 egg whites

Serves 4–6

Combine strawberries and water in a saucepan, bring to a boil. Reduce heat and simmer 15 minutes.

Add sugar and stir constantly over heat, without boiling, until sugar dissolves. Cool mixture. Stir in lemon juice. Place mixture in the bowl of a food processor and process until smooth. Pour mixture into a rectangular pan 13 x 9 in (33 x 23 cm) and freeze until partly set—about 1 hour. Remove mixture to bowl of a food processor, add egg whites and process until combined. Return to pan, cover and freeze.

Mango Sorbet

2¹/₂ cups (1¹/₂ lb/750 g) chopped mango flesh
2 cups (16 fl oz/500 ml) water
1/2 cup (4 oz/125 g) superfine (caster) sugar
1 tablespoon lemon juice
2 egg whites

Serves 4–6

Follow directions for Strawberry Sorbet.

Mango sorbet; strawberry sorbet; lemon sorbet

From left: blueberry ice cream; raspberry ice cream; mango ice cream

Custard Base for Ice Cream

1 cup (8 fl oz/250 ml) milk
1 cup (8 fl oz/250 ml) light (single) cream
2 egg yolks
2 tablespoons superfine (caster) sugar

Serves 4

Combine the milk and cream in a saucepan and heat until almost boiling. Whip egg yolks and sugar until light. Continue whisking while pouring milk mixture into egg yolk mixture. Return to saucepan and cook over low heat, stirring constantly, until mixture thickens. Cool and chill thoroughly before using. For flavors, see following recipes.

Mango Ice Cream

3 large mangoes, peeled and cut off pit
2 tablespoons orange juice
Custard Base for Ice Cream (see recipe, above)

Place mango flesh and orange juice in the bowl of a food processor, process until smooth. Add to custard mixture. Pour into a rectangular pan 13 x 9 in (32 x 23 cm). Freeze until almost set. Remove from pan and place into bowl of a processor or electric beater. Process or beat until smooth. Return to pan and freeze. Alternatively, use an electric ice-cream maker and follow the manufacturer's instructions.

Photograph pages 226–27, "Poolside Snacks for a Crowd," clockwise from front: smoked salmon and shrimp open sandwich (page 70); rare roast beef with béarnaise on rye (page 68); chicken and walnut on rye (page 63); ham, asparagus and mustard cream open sandwich (page 66); prosciutto and sun-dried tomato focaccia (page 63); fruit cocktail frappé (page 237); watermelon frappé (page 237); pineapple–mint frappé (page 237); pesto cheese (page 222); mustard and port cheese (page 221); date and pistachio cheese (page 222); herb and garlic cheese (page 222)

Raspberry Ice Cream

1 cup (8 oz/250 g) raspberries
1 tablespoon lemon juice
Custard Base for Ice Cream (see recipe, this page)

Follow directions for Mango Ice Cream, substituting raspberries and lemon juice for mangoes and orange juice respectively.

Blueberry Ice Cream

1 cup (8 oz/250 g) blueberries
1 tablespoon lemon juice
Custard Base for Ice Cream (see recipe, this page)

Follow directions for Mango Ice Cream, substituting blueberries and lemon juice for mangoes and orange juice respectively.

Drinks

Outdoor entertaining calls for drinks that are essentially cool, light and uncomplicated. Often the "thirst-quenching" factor is of paramount importance, especially if you are entertaining out-of-doors under the hot summer sun. Therefore, you will need to give a lot more thought to drinks than if you were simply entertaining indoors. The following pages outline the major considerations.

The variety of available wine types can be confusing. So can knowing which foods to serve with a particular wine. This chapter describes the most popular kinds of wine for outdoor entertaining, and provides hints as to which foods they best accompany.

There is also information on how much alcohol—including beer and spirits—you need to provide per person, and how best to keep drinks cold.

For nondrinkers and younger guests, there are ideas for delicious concoctions of fruit, milk, yogurt and ice cream, as well as recipes for iced and herbal teas.

Opposite, from left: fruit cocktail frappé (page 237); pineapple–mint frappé (page 237); watermelon frappé (page 237)

WINE

Crisp, fruity whites are the most popular choice for outdoor meals, and current favorites for fresh-tasting wines are Chardonnay and Sauvignon Blanc.

Chardonnay has become exceedingly popular during the past few years. It is the grape variety from which France's famous white Burgundies are made. Chardonnay can be made in a variety of styles, from a lean, silky wine with delicate grapefruit and lemon flavors to rich, full-bodied and fruity, with the distinctive sweet vanillin smell and taste of oak. It can be enjoyed with a wide variety of foods. The luscious richness of Chardonnay goes well with pasta and rice dishes, seafoods, pâtés and smoked meats. Because of their depth of character, Chardonnays with a few years' bottle age will complement a wide range of cheeses, from creamy Brie and Camembert to mature Cheddar and blue cheeses. Hints of melon or tropical fruit can be found in many Chardonnays, so the wine can accompany most fruits and fruity desserts.

Sauvignon Blanc has a distinctive aroma of freshly cut grass and a flavor of melon or citrus. Whether it is made in France, California or Australia, most Sauvignon Blanc wine is easy to drink while at the same time offering interest and balance. It is excellent served with salads, chicken and seafood dishes.

Other popular white wines include Chenin Blanc, Pinot Blanc, Italian Pinot Grigio, Goave, Orvieto and Frascati.

Wines made from the true white Riesling or Johannisberg Riesling grape of Germany and Alsace are rarely disappointing, and sometimes they are magnificent. Today's Rieslings are fresh-tasting wines with floral aroma and long, complex citrus characters on the palate. Riesling ranges in style from bone-dry through a pleasant fruitiness to richly sweet and complex late-harvest wines. Young Riesling is an excellent apéritif, and the delicate bouquet and lemony crispness of dry to medium-dry Riesling complements fish, salads and finger food.

Sweeter spätlese and auslese styles of Riesling can be enjoyed with a wide range of outdoor food and should not be confined to the dessert course. Try these with rich hors d'oeuvre like smoked fish, pâtés and terrines, and with main-course salmon, lobster and crab. Because they finish with a touch of crisp acidity, these sweeter Rieslings complement fresh fruit or fruit tarts.

Luscious without being sweet, aromatic and spicy with a bouquet of rose petals, Gewürztraminer is the white wine that best accompanies Oriental cuisine, including barbecued spiced sausages and kebabs, smoked pork and duck, Thai, Indian and Malaysian foods.

For a special celebration, Champagne or sparkling wines may be served throughout the meal. Depending on the production techniques used to make them, sparkling wines are now available at a wide range of prices and from a number of countries—Spain, Italy and the US, in addition to France.

Premium Champagne, produced by the *méthode champenoise*, must be produced within the delimited Champagne region of France. These are wines for elegant dinner parties. A medium-priced range of sparkling wines is made to a very high standard, often employing the *méthode champenoise*. Inexpensive sparkling wines are made by a less costly process and can be bought by the case for an *al fresco* party or picnic. They can still be delicious, technically well-made wines which will impress your guests with a sense of special occasion without blowing your budget; they're the perfect base for sparkling fruit punch.

Rosé and blush wines are gaining ground as perfect wines for outdoors, tasting clean and fresh, and looking lovely in the glass on a warm summer day. Typically, these wines are medium dry with relatively low alcohol and are quaffable—just what's needed for most outdoor food, from cold and smoked meats to spicy Oriental foods and tropical fruits.

The universal benchmark for light red wine is Beaujolais, made in the French area of the same name. Don't be fooled by sound-alikes; there is simply no substitute for the fruity flavor of true Beaujolais. It is a "drink-anytime" wine that is light enough to accompany salads, yet sufficiently robust to go with lamb, beef and fowl. Whichever light red you choose, make sure it is served chilled.

For *al fresco* dining, avoid full-bodied, tannic reds, such as Cabernet Sauvignon, and enjoy a softer Cabernet Merlot blend or a spicy Shiraz.

BEER AND SPIRITS

Wine is the preferred choice of most modern hosts, but if your beverage is beer, spoil your guests with a selection of boutique brews and exclusive ales rather than serving them the more common varieties. Cans are easier to chill and to keep cool but bottles look better.

Nobody expects you to have a portable, well-stocked bar for dining out-of-doors, so if

Red wines benefit from being opened in advance to "breathe." An old wine, or a wine of great delicacy, should be given only a brief breathing time, but most commercial reds will soften and become richer in flavor if they are poured out into a jug or decanter an hour or two before they are to be drunk.

you decide to serve spirits, keep the selection to a minimum. Offer no more than two spirits, depending on the known preferences of your guests. Contrast a "dark" with a "white" spirit, giving them a choice of bourbon or vodka, scotch or gin, brandy or white rum.

Limit the choice of soft drinks for those who prefer nonalcoholic drinks for mixers, but ensure you have plenty, for on a warm day, most people will prefer their drinks on the weak side and more will be consumed by the soft drinkers. Make sure the mixers are very cold, and chill the liquor bottles, too, or you'll be rushing out for more ice.

Old-fashioned punch recipes are potent. One recipe goes: 3 parts rum, 2 of brandy, 1 of lemon juice, 4 of hot water, sugar to taste. Fruit punches today should offer more flavor and be less potent—or without alcohol at all.

NONALCOHOLIC DRINKS

Wine and spirits play an important part in entertaining, but on hot summer days they are not always wholly appropriate. Many people merely wish to quench their thirst when dining outdoors and, particularly if lunch, a picnic or steering a boat in the heat of the day is involved, prefer to avoid alcohol altogether. If children are among the party, the need for nonalcoholic drinks is paramount.

Among the easiest drinks to prepare are freshly made fruit and vegetable juices. Here, a blender and a citrus juicer or juice extractor will prove themselves invaluable. You are going for quantity here so, unless yours is a very special occasion, take advantage of seasonal items, rather than expensive, out-of-season exotica.

From left: fresh orange fruit cordial (page 234); lemonade (page 234); fresh strawberry fruit cordial (page 234); fresh lime fruit cordial (page 237)

Experiment with combinations—apples and pears, carrots and oranges, peaches and strawberries, tomatoes and limes (add some ground, roasted cumin seeds to this one)—determining the best proportions ahead of time. Not all combinations work well and may not marry with the food you are serving, so don't be tempted to mix things on the spur of the moment. Children tend to prefer things plain—a single fruit only, rather than a combination that may look colorful but be lacking in taste appeal.

A nonalcoholic fruit punch can be lovely but, once again, go for a tried and tested recipe rather than taking a hit-or-miss approach with a bewildering array of ingredients, the combined effect of which can be thoroughly unpleasant. Always chill your punch with chunks of ice; if ice cubes are too small they will quickly melt and dilute the mixture.

Place the juice(or punch) in a chilled pitcher in the refrigerator until it is needed. Like wine, the pitcher can sit on a bed of ice in a large bowl when you are outside, to keep it cool as long as possible. And don't forget that one of the most beautiful of all drinks, reminiscent of afternoon teas on the lawn in days gone by, is a homemade lemonade spiked with plenty of mint.

For something erring on the side of wicked but wonderful rather than super-healthy, a smoothie can be a sumptuous treat. Serve these milk/cream/ice cream or yogurt and fruit concoctions with a light meal in place of a dessert, in tall glasses garnished with berries and sprigs of mint. These are popular with adults and children alike.

Equally delectable, refreshing and healthy is a lassi, a yogurt drink that is synonymous with Indian cuisine but as much at home with the food of other nations. You can make it with plain yogurt, with or without fat. The most basic recipe to serve four people requires 1 cup (8 fl oz/250 ml) of plain yogurt and 3 cups (25 fl oz/750 ml) of ice water. Place in a blender and combine briefly until smooth or place the yogurt in a bowl and add the water very slowly, beating the mixture with a whisk or fork. A salty version includes a little salt and freshly ground pepper to taste. For the sweet-toothed, add 3 tablespoons of sugar to the basic mixture and a few drops of orange-flower water or other essence of your choice.

Iced tea is one of those things that most people don't bother to make properly (most seem to manage better with iced coffee). You don't simply cool hot tea and toss in some ice cubes; if you do, you'll find yourself with a cloudy brew and a pronounced taste of tannin. For a beautifully clear concoction, add cold water to about three times the quantity of tea you would use to make the hot brew, and let it stand overnight in the refrigerator to infuse. Iced tea can be served at any time—morning, noon or night.

There are many herbal and fruit teas available that are ideal, made with cold water at the end of a light, summery meal outdoors. And you could try adding a sprig or two of rosemary to an ordinary pot of Indian or black China tea (served hot). This is particularly soothing if the glare of sunlight has given anyone a slight headache.

When you have little or no time at all to prepare cold drinks, bitter lemon, tonic and soda water, tomato and orange juices, ginger beer and mineral water served well chilled with ice and slivers of lemon or lime are perfectly acceptable and sit happily with all manner of food. Make sure you have plenty of crystal-clear, fresh ice on hand. If you have run out of space in the freezer, layer the bottles with ice in a large bucket or plastic garbage bin.

Always have unsweetened juices on offer for children. Excessively sweet or fizzy drinks should be avoided except for very informal occasions and for children who can't live without them. Not only are they usually oversweetened and bad for teeth but also they are usually strongly flavored and overpower the flavor of the food.

For something a little more elegant, a frappé or fruit juice added to shaved ice at the last moment and served in a martini glass is a stylish drink to serve poolside with canapés and open sandwiches. Children, understandably, love them too.

It's important to err on the side of generosity with supplies of cold drinks—most will not spoil, after all—and very active children running about on a hot day (or people who have trekked a long distance to the picnic or barbecue site, for that matter) can easily consume three or four glasses, while their parents linger over a long lunch. Teenagers, in particular, can drink amazing quantities of liquid. Aim for variety and quantity, and you won't go wrong.

CHILLING BEVERAGES

Successfully chilling large quantities of drinks requires forethought and planning. If the outdoor party is at home and you entertain

Opposite: frozen berry daiquiri (left and right, page 237); lime daiquiri (center, page 237)

regularly, a separate bar refrigerator is a good idea. A tub full of ice cubes is the effective, old-fashioned way of keeping bottles cool. Put the bottles in first, then pour the ice over them.

How chilled bottles are transported depends on the number of guests and how long it takes to reach the venue. For a small family picnic, there are a number of insulated "bottle bags" on the market that will keep their contents at drinking temperature for hours. Then there are a host of elegant and casual carriers made expressly for keeping beverages cold.

When serving a crowd, experienced picnickers carry their bottles in large coolers with ice or, preferably, "freezer bricks." Opened bottles are returned to the cold box or kept in ceramic or plastic "wine wells" between glass refills. If you want to bring magnums of wine or "bag-in-a-box" wines, remember that they take longer to chill than regular bottles. The sturdy cardboard pack on a wine cask is a good insulator, so allow six to eight hours in a domestic refrigerator.

If you have a glut of fruit on your garden citrus tree, set to work. Cut lemons, limes and oranges into slices and store them in the freezer ready for cool summertime drinks. Also, freeze orange wedges. These make healthy ice pops for guests' children on a hot day. The microwave is very useful for making sure you extract the maximum amount of juice from citrus fruits. Heat each piece of fruit on HIGH for about 30 seconds, and let stand for a while before squeezing.

GLASSES

A picnic is not the place for your best crystal, but you don't have to drink from paper cups and peanut-butter jars. There are plenty of good, robust, stemmed glasses available at prices that won't break the budget. Broken glass in a swimming pool or around a picnic area is a no-no, and plastic glasses are light and unstable, so for poolside barbecues, keep a stock of those excellent hybrids of glass and plastic, which feel like glass but are practically unbreakable.

QUANTITIES

How much drink will be needed? For wine, count on needing half a bottle per person. If the occasion is a leisurely one, extending for 3 or 4 hours on a balmy weekend afternoon, allocate more wine, but make sure that there is an equivalent amount of mineral water and soft drinks on hand. Some of your wiser guests may choose to mix wine and mineral water to make their own spritzers.

For beer, four to six bottles per person should be sufficient, unless you know you have some heavy drinkers in the party. If you limit the choice of liquors to two, then each bottle should serve 25 shots, so figure on a bottle for every five people. Heavy drinkers may regard these suggestions as miserly, but

it's a fact that outdoor eating encourages moderation. For the same reason, ensure you have plenty of mineral water, soft drinks and mixers.

Lemonade

3 cups (24 fl oz/750 ml) water
zest of 3 lemons
1 cup (8 oz/250 g) sugar
2 cups (16 fl oz/500 ml) fresh lemon juice

Serves 4–6

Combine water and lemon zest and bring to a boil. Remove from heat and stir in sugar until dissolved. Let stand for 15 minutes. Add lemon juice and chill thoroughly. Strain and serve over ice with lots of fresh mint and slices of lemon (photograph page 231).

Fresh Strawberry Fruit Cordial

2 cups (1 lb/500 g) strawberries
2 tablespoons lemon juice
1/3 cup (2 1/3 oz/75 g) sugar
2 1/2 cups (20 fl oz/625 ml) water

Makes 4 cups (1 qt/1 l)

Place strawberries in the bowl of a food processor and process to a smooth purée. Stir in lemon juice. Combine sugar and water in a saucepan. Place over moderate heat and stir, without boiling, until sugar dissolves. Chill sugar syrup. Combine strawberry mixture and syrup and let stand for 15 minutes, at least, before straining into a jug or bottle and chilling. Serve with lots of ice, a dash of vodka and soda water (photograph page 231).

Fresh Orange Fruit Cordial

2 1/2 cups (20 fl oz/625 ml) water
zest of 2 oranges
1/3 cup (2 1/2 oz/75 g) sugar
1 1/4 cups (10 fl oz/315 ml) orange juice

Makes 4 cups (1 qt/1 l)

Combine water and orange zest in a saucepan and bring to a boil. Remove from heat, add sugar and stir to dissolve. Leave to stand for 15 minutes. Add orange juice and chill thoroughly. Serve with lots of ice and soda or mineral water (photograph page 231).

Smoothie

Fresh Lime Fruit Cordial

2¹/₂ cups (20 fl oz/625 ml) water
zest of 3 limes
²/₃ cup (5 oz/155 g) sugar
1 cup (8 fl oz/250 ml) lime juice

Makes 4 cups (1 qt/1 l)

Follow directions for Fresh Orange Fruit Cordial on page 234 (photograph page 231).

Smoothie

¹/₂ cup (4 oz/125 g) strawberries, hulled
1 banana, peeled
¹/₃ cup (3 fl oz/90 ml) plain yogurt
1 tablespoon honey
1 cup (8 fl oz/250 ml) low-fat milk
3 ice cubes

Serves 1–2

Place all ingredients in a blender and process until smooth.

Fruit Cocktail Frappé

3 cups (24 fl oz/750 ml) orange juice
2 cups (16 fl oz/500 ml) apricot nectar
1 cup (8 fl oz/250 ml) pineapple juice
1 cup (8 oz/250 g) sugar
1 cup (8 fl oz/250 ml) water
2 cups (16 fl oz/500 ml) ginger ale

Serves 12

Place orange juice, apricot nectar, pineapple juice, sugar and water in a saucepan, stir over low heat until sugar dissolves, allow to cool, transfer to a bowl. Add ginger ale, and freeze until partially set or completely frozen. Blend in blender or food processor until mushy. Serve immediately (photograph page 228).

Pineapple–Mint Frappé

6 cups (1¹/₂ lb/750 g) peeled, cored and chopped pineapple
1 cup (1 oz/30 g) mint leaves
¹/₂ cup (4 oz/125 g) sugar
3 cups (24 fl oz/750 ml) mineral water

Serves 12

Place pineapple in a blender or the bowl of a food processor and process until very finely puréed. Add mint and sugar and process for 10 seconds. Transfer pineapple purée to a bowl and add mineral water. Place frappé in freezer and freeze until partially set or completely frozen. Blend in blender or food processor until mushy. Serve immediately (photograph page 228).

Watermelon Frappé

6 cups (1¹/₂ lb/750 g) seeded watermelon flesh, cubed
1 cup (8 oz/250 g) raspberries
1 cup (8 oz/250 g) strawberries, hulled
¹/₂ cup (4 oz/125 g) sugar
1 cup (8 fl oz/250 ml) mineral water
2 cups (16 fl oz/500 ml) lemon–lime soda

Serves 12

Place watermelon, berries and sugar in blender or bowl of a food processor and process until puréed. Transfer fruit purée to a bowl and add the mineral water and lemon–lime soda. Place frappé in freezer and freeze until semi-set or completely frozen. Blend in a blender or food processor until mushy. Serve immediately (photograph page 228).

Lime Daiquiri

2 tablespoons (1 fl oz/30 ml) white rum
juice of 1 lime
2 teaspoons sugar syrup

Serves 1

Pour the rum, lime juice and sugar syrup into a cocktail shaker over crushed ice. Shake well and strain into a cocktail glass (photograph page 232).

Frozen Berry Daiquiri

2 tablespoons (1 fl oz/30 ml) white rum
¹/₃ cup (3 oz/90 g) mixed berries
1 cup (8 fl oz/250 ml) ice

Serves 1

Place the rum and berries in a blender with the ice. Blend and pour into a cocktail glass (photograph page 232).

Pacific Punch

¹/₂ cup (4 oz/125 g) sugar
3 oranges, thinly sliced
juice of 4 lemons
2 cups (8 oz/250 g) diced fresh pineapple
¹/₂ cup (4 oz/125 g) diced strawberries
8 cups (2 qt/2 l) dry white wine
3 cups (24 fl oz/750 ml) sparkling wine

Serves 20

Combine all ingredients and chill. When ready to serve, add wine (photograph page 235).

When making cocktails and mixed drinks, always have plenty of fresh, crystal-clean ice on hand. Use only quality branded products. Measure ingredients accurately; a good cocktail depends on exact proportions. The best cocktails usually contain only one base spirit. Avoid complicated cocktails containing many spirits.

INDEX

Page numbers in italics indicate photographs

ACKNOWLEDGMENTS

Weldon Russell would like to thank the following people for their help with the production of this book:

Appley Hoare Antiques; Australian Craftworks; Barbeques Galore; Bohemia Crystal; Craig Brown; Butler & Co; David Cameron; Corso de Fiori; Country Road Homeware; David Jones, Brisbane, for loan of props; Sandy de Beyer; Feature Cane; Julia Gamble; Gekko's Restaurant, Brisbane, for use of locations; Glass Artists Gallery; IVV, Italy; Jupiter Antiques, Brisbane; Krosno; Les Olivades; Milton Brisbane for supplying crockery; Noritake Pty Ltd (Australia); Oneida Silverware; Park Road; The Parterre Garden; Royal Copenhagen and Georg Jensen Pty Ltd; Royal Doulton Australia Pty Ltd; Tekno Ceramics; Waterford Wedgwood Australia Ltd; Gayle Yates.

Mark Burgin (photographer) and Jacki Passmore (food stylist) for the photographs on the following pages: 10–11, 30, 33, 39, 51, 55, 66, 67, 68–69, 93, 94, 95, 100, 101, 103, 105, 109, 113, 114–15, 116, 118, 119, 121, 128, 134, 135, 138, 139, 143, 148, 149, 151, 152, 153, 154, 155, 157, 158, 162, 163, 176, 183, 187, 188, 189, 190, 191, 192, 194, 195, 196, 198, 199, 200–201, 202.

Rowan Fotheringham (photographer) and Carolyn Fienberg (food stylist, assisted by Joanne Forrest and Donna Hayes) for the photographs on the following pages: front cover, 1, 2, 3, 4–5, 6, 16–17, 22–23, 40–41, 61, 70, 78, 79, 90–91, 106–107, 112, 120, 122–23, 124–25, 140–41, 144–45, 156, 160–61, 164–65, 168, 184–85, 197, 203, 204–205, 209, 215, 218, 221, 226–27, 228.

Rowan Fotheringham (photographer) and Consuelo Guinness (food stylist) for the photographs on the following pages: 8, 58–59, 74–75, 171, 214.

Mike Hallson (photographer) and Jacki Passmore (food stylist) for the photographs on the following pages: 98, 99, 110–11, 114, 117, 129, 131, 132, 159.

The Image Bank (Marcelo Enderle) for the endpapers photograph.

Ashley Mackevicius (photographer) and Suzie Smith (food stylist, assisted by Heather Tindale) for the photographs on the following pages: back cover, 9, 15, 24, 25, 26–27, 28–29, 34, 36–37, 42, 43, 44, 45, 46, 47, 48, 50, 53, 54, 57, 60, 63, 64–65, 71, 72, 76, 77, 80–81, 82, 83, 85, 86, 89, 92, 96, 108, 126, 127, 130, 136, 137, 142, 146–47, 166, 167, 169, 170, 172–73, 174, 177, 178, 179, 180–81, 182, 186, 193, 206, 207, 208, 210, 211, 212, 213, 216, 219, 220, 223, 224–25, 229, 231, 232, 235, 236.

Weldon Trannies for the photograph on page 12.